# Constraining Government

# Constraining Government

Zoltán Balázs

LEXINGTON BOOKS
*Lanham • Boulder • New York • London*

Published by Lexington Books
An imprint of The Rowman & Littlefield Publishing Group, Inc.
4501 Forbes Boulevard, Suite 200, Lanham, Maryland 20706
www.rowman.com

6 Tinworth Street, London SE11 5AL, United Kingdom

British Library Cataloguing in Publication Information Available

**Library of Congress Cataloging-in-Publication Data**

Names: Balázs, Zoltán, author.
Title: Constraining government / Zoltán Balázs.
Description: Lanham : Lexington Books, [2021] | Includes bibliographical references
    and index. | Summary: "This book argues for the case that governments develop with
    inherent constraints. These constraints support the case for the normative political
    theoretical defense of moderate governing"—Provided by publisher.
Identifiers: LCCN 2021002619 (print) | LCCN 2021002620 (ebook) |
    ISBN 9781793603807 (cloth) | ISBN 9781793603814 (epub)
Subjects: LCSH: Political science—Philosophy. | Executive power. |
    Constitutional law.
Classification: LCC JA71 .B2746 2021 (print) | LCC JA71 (ebook) |
    DDC 320.01—dc23
LC record available at https://lccn.loc.gov/2021002619
LC ebook record available at https://lccn.loc.gov/2021002620

# Contents

# Preface

This book is a sequence to my previous one: *The Principle of the Separation of Powers: A Defense*, published by Rowman and Littlefield in 2016. In it, I attempted to revise the classical doctrine, defending it against recent criticisms and offering a constructive conception of it. Writing that book, I was already pondering a more general account of constrained governing.

Our common political theoretical tradition knows and cherishes the idea of moderate government; yet, I found this tradition somewhat arcane, rather exhortative, analytically less rigorous, and technically less refined than mainstream contemporary theories of governing. Typically, the latter conceive of governments in terms of institutions, procedures, functions, and offices. Political philosophy adds to this the normative moral principles of justice, human rights, equality, fairness, as well as more political principles, such as the rule of law, legitimacy, security, and popular sovereignty (democracy), whereas legal philosophy is preoccupied with the constitution, again, mainly in terms of institutions and procedures.

Recent scholarship in realist political theory has been stressing the personal-political dimension of governing, both inspired and worried by the rise of authoritarian regimes, but also in acknowledgment of the realities of politics in general. Now whereas for the institutional-procedural approach to governing the very existence and operation of institutions and procedures seems to entail a kind of natural limitedness of all these agents, entities, and games; once governing is interpreted as a specific activity, more precisely, as constituted by human persons doing various things, which they, or those who talk about them, describe as "governing," such a natural and inherent limitedness does not seem to obtain. The central argument of this book is that notwithstanding this impression, such limits and constrains do exist, and by exploring and exposing them, we are in a better position to defend, and eventually, to protect them.

I said that classical theories of moderate government, such as Montesquieu's, tend to be less rigorous and amenable to formalization and an axiomatic treatment. But they have the advantage of being more open and accessible to the general public. This is a value that must be cherished and preserved, and my way of exposing the conception of this book has been tailored accordingly. Nonetheless, they are in need of, and they do deserve, more focused and sharpened restatements. This is my ambition, nothing more—and nothing less.

I am thankful to my colleagues who helped me with this endeavor at the Corvinus University, Budapest, and the Political Science Institute of the Eotvos Research Network, Budapest; as well as to my reviewers for their useful comments. Team at Rowman and Littlefield was very generous throughout supporting this project, for which I am indebted to them greatly.

Readers are encouraged to communicate their comments to zoltan.balazs @uni-corvinus.hu.

# Introduction

This book is exploratory. It has conceptual, descriptive, and normative aims alike. It seeks to understand what it means to have a government with constraints, to understand governing as a constrained activity. A better and persuasive account of the inherent constraints of governing, at least within the Western tradition broadly understood, is also meant to provide normative arguments for the defense of the conception of constrained governing. Evidently, if it proves to be impossible to govern without constraints, then this conclusion is itself an argument against efforts to do so.

It is not presumed that all mankind has always desired such governing and such governments. However, it is presumed that on a historical scale, people of many societies and polities—across deep cultural, religious, and ideological divisions and splits—desired to see their interests, lives and properties, faiths and families of individuals, and their small circles be protected efficiently, against each other but eventually also against the government itself.

It sounds an impossible task, a squaring the circle to have the agent responsible for protecting us to observe limits and constraints without robust opposing powers because such powers are exactly those that we wish to be protected against. We fear of the power of the rich, of the strong, of the majority, of the other with a different faith. Yet there is a lamentable history of governments of the rich, of the strong, of the ultimate truth, of the elect, and so on. Is there a way out of this dilemma?

Political theory has offered a number of ways. In view and in response to what seems to be, or what is conveniently called in political science and in political journalism a "populist/authoritarian" surge in democracies, including not only the "developing" ones but the most consolidated ones, political theorists have begun to recall and reconsider these ways. For instance, in a recent article, William A. Galston, a noted realist political theorist, argues that the "colossal" changes on the democratic landscape cannot be fully explained by the undeniably important economic crisis and the social shifts occurring partly as a result of the crisis but partly as a result of the triumphant globalization of the national economies.[1] These shifts have already established, or contributed to a new sort of alienation between governments embedded in and educated by the post-nationalist era and large masses of their citizens, which finds its expression in new cleavages, value conflicts, and emotional frustrations. Thus,

> governments across the West face growing public ire. Many citizens, their confidence in the future shaken, long instead for an imagined past that insurgent politicians have promised to restore. As popular demand for strong leaders grows, rising political actors are beginning to question key liberal-democratic principles such as the rule of law, freedom of the press, and minority rights. The door seems to be opening for a return to forms of authoritarianism written off by many as relics of the past.[2]

Virtually, Galston admits that we are dealing here with a paradox. On the one hand, the principles of popular sovereignty (he calls it republicanism) and democratic majority make room for an unlimited government. On the other hand, therefore, limitations are necessary: by constitutionalism, he means to establish the very idea of boundaries, and by liberalism, he means to demarcate the private sphere of individuals from the sphere and competences of governments. He asserts us that these four principles can be consistently upheld and followed. Of course, the story begins as soon as any of them becomes controversial. Galston himself indicates that "popular sovereignty" is a highly technical and abstract concept, which can be used in political rhetoric in various and contradictory ways, depending on how the generic concept of the "people" is understood. Therefore, we should not expect political theory to provide us with a simple and ultimate solution to the consistency problems that inevitably arise. Galston, a realist, in other words, a skeptic of ideal political theory, and the role political theory could or should have in politics, has no objections to this conclusion. However, he is still doing political theory when he assumes and suggests that these principles are best held up and defended together, in practical politics as well. He hopes that threats to the existing, by default good, but in many ways corroding and ailing political system, can be avoided in this way. Hopes need, however, a more solid justification, and Galston does not provide this here. The two pairs of principles (popular sovereignty and majority versus constitutional limits and demarcations) tend to clash and make the problem of how to constrain governments that are there to protect us against all sorts of power that constrain our freedom and freedoms admittedly difficult to solve.

However, the realization of this difficulty does not require sophisticated political philosophy. It is part and parcel of everyone's political life and experiences. Nilly-willy, most people must reflect on these problems, when it comes to paying their taxes (spent on things they may disagree with), sending their children to school and exposing them to various teachings, taking security risks in the streets for reasons they has no control over, and so on. Ordinary people have the same ambivalences, contradictory expectations and feelings as political theorists and philosophers have about the difficulties of reconciling private autonomy with collective authority. The very fact of there being a government makes us feel secure but it also worries us, and this ambiguity provides us with the first incentive to look for a reasoned and salient conception of how governments and governing can be constrained.

In the history of political thought, the polemics between the representatives of the Lockean theory of representative/popular government and those of the Humean skepticism about the usefulness and justifiableness of this theory is well-known. The disagreement reflects a deep difference regarding political theory and its vocation. According to Paul Sagar, Hume

> aimed to call into question, and then realign, our underlying conception of what political philosophy is and can do. If one viewed the role of political philosophy as being the issuing of pronouncements as to the legitimacy of human social practices, predicated upon an external and ultimately superior standard of justification, whilst specifically making consent the condition by which the legitimacy of political authority was achieved, then one must claim that any government not actually consented to by its population was *ipso facto* illegitimate.[3]

This would mean that there has practically never been a legitimate government: this is, of course, an almost absurd, but certainly useless, conclusion. The idea of tacit consent is no less unrealistic and unconvincing. Such political theoretical speculations are incapable of justifying obedience. Thus, "philosophy's role was to help us better understand our state of affairs, in particular to better appreciate the nature of our values, whilst being aware that such values must, and could only ever be, our own creations."[4]

Nonetheless, there is a normative and constructive tail attached to this largely critical Humean view. All governments, notwithstanding their origins and legal legitimacy, must observe public utility. It follows that governmental oppression can be legitimately resisted if people's interests are seriously harmed. But obviously, neither "utility" (especially public utility), nor "interests" are politically innocent or neutral concepts. They have a normative dimension, as they entail a prohibition (to harm) and a prescription (to respect). These may be more fundamental and morally trivial than the more "political" conception of Locke: "in political theory prior to the engagement of practical politics as it happens to be given by the practice of the age, sovereignty is not a primary or useful category of political analysis from Hume's perspective."[5] However, they remain to be robustly normative, as they are meant to provide us with some arguments against the policies of the government.

Since Locke's and Hume's days, our political vocabulary has been enriched by various other conceptual frameworks that have contributed to a more complex view of the social world, over which the political sphere has a unifying but not an overwhelming authority. Sheldon Wolin observed:

> The cultivation of political understanding means that one becomes sensitized to the enormous complexities and drama of saying that the political order is the most comprehensive association and ultimately responsible as no other grouping is for sustaining the physical, material, cultural and moral life of its members.[6]

But he also noted that "whether the primary [political] theoretical task be one of explanation or critical appraisal, the theorist will want to locate 'divisions' in the human world and embody them in theoretical form."[7] His own examples were religion and economy (or religious and economic activities). Roughly, then, the commonplace observation that our activities, some of which are basically types of interactions with other individuals, are subject to various sorts of authorities, standards, principles, values, norm codes, communicative mediums, and so on itself suggests a sort of a delimiting, demarcating logic inherent to modern social life. This logic entails that the government is an agent active somewhere out there, with which it is not normal or natural to identify ourselves without remainder. Thus, we have more means at our disposal to describe what governing does *not* involve, and if our description is robust, realistic, and consensual enough, then we already have a normative argument as well. However, it does not follow that modern societies (again, at least in the Western tradition) are intrinsically more protected against tyrannies, and indeed, the past two centuries have produced various political theories aiming at the justification of them (some of them will be discussed in the next chapter). We still need some sort of a political theory or philosophy that grows out of our ordinary experiences of and with our governments, and that is sufficiently realistic and reliably normative.

Thus, a sound and convincing political theoretical conception presupposes a perspective that can be taken and shared before proper philosophy can begin. This perspective is of course not something out there, nor can it be constructed in the way the famous Clapham omnibus passenger was invoked in the British law, nor is it, needless to say, the hypothetical person in the state of nature or in the original position. There is a more convenient proxy to such a perspective, I assume, and this is that of the reader or watcher of the stories on governments, on their rises and declines, as they have been expounded in some of the most well-known classic pieces that have formed our pre-political conceptions of governing. Thus, before addressing some more properly theoretical accounts of how governments should or should not be constrained, I shall invite the reader in the *first chapter* to reflect on this issue by revisiting the *Antigone* and *Measure for Measure*. It no longer requires a detailed justification of inserting literary works into a discussion of political theoretical problems. Sophocles' and Shakespeare's oeuvres have been particularly seminal in this respect. It is especially the *Antigone* that has been extensively commented on by influential political theorists, whereas Shakespeare is perhaps more popular among historians of political ideas, and *Measure for Measure* has received particular attention for the complex political context it was written in. My intention is to cite and use them as representatives of an ordinary citizen's point of view who happens to be considering the paradox of governing discussed about. Whereas the *Antigone* is particularly apt for introducing us to the problem of how to justify governments, how to draw its competences, and how the best intentions of the government lead to tyranny, that is, unconstrained governing, *Measure for Measure* provides us with excellent insights about what order and disorder means, and how to delineate and distinguish the two states of affairs. A much greater potential resides in the two plays, and they will be extensively cited in the subsequent chapters, according the various topics they will cover.

The *second chapter* takes the reader just into the middle of political theory. It will be shown how certain political concepts, often images, that have greatly influenced political thinking in general, nurtured by various political theories, make an explicit or implicit case for an unconstrained government will, nonetheless, end up with illuminating hidden constraints. The argument is basically, thus, a contrario one. The chapter is in two parts: part I discusses types of political theories and argues that neither the so-called normativist/moralist, nor the descriptivist/realist school is sufficiently close to the ordinary way of thinking about the government. Instead, conceptualism is proposed as an alternative. Once accepted, it provides us with a special focus to highlight new dimensions of the four theories to be discussed afterward. These are the following: first, the Leviathan as the de-politicized zone between government and the citizens also known as the state; second, the Supreme Leader concept as the compression of the government into a person; third, the corporatist conception of society as a whole replacing the government; and fourth, the "Watchmaker Government" (my own term), which is essentially a distributive agency, taking care of the commonwealth grounded in consensually accepted principles of distribution. Each conception contains an unintended restriction on what the respective government is able to do. These restrictions make sense once the leading image is fully developed. The state cannot be what it is meant to be unless it constrains the political omnipotence of the government; the leader is constrained by the personal loyalty ties; the society is workable only if the ideas of harmony and wholeness are somehow shared by everyone; and the distributive government is defenseless against the real challenges of counter-ideologies and the power motives of its own masters.

The *third chapter* is an attempt to reflect on the common understanding of governing as an activity performed by visible and concrete persons. Whereas the "state," or the mentioning of it, suggests impersonality, institutionalized agency, governments are elected, thought to be accountable and responsible for humanly intelligible deeds and decisions. All this because governments—as such, also somewhat impersonal and institutionalized—are basically run by politicians, political leaders with a public face. However, every responsible person has such a face, and it follows that governing is to a great part a personal business: the rise of what is called populism is partly nothing but a rediscovery of this aspect of politics. This explains why politics is, in fact, much closer to us than the institutionalized, routinized, but also sacralized and mystified image of modern governing suggests. But then it is also true that politicians who run the government are like everyone else. Therefore, it is reasonable to consider what moral philosophy has taught us, namely, that our moral (to be more precise, our norm-following) behavior entails the necessity and inevitability of constraining ourselves for sake of our reputation, prestige, and fame—apart from the loftier but arguably less common motivation of desiring to live a virtuous and good life, so dear to Aristotelians. To understand why constraining ourselves is a necessity and inevitability, the experience of shame appears to be particularly important. Plato and his dialogue *Charmides* will help us look to the roots of shame, which will be found in our self-knowledge. Knowing ourselves is not a very high ideal, it is a practical necessity; and knowing ourselves implies realizing that we do not know everything. We strive and struggle for knowing ourselves as much as possible to be able to control our public image and avoid shame, yet perfect knowledge is impossible. Thus, there is a temptation for such a perfection, in a politician's case, for the perfect control of her image, which is a safe way to tyranny; and there is a temptation to abandon all hopes to control anything, which is a safe route to indifference, and in the case of a politician, to anarchy, whimsicality, arbitrariness, and vacuity—to be able to avoid both extremes amounts to have moderation, a cornerstone of all political theories of constrained government. Checking politician's reactions to their public image, to shame, and to self-control is a reliable compass of whether transgressions of constraints are occurring.

In the *fourth chapter*, the transition from the personal aspects of governing and its constraints will be examined, after having discussed and developed three distinctions that are hopefully trivial and natural enough so that the ordinary perspective and mode of reflection is preserved. The first distinction is between character and office, the second is between normal and exceptional times of governing, and the third is between political governing (or governing as commonly understood) and anti-governing, which refers to the natural self-governing activities all people in their private lives perform and wish to protect. These distinctions serve, again, as beacons showing where the constraints lie, though hidden. Through the main figures, the legislator, the executive leader, and the judge, I shall discuss how these distinctions are discernible and become effective. This helps us decide whether those in the government responsible for legislation, or running the bureaucracy and "leading the commonwealth," or making the final judgments over individuals are doing their jobs properly or improperly, respecting or transgressing the limits of their offices, of their historical call, and of their sphere of competence.

In the *fifth* and last *chapter*, I shall present a more normative version of a constrained government, based on the insights and considerations of the previous chapters. First, I shall argue that against the single-image conceptualism of the political theories discussed in the second chapter, we may look for a kind of conceptualism that is richer and more complex. Harmony, balance, and order are the qualities, or meta-qualities that help us understand why and how various political regimes can be said to have constrained governments. This pluralism allows for a wider historical and cultural perspective, never losing sight of the main concern, namely, to resist the tyranny and despotism of unconstrained governments. Second, confronting directly the idea of moderate governments as expounded by Montesquieu and his recent commentators, I shall argue that moderation as such is not a political principle, not even a compass for governing. But it is possible to argue for a "political conception" of a harmonious and balanced pluralism of political principles. Finally, I shall briefly deal with the principle or doctrine of the separation of powers and argue that even though it has come under attacks from several angles in political theory, apart from its defensibility or indefensibility as a substantial political theory, the doctrine is useful for illuminating the constraints of government discovered in the political conceptions discussed in the second chapter. Those conceptions are all distrustful of, or even straightforwardly against the separation of powers; when and if their full power is applied to the legislative, executive, and judiciary branches (as traditionally understood), their inherent constraints become more easily discernible.

I hope to be able to show and convince the reader that the conception of constrained governing and governments is a viable and attractive perspective to defend private and public freedom, and resist various sorts of tyrannies, of whatever kind, without the need of an axiomatic and deductive method. Sophocles and Shakespeare are reliable and excellent cicerones along this journey, providing not only political theorists but ordinary people with sound insights and questions that we all need to be asked once or more during our political life.

## NOTES

1. William A. Galston, "The Populist Challenge to Liberal Democracy." *Journal of Democracy* 2 (2018): 5–19.

2. Ibid., 7–8.

3. Paul Sagar, "The State without Sovereignty: Authority and Obligation in Hume's Political Philosophy." *Opinion of Mankind* (Oxford, Princeton: Princeton University Press, 2018), 103–38, 132.

4. Ibid., 134.

5. Ibid., 138.

6. Sheldon Wolin, "Political Theory as a Vocation." *The American Political Science Review* 4 (1969): 1062–82, 1077.

# Chapter 1

# *Antigone* and *Measure for Measure*
## *The (Re)Birth of Government*

## INTRODUCTION

In this chapter, I invite readers to consider and reflect on two masterpieces of Western literature and observe how governments operate in them. There is a growing awareness of the importance and usefulness of literary works for political theory.[1] Some classic themes of political thinking have always been heavily influenced by explorations done by novelists, for instance: the best example is perhaps utopia and dystopia. The difficult relationship between moral and political principles and values has been widely studied by help of drama, especially the ancient classics. For the systematic study of governments and governing, however, plays are rarely used, though there are partial exceptions. *Antigone* and *Measure for Measure* are arguably such exceptions, though their potential has perhaps not been fully exploited yet. The way they are to be analyzed here is the one I outlined in "Introduction." They serve as a proxy to the pre-political perspective of anyone who begins to reflect on how governments are and should be constrained.

It is worth nothing that the opposite direction has been also suggested, namely, to study canonical texts of political philosophy as literary text, of course, not for the sake of entertainment but in order to unearth more profound lessons for philosophy.[2] In the next chapter, I shall discuss the political theoretical importance of imagination in more detail: the imaginative force of Hobbes' theory, in particular, has already been noted by recent commentators.

Understandably, some genres have proved to be especially suitable to explore problems of political philosophy: novels (in classic times: eposes) and plays, especially but not exclusively tragic ones, provide the better framework for this than do other genres. The term "exploration" is key here. Of course, any literary genre can find some place within politics (poems have been one of the most memorable—because easily memorizable—carriers of national and other political sentiments) but theoretical reflection needs more spacious room, which only novels and plays can offer. Further, dramas have a special advantage over novels: they are more capable of reaching out to and inviting the audience or the readers to ponder about the issues discussed by the characters, giving them not only a more personal stake but more success-fully implying that political thinking is more tightly connected to acting than many other types of philosophical reflection.

In analyzing the *Antigone*, my method will be a close reading without political theoretical preconceptions, yet with a contemporary mind that is interested in learning about what Sophocles might suggest as the primary and internal causes of the fall of Creon's government. If a government falls for internal reasons (no war, foreign conquest, or natural catastrophe brought it down)—and of course, what constitutes a "fall" is itself a matter up for dispute—then we have a prima facie assumption that the cause of the fall had to do something with its own actions. Further, it can be hypothesized that some of its actions were wrong for having transgressed borders that they should not have had. It is this hypothesis that serves as a guiding light for the forthcoming reading.

In the case of *Measure for Measure*, my method will be a bit different. Shakespeare's play is not a tragedy, though Angelo's government does "fall" in some sense, yet the Duke's governments (both the pre-Angelonian and the post-Angelonian) do not, hence asking the questions relevant to political theory need a more solid theoretical grounding. Order and disorder are in themselves common and easily intelligible concepts, in political theory, espe-cially when it comes to founding a government and justifying political rule, these concepts should be better explained. I shall use Hobbes and Mandeville as guides here. However, the distinction between order and disorder remains an important beacon for understanding what governing means to ordinary citizens as well, and for this reason, it constitutes an inherent constraint of what governments are supposed and permitted to do.

## ANTIGONE

The *Antigone* is one of the most famous tragedies in the world. Especially since the Romantic age, Antigone has gradually become a symbol of indi-vidual resistance, up to the point that a poet like Goethe would have censured some lines of the play contradicting this picture (Antigone: "Had I been a mother of children, and my husband been dead and rotten, I would not have taken this weary task upon me against the will of the city" 961–964).[3] Others, like Hegel, render Antigone a bearer of private ethics as opposed to the public and political ethos of the polis.[4] Post-Hegelian criticism, however, often disputes this distinction. There is now a wide variety of interpretations that make their own favorite distinctions or argue that it is exactly the shifts between distinctions that dynamizes the tragedy: I shall refer to those relevant here later. The *Antigone* has thus become a text used for testing various philosophical positions, and the strength and convincing force of other disciplines, most notably of psychoanalysis. But it is also arguable that Sophocles himself put his own political and moral ideas into different mouths in the tragedy, and that the core problem of how to bury the dead might have sounded somewhat obsolete to the Athenian audience of the time, too.

Interpretations are, thus, a legion and most of them contribute something interesting to the discourse of their own day. I shall use the text to understand more accurately how governments evolve because that is my concern, which, as I argued in the Introduction, has its own current context. The basic idea is that the multidimensional nature of government becomes discernible by a close reading of the play from the political theoretical perspective. Hence, the reading I offer here puts Creon into the center: Antigone recedes somewhat to the background.[5] The main message will be that the *Antigone* makes a surprisingly complex case for how a government should and could be constrained and it shows how the particular limits within which power is exerted legitimately are transgressed, causing the collapse of the government.

## Creon's History

The *Antigone* is the concluding part of the Theban trilogy, though it was written first, and the first part (*Oedipus the King*) perhaps more than a decade later. Sophocles seems to have been deeply and enduringly fascinated by and concerned with the issues raised by the rise and fall of the Labdacus Dynasty. Since the order of the plays in terms of their genesis and the historical sequence of the events told by them do not correspond to one another, it would be futile to seek for a philosophically coherent conception of the main issues (not to speak about the limits of expounding a "conception" in the form of a drama). This makes it easier to skip over the question of how *Antigone* should be read in the light of the other two plays: it could and should stand in and for itself. However, since the myth that formed the raw material for the three dramas had existed in its entirety before Sophocles began to write, we cannot simply dismiss the question of coherence. For instance, the figure of Creon is centrally important in the *Antigone*. He is the only person who (or whose image) undergoes a profound change: entering as a right-minded, well-trained, though a bit harsh ruler, becoming a tyrant, and falling miserably in the end. The Creon of the *Oedipus the King* is different: he is an obedient and loyal subject of the king who must suffer his sovereign's unjust suspicion. Even his life is in danger when Oedipus who begins to rage against everybody guesses that a plot is underway to subvert his rule, with Creon involved in it. Then, in *Oedipus at Colonus*, Creon is an envoy of the polis demanding the return of the king to the outskirts of the city (but not allowing to enter it), and to achieve this purpose he attempts to kidnap Antigone. The blackmail attempt is hindered by Theseus, the king of Athens. Creon is ruthless here, but not selfish: he represents, defends, and tries to enforce the interests of his city.

Is it possible that the later Sophocles thought that Creon's character and behavior in the *Antigone* needs some further explanation? And if yes, then can we absolutely disregard the later play when we try to understand the former one? In any case, it is possible, I submit, to look upon Creon in the *Antigone* as a character who has a history, though to be told only later, which is especially pertinent to the problem of his conception of government.[6] By any means, Creon was witness to the rise and fall of Oedipus, the king of Thebes whose tragedy surpassed human dimensions. Later he represented the city on a difficult diplomatic mission, though he failed to achieve his purpose; and then defended it with his fellow citizens against Polyneices. It is always to be remembered, though, that all these figures are members of a doomed the family to which he, as husband (brother-in-law, uncle), also belonged. This made it even more necessary and urgent to emphasize the complete rebooting of the government, to found it anew.

## Creon's Government: The Birth

Thus, as Creon first enters, we may guess that Sophocles had already thought of him as someone with a history in former government of Oedipus, and an experience with governing (he was—or will be in the *Oedipus the King*—also the envoy to Apollo's temple entrusted with the mission of enquiring about the causes of Thebes's unfortune). He holds positions in the era marked by the two brothers' feuds. Nonetheless, that government and those times are over, all male heirs to the throne are dead, except for him. He enters, then, if not triumphantly but with great self-confidence, outlining his program and his philosophy of government.

His first words of praising the gods who have "shaken" the city but "brought her through again to safety" (180–181) are religious in form but rather perfunctory, appearing to be mere lip service to the gods. Creon immediately gets to real business, first, by settling any questions regarding the legitimacy of his authority. He announces that no one else but him has the right to the throne of Thebes. There is, however, something portentous about his stressing the fact the "here I am, holding all authority and the throne, in virtue of kinship with the dead" (191–192). Being a kin to the dead is a tie that may become a burden in the future, though presently it eases his accession to the throne greatly. Ties to the dead are sometimes difficult loosen and eschew when it proves necessary. Creon seems to sense this because he drops the issue immediately, as quickly as he left the gods and their world at the beginning of his address.

So lest anyone may think that ancestral legitimacy is all that matters, Creon continues with words that must have sounded familiar and surely sympathetic to the Athenian audience: "It is impossible to know any man—I mean his soul, intelligence, and judgment—until he shows his skill in rule and law" (193–195). These are heavyweight political words (skill, rule, and law) and unconditional promises made in awareness of every human capacity (soul, intelligence, and judgment). As was argued, even though the *Oedipus the King* was written much later, the idea that governing is also sort of an exploratory endeavor by which a man can come to the full consciousness of his abilities and others can also know him only in this process was present in the *Antigone* as well. It is in politics, in leadership that the old counsel—nosce te ipsum—can be practiced. Oedipus had to learn awful things about himself: Has he ever reached knowledge? Was the act of blinding himself a symbol of having gained wisdom? Or rather a desperate mirroring of the unfathomable and invisible (blind?) "knowledge" only gods can have? Whatever conclusion we are inclined to accept, Creon's approach appears to be much more plausible and psychologically sound. Even if power tends to corrupt, a morally strong character can resist it, revealing its strength exactly by this resistance. Besides corruption (itself a very abstract notion), we do not know yet what dangers a politician must face, what temptations he must resist. Creon's words are thus, pleasing and right-minded as they may sound to the citizens of a democracy, still a bit hollow. He wishes to govern by rule and law, and he knows he will be known in virtue of them. But we need something more.

And Creon delivers, stating and solemnly announcing the supreme ruler must be fearless, never keeping "his tongue under lock and key", (200) adding that "anyone thinking another man more a friend than his own country, I rate him nowhere" (202–204). A good leader, Creon proclaims, must be courageous in defense of the city, and the supreme principle of his judgment (laws and decisions) should be based on the good of the city. From these principles, he derives and by them he justifies his well-known decree about honoring Eteocles' body and dishonoring Polyneices' body. We are, thus, given the principle of government (the public good) and the ultimate measure of virtuous leadership, namely, courage and tenacity in speaking up for and defending this principle. This, again, must have resonated well with the audience in the Athenian theater, since that was the baseline for every "demagogue," that is, for anyone aspiring to be a leader in a democratic government. Fear of speech amounts to silence, silence hides second thoughts, and second thoughts are subversive of democracy: contemporary democratic theory is no less fascinated with undistorted communication and free speech than Creon was. At least in words.

Creon's first speech is, thus, impeccable. He takes care to justify his rule by what we would call traditional legitimacy but immediately hands over authority to the public, to the city ("you shall know me by my deeds"). Finally, he establishes a political measure for everyone (courage to speak) and the principle of government (the good of the city). By these standards and principles, the institution of government becomes a joint issue of the citizens and their leaders and the supreme leader. It would be difficult to find a more concise and appealing conception of what leadership and governing consists in.[7] The lesson is that government is born with limits, in a certain language and with a topical unity. The government is limited insofar as its business (the good of the city) is a restricted one, and that there are publicly accessible and controllable measures and principles by which it is bound. The "language" is itself a sort of constraint, because in matters of government, there are no secrets, no magic, no special connection to the gods. Creon speaks about the providential outcome of the civil war: though he wishes to honor Eteocles' body, it is not the body but the person and his merits that is important. Further, it is the person as a citizen and not as the member of the accursed family that counts: Creon seems to be satisfied with the fate having meted out the same end to both brothers. On a positive account, the language is restricted to law, rule, and leadership that, in turn, gives a unified character to the government.

Athenians were well aware that ancient Thebes was not a democracy, but this makes the point even more forceful. Governing, no matter whether democratically, aristocratically, or monarchically, has publicly controllable standards, is related to the quality of leadership, and is intrinsically a public affair.

## Antigone's Challenge: Political Theology

Open issues settled, principles determined, and measures and constraints established: Creon's next step is to proclaim his law about honoring those who have fallen in defense of the city. What else could have been more honorable and worthy of respect than dying for the polis, the community of citizens? The highest good must be contrasted with the lowest evil, namely, assaulting the community. Notwithstanding the fact (probably known to everybody though not explained in the play) that Eteocles broke the promise to share the throne with his brother who demanded justice, a war launched against one's own city is absolutely inacceptable. This is Creon's justice and the Athenians were in all probability in agreement with him.

As everyone knows, here is where Antigone's claim intrudes. She does not dispute Creon's right to the throne and his right to rule. She does not directly call into question the principles Creon cites. What she refers to are the unknown and unfathomable laws of the gods:

> I did not believe / your proclamation had such power to enable / one who will someday die to override / God's ordinances, unwritten and secure. / They are not of today and yesterday; / they live forever; none knows when first they were. (496–501)

Creon's reaction is summary, but his motives and arguments are complex. What Antigone represents is, in the first place, the past, the obscure, and rights of the dead, the rights of death. Apparently, she wants to bury the dead yet thereby she also wishes to make an ugly and chaotic past be remembered. Burying both brothers means that Thebes will continue to be tightly bound with the Labdacus Dynasty with all its bloody history that resulted in civil war, making the inner feud of the family a menace of whole Thebes. This would subvert Creon's whole founding act based on his moral principles and political ideals. In Vernant's interpretation, we are witnessing a clash between two conceptions of religion and its influence on politics:

> Conflict between Antigone and Creon . . . is not an opposition between pure religion, represented by the girl, and total irreligion, represented by Creon, or between a religious spirit and a political one. Rather it is between two different types of religious feeling: One is a family religion, purely private and confined to the small circle of close relatives, the philoi, centered on the domestic hearth and the cult of the dead; the other is a public religion in which the tutelary gods of the city eventually become confused . . . with the supreme values of the state.[8]

Bonnie Honig makes a similar claim, though she thinks that the bedrock of the conflict is a clash between Antigone representing the old Homeric ethic, which Athens does not recognize any more, and Creon's absolutist, but in its foundation, democratic ideal of politics:

> Creon on this reading represents not sovereignty run amok, or not just that, but more pointedly the fifth-century democratic polis that appropriated funerary practice for polis needs. [Criticizing M. Nussbaum, she writes further that] [r]eading procedurally, interpreters such as Martha Nussbaum see no evidence of democratic leaning in Creon, who after all does not deliberate nor consult with the people or the elders and is hard pressed to take counsel from anyone. But Creon metonymizes democracy substantively. His ban on lamentation and his repeated emphasis on the harms of individuality represent the fifth-century democratic view.[9]

It is easy to argue, then, that the conflict can be interpreted in contemporary political theory as being between to political theological conceptions, for what is at stake is, in J. Strauss's words, "to imagine the origins and limits of the political state." The *Antigone* can thus be read

> as a struggle to understand the shape, limits, and meaning of the city at one of its defining moments, a reflection on the rise of the state from the viewpoint of a privileged representative and at a time when the polis was just emerging from its birth phase.[10]

Antigone's claim (however implicit or virtual it remains, ever to herself) is very strong. What she does amounts to calling Creon to revoke the political theology that underpins his philosophy of governing. His political theology was a sort of a *theologia naturalis*: the gods are nothing more but the guarantors of the authority of the laws made in accordance with the publicly accepted norms of morality. Now accepting *her* political theology would be tantamount to the continuation of governing by vague and obscure laws, "unwritten" albeit "secure."

On the one hand, contemporary readers may indeed think that the divine law to which Antigone refers and in defense of which she dies was widely shared and respected in Sophocles' time. Religion was integral to the lives of all citizens of the polis. When the gods punish the defiant Creon severely, the divine law seems to be vindicated. Later, in *Oedipus the King*, we have even stronger religious themes: the epidemic is inflicted on Thebes by Apollo who demands purification. Finally, in *Oedipus at Colonus*, we have the king being transmitted or transposed into another world, in his strangely personal apocalypse. The gods never appear in these plays, yet it is they who rule the world and all human affairs and on whom the fate of the city depends. Notwithstanding the secular political democracy of Athens, immortalized by Pericles, the Athenians themselves were deeply religious. The *Antigone* must have been a powerful reminder of the importance of their own religious devotion, piety, and feelings.

On the other hand, many commentators, some of them cited earlier, contend that Sophocles (and his Athenian audience) seem to have been suspicious of such religious explanations and contextualization of events.[11] Challenged on theological issues, however, Creon has no choice but to defend his views by similar arguments. Hence, he cites the gods, too, claiming that one cannot imagine them to be unjust. His theology, as was pointed out, is purely moral and natural, reminiscent of the later Scholastic-rationalist, and later natural law-based, and even later the rationalist-deistic Enlightenment theory: the gods (or the God) can and must be assumed to have consented to and approved of the principles of morality as common human minds can conceive them (as their Creator). Is that sufficient to counter Antigone's unwritten but secure laws? Sophocles gives no final clue or answer. Nonetheless, the play is a powerful reminder for any government that theology, or commonly shared theological views, however obscure or even secular (non-religious) they may be, are a fundamental challenge to the justification of its legitimacy. The sympathy for Antigone may be an emotional response to her heroism, courage, innocence. But partly it stems from the inherent rightness attributed to her cause, namely, that the dead deserve a proper treatment. We may be less concerned with the sacredness of dead body today, yet however secular our world may be, where certain religious customs and traditions seem to have lost much of their sacred nature, violations of symbols, for instance, those that are strongly linked with national feelings, may be equally relevant to determining what a government is allowed to do.

## The Fundamental Boundary: Life and Death

Even if we are not particularly worried about how the state and its bureaucracy treats the dead today (though some decency and respect is generally expected), the state's authority over life and death remains, understandably, a central issue in modern politics, too. The *Antigone*'s topic is a dead body, yet the stake is the state's right to add more bodies to the dead. In that respect, all governments that claim that right (including modern ones) extend their authority over death and, in a crucial sense, desire to overcome it. In J. Strauss' view,

> it would seem that Creon, as representative of the *gegrammenoi*, or written laws of the state, had prevailed, historically at least, over his niece and the dark, unrecorded mutterings of the dead.[12]

If we consider the trilogy as a unity, then it simply tells the story of an old, mythical dynasty dying and slowly perishing from the face of the earth. And with them, all their problems of purity and impurity, curse and blessing, secrecy and mystery, uncanniness and murkiness, theology and rituals, incest and suicide, longing for death and for fame. As many commentators have pointed out, this is also an old aristocratic society vanishing and a new, democratic society emerging.[13] Was the play intended to be an educative work, a posthumous tribute to the dead, at the same time, their final burial in the hearts still remembering of the heroic past?

On this reading, Creon's tragedy consists in nothing more but that he was caught by the daemons of the sinking world, a revenge of Laius via Oedipus via Antigone via Haemon, his inability to set himself free of the old familial ties. Creon does not die but becomes petrified like Lot's wife in the Bible who clung to the old city. Unlike Oedipus who, though in exile, still had the magical power to curse, Creon becomes a ghost as it were, a living memory of an age when gods made the decisions and *governed*, by impenetrable principles and codes, the world of humans. His rejection of Antigone's political theology was without credit, the curse of the Labdacid Dynasty reached and caught him.

However, nothing of this invalidates his principles. His political theology is sound. The old mythical sort of government must have been already alien and long gone to Sophoclean Athens. The gods had by then already retired and were necessary to explain only the past. Notwithstanding pious practices, rituals, and their emotional importance (remember the uproar caused by mutilation of the Hermae in Athens and the political consequences), mystery and magic were gradually being removed from governments. Put very succinctly, with the fall of Creon, Thebes is finally liberated for a different life. Antigone dies and hers is a tragic and heroic death, whereas Creon does not commit suicide, nor calls for any further heroic action, does not invoke any god as Oedipus did (calling Apollon the author of his misery) though his grief is as excessive Antigone's whom he chastised for that. Bonnie Honig concludes, therefore, that Creon remains committed to

> his sovereign mission to wean Thebes from vengeance and end cycles of violence. On this reading, Creon, who seems to be utterly destroyed, does not quite lose himself. He does not yield to the passions he sees as most destabilizing to the city and so he ends the play as he began, pressing himself into service on behalf of the public good, modeling what he now sees as the appropriate comportment in mourning for Theban citizens.[14]

Despite all tragic losses, Creon's tragedy has a liberating effect. Freedom for governing presupposes freedom from the gods.

However, matters are more complicated than this reading has it. The historical and social readings have their convincing force with regard to the *Antigone*, but the problem remains. Contemporary political theory admits the importance of political theology. The influence of religious thinking has not waned entirely. National sentiments, fears, resentments, identities, and old customs exert a constant, sometimes spectacular influence over politics. The muttering dead may stay with us as fearsome political enemies. We should trust Sophocles and consider him making an ever-relevant political point about governing a religious society.

Let us therefore reconsider Creon's law and decision not to permit the burial of Polyneices. The justification is clear (good and bad, right and wrong must be distinguished from one another and judgments must be made accordingly), yet the target is somehow unnatural. The target is the body and not the person.

We have very limited access to the Athenian minds of Sophocles' age, but it seems they must have been flexible enough to understand things from different angles: the co-existence of comedies and tragedies is a good indicator. It would have been very easy to write the *Antigone* as a comedy, with, say, the sisters bribing the guard or guards or steal the corpse or use some cunning tricks. There were divine trickster figures in abundance to justify such an action for more pious eyes.[15] Notwithstanding the rightness of Creon's principles and the soundness of his approach to governing, he seems to be developing some inordinate and excessive preoccupation with the corpse of Polyneices. In one way, for sure, Antigone herself appears to be excessive in that respect but at least she has her own very dark and troubled history, from her own birth to the deaths of her family members.[16] But whence Creon's obsession with the body?[17]

Since Michel Foucault's explorations in the history of the body and especially since he introduced the concept of biopolitics, the interest in the relationship between political power and the human body has been growing. Classic texts have served well this interest because many of them do put the body into the focus, from the Iliad (Hector's body being desecrated by Achilles) to the Athenian dramas. In the *Antigone*, we have three bodies: two dead ones and another one, that of the heroine, also destined to become a dead one.[18] She must suffer death but in an unusual fashion. Creon sentences her to death but at the same time wants to keep his own hand and the public hands pure of blood. Antigone "must" execute herself. His handling of bodies is, therefore, inconsistent. He both claims power of them and then recoils again. Is this because he feels and fears to enter some terra incognita? But how can one draw the boundaries of something one does not know? And it is not just Antigone over whose body, and consequently, over whose life he does not really decide. Leaving Polyneices's corpse out there, beyond the walls of the city, for the nature (dogs and birds) to consume it, amounts to both dishonoring it (an act within the city) and actually not doing anything about it (a nonaction outside of the city). No active desecration occurs, only a guard is left there to observe what happens. And as it happens, the body is covered with dust first by unknown hands (was it Ismene? some commentators speculate she was),[19] and secondly, by Antigone. Creon is outraged. But his rage is in some sense a relief. It is a relief to have a living person to replace the body of the deceased one, over whom no earthly ruler has power. Creon has entered an unknown terrain and he was frightened. He retired and now he has someone to sentence to death. It is not the corpse that matters anymore, thanks to the gods, but a living body. The inconsistency is not solved, however. Antigone's action is the test of *his* power, yet it stems from an unforeseeable event. The stubbornness and revolt of Oedipus' daughter is a much-needed and god-sent occasion to strengthen his power. And yet again: Is Antigone not a gifted gift, so to speak, touched by the gods whom Creon did not want to hear about? He tested the gods and won; and yet he is already poisoned with superstition. And he begins his transformation into something completely different from what he wanted to be.

Creon's fall repeats the fall of Oedipus. But while Oedipus belonged to the aristocratic tradition according to which the well-being of the city depended on the goodwill of the gods that, in turn, depended on largely mysterious past events and actions beyond human control, Creon's rule was meant and intended to be a preparation for a democratic government. His skills and character, as well as clearly formulated principles were essential to good government and to achieving public good. But he was inconsistent. He wanted to draw a clear line, a boundary between his city and the outside world, claiming that the "ship of the state" needs to be protected against the elements of nature, yet he extended his rule outside of the city both literally and symbolically when he ordered to leave the body outside and have Antigone be cast out.[20] That was against his own principles. He was unwilling to touch the dead but became preoccupied with them, making them inadvertently central to his secular rule. There is, of course, no general rule how *not to* transgress the boundaries of the state, of the polity. The story of Creon's government does not tell us more than a general and perhaps "impractical rule" that one should beware oneself of the dead, of what is outside of the city. But the dead live in a negative way, their most important message being precisely the fact of life and *its* boundary, namely, death. This is nothing more but the idea of constraint, not as a constitutionally or legally, not even politically or philosophically definable concept but rather as a problem. Contemporary debates on abortion, euthanasia, the claims of past generations for justice, and the like, all of which concern questions of life and death, as well the inscrutable intentions and motivations of the departed, demonstrate that Creon's dilemmas, and the splits that he was unable to bridge, are very much ours. Governing means to be able to manage and literally survive these splits, rather than solve them, and the only lesson that can be drawn from the *Antigone* appears to be that governing is massively constrained by the fears and hopes that our bodily life carries.

## The Political Constraints

Creon's "address to the city" is, as I argued, a sovereign monarch's political program, yet it contains very strong self-constraining elements. What we are witnessing in the play is how Creon transgresses each of his standards: his character, his principles, and the public good.

*First,* Creon's ambitions to prove a virtuous leader are all frustrated. He resolves to be a tenacious and brave leader but—in Aristotle's terms—he deters from the middle route and falls victim to the extremes. This a classic explanation of his fall, one that is well summarized by R. Rehm:

> Creon participates in the canonical boundary violation that the Greeks called hubris (going too far), which does violence to the order of things and is punished accordingly. Although the word is never applied to Creon in the play, he twice accuses Antigone of this outrage . . . for "transgressing the laws that had been laid down" by him (481), and for threatening his sense of masculine control, "for now I am no man, but she is a man" (484). Whatever Antigone's challenge to Creon's law and authority, it does not extend to the realm of the gods. Creon, however, assumes the dangerous status of a theomachos (battler against the gods), indicated by the natural and supernatural responses to Creon's edict. The tyrant's fall establishes all too clearly that the deities above and below are appalled at his actions and exact their vengeance accordingly.[21]

It is instructive to observe how Creon, almost immediately after finishing his grand speech, reacts to the news brought by the sentry who, in great excitement and fear, reports about the violation of his ruler's order. The Chorus comments that the circumstances may indicate divine intervention. First, Creon can hardly control his rage, and begins to talk about his authority being already challenged by some muttering citizens, and that his enemies paid someone to perform the ritual. Greed and resistance, according to Creon, are the motives behind this action; it has nothing to do with divine powers. Then he suspects the sentry's involvement in it, an idea that occurred to Oedipus as well, when Creon was the one under suspicion. It seems that the logic and concerns of power make an immediate effect on the leader's psyche, slowly starting to change his character. The sentry leaves with saying (aside) that he would never return for fear of his life.

Next, Antigone is showed in and accused of having committed the forbidden act. Creon's interrogation of her is fair. Apparently, he regained his composure—he is now an impartial judge. However, Antigone's fearless speech of defense in which she (as was argued) leads a full assault on the political theological foundations of Creon's conception of law and order, puts Creon out of his emotional balance and transforms him into a masculine beast for a moment: "I swear I am no man and she the man / if she can win this and not pay for it" (528–29). Then he overcomes his emotions once more and tries to defend his principles, referring once again the difference between what is good and what is bad. However, to Antigone's steadfast defiance, Creon has, again, nothing to respond but that "When I am alive no woman shall rule" (578).

It is not necessary to follow and comment on Creon's transformation and fall into hubris to the very last moment. Upon hearing Teiresias's words announcing death in his house, Creon seeks for comfort in his own character:

My mind is all bewildered. To yield is terrible. / But by opposition to destroy
my very being / with a self-destructive curse must also be reckoned / in what is
terrible. (1168–71)

Yielding is terrible because it would amount to his losing what he thinks is
his courage. He does yield but then his own authority will have crushed him.
However, should he have decided not to yield, nothing would have remained
of him, hence the reference to the destruction of his being.[22] What we see
now is how moral virtues become idolized, thereby distorted and take over
the rule: what happens to Creon is a peculiar but psychologically well-estab-
lished phenomenon. A character becomes a mask that captures the politician.
Virtues like tenacity or perseverance change into masters to be served rather
than goods that serve one's happiness. But that is the nature of power: it
consumes, it devours, it absorbs the virtues. They are no more effective constraints. The lesson is somewhat surprising: an effective constraint on government, at least its personal-leadership aspects, is not a sort of moral education
that politicians are well-advised to undergo, with the aim of forging a character capable of resisting corruption, fear, and chaos. Rather, it is perhaps
better to prepare leaders, or they are better advised to prepare themselves to
be attentive to the temptations of virtue ethics, lest they fall prey to the idol-
ization of virtues. In chapter 3, the problem of how the character is related to
politics and governing will be analyzed in more detail. To anticipate the main
argument: the lack of self-control that becomes so conspicuous in Creon's
case arises not from his overconfidence of his own moral character traits but
partly from his desperate attempts *to practice* them. He believes to know
himself, but his knowledge is seriously deficient: politics does not help, on
the contrary, it diverts him from self-knowledge without which he is unable to
govern himself. It is very telling that Creon never refers to sophrosyne, or the
virtue of moderation, that is essentially related to knowledge, including self-
knowledge: all the masculine, outward-oriented virtues of courage, tenacity,
truthfulness remain hollow and sham without being rooted in and guided by
self-knowledge, the nature of which remains to discussed later.

*Secondly*, Creon wishes to hold up Thebes's good as the ultimate standard
of his government. On this account, again, his failure is instructive. The
Athenians must have applauded the idea, yet Sophocles draws ambiguous
consequences from it. There are two crucial points made in the drama.

The first is related to free speech. Creon declared that as a leader he cannot
and should not keep "his tongue under lock and key." The virtue of courage,
required of the leader, implies taking the risk of speaking. For speaking is
an inherently interpersonal, and in ancient Athens, a crucial political issue.
Plato's philosophy and Thucydides's history of the Peloponnesian War
are the memorable testimonies to this. Sophocles joins the consensus. In a

democracy, what Creon demands for himself is expected of every citizen. Significantly, in the first encounter between him and Antigone, she confronts Creon with the news that the people of Thebes keep "their mouths shut for the fear of you" (556). Creon disbelieves. A bit later however, Haemon makes a similar, though more poignant argument in defending his fiancée, bluntly saying, "The entire people of Thebes says no to that" [i.e. that Antigone is wrong] (793) to which his father retorts: "Should the city tell me how I am to rule them?" (794). Creon is of course suspicious about the objectivity and truthfulness of Antigone's and Haemon's reports, and the dramaturgy is excellent, but the political point must have been straightforward to the audience. Fear and silence make for a bad government because the only voice that remains is that of the ruler who will have no other choice but to listen to his own soliloquys. Freedom of speech becomes *his* freedom of speaking but not communicating which would require partners.

Once again, Sophocles is ingenious in connecting the problem of freedom immediately to the fatal political mistake Creon makes. Not allowing to tell the city him how to rule it, Creon is led to proclaim in a rhetorical question that "Is not the city thought to be ruler's?" (800). This is where the political abyss opens and Creon falls into it. This is the thought and the voice of the tyrant.

Commentators who are interested in the issue of tyranny being "discussed" by Sophocles tend to miss the real force of the argument. Martha Nussbaum, for instance, analyzes the dialogue or polemic between Creon and Haemon and contends that Haemon does not challenge Creon's political conception and philosophy (referring to the metaphor of the ship: "our pursuit of the good must devise ways to keep us safe from natural disaster") but draws a practical lesson from Creon's failure to listen: "it is important in pursuit of one's human ends, to remain open to the claims and pulls of the external, to cultivate flexible responsiveness, rather than rigid hardness." Therefore, Creon should have possessed the virtue of "practical wisdom that bends responsively to the shape of the natural world, accommodating itself to, giving due recognition to, its complexities."[23] (The natural world is an extension of the metaphor of the ship; what is complex is the city and its citizens.) Thus, Creon's failure flow from his disrespecting the non-political needs and factual world of Thebes—in modern language, the private sphere. Valerie Reed comments: "in Nussbaum's reading, the flaw in Creon's character lies precisely here, in his inability to acknowledge the possibility that oikos and polis both represent separate, legitimate yet conflicting, positions."[24]

Obviously, however, neither Antigone nor Haemon represent the private sphere of the city. Although Antigone cites love as her guide, that is an inherently political sort of love directed to her fallen brother (the enemy of the city). Both are public personalities, close relatives of the king, and as Creon

senses, they are the tests of the impartiality of his rule. Analyses of the tragedy have noted that the proper burial of the dead was the job of male citizens,
hence Antigone's action was itself a break with the customs. In any movement of hers, there is a political aspect, perhaps despite her own intentions:

> Every turn that Antigone makes toward her home is also a turn away from
> it; every act that she performs on behalf of her oikos duty also acts, in some
> sense, against that duty. And in this way, she embodies a different kind of
> Unheimlichkeit—a radical uncertainty, and not just a perpetual becoming
> homely, that is suggested throughout the play and cemented by the singularity
> of her death.[25]

Both cite the public opinion of Thebes against Creon, willingly taking the
political risk of contradicting the sovereign leader of the city. Thus, the idea
of Antigone and Haemon protecting the rights of the family, of privacy, of
the non-political, is hardly defensible.

Therefore, the implicit constraint of Creon's government is inherent to the
political construction of it. Both Antigone and Haemon speak their minds,
and by implication, everyone else is supposed to do so. No government likes
contradiction, especially those that govern by commands to which every
government is inclined that conceives of itself as a ship navigating in rough
waters. Silencing the voice of citizens has, however, the inevitable consequence not of turning against them (*their* good is still *the* public good) but by
making them non-human beings. To Creon's outcry ("Is not the city thought
to be the ruler's?") Haemon (Sophocles) gives the perfect reply: "You would
be a fine dictator of a desert" (801). Thereby he nails the point: a tyrant
always rules a desert, never a city.

Besides the point about free speech, without which the city becomes a
desert, Creon's adherence to the principles of morality is also subverted and
a demolished. He declared to base his order of honoring/dishonoring the two
brothers on the principle of good and bad understood as being for and against
Thebes, implying that the city is intrinsically good because the gods dwell
in it, and she is protected by them. It would certainly be too much to expect
a modern ethical or political-ethical conception being on Creon's mind and
moving him, but it is undeniable that he is at pains to justify his law and his
actions by clear reasons, accessible and acceptable to any citizen. On these
grounds, he is challenged, once again, by Haemon.

When Creon meets him for the first time, his son approaches him with
words of respect, yet his father is visibly (or audibly) anxious and feels
compelled to defend his decision in a lengthy address, without having been
questioned in the first place. Creon seems to expect, however, that personal
love is one of the strongest emotions, something that he cannot overcome by

arguments. He must prevail, nonetheless. His strategy is to convince his son about the importance of power, rather than of his principles. First, he warns him of the possibility of having a bad wife: "the embrace grows cold / when an evil woman shares your bed and home" (704–705). Shortly after this thought, however, he slips into the rhetoric of power: "For he who is in his household a good man / will be found a just man, too, in the city" (715–716). A just ruler is, according to this argument, a man in control of his household. To make him understand the logic and imperatives of power, Creon must, however, abandon the idea of ruling by principles (of good and bad, just and unjust): "The man the city sets up in authority / must be obeyed in small things and in just / but also in their opposites" (720–722). "The opposites" is sometimes rendered more explicitly as "unjust." What counts, in the end, is obedience, something that Creon goes on to extol almost fervently. One may or may not agree with his conclusions, or perhaps admit the realism of power that must be used once reasons prove weak, not because they are senseless but because they are hard to accept; nonetheless, giving up reasons and reasoning amounts to the betrayal of the belief in the self-evidence and compelling force of principles. Betrayal is, however, also a sort of transgression, something that others—like Haemon—can notice immediately. They may themselves be traitors to their own principles (Haemon's reasoning is also either inconsistent or mere rhetoric, his reasons may serve his own personal interests), yet any government and its rulers must reckon with the fact that abandoning or suspending principles and switching to naked force is a dangerous transgression. It is revolting, no less than the revolt they may wish to put down. As a matter of fact, Haemon himself nowhere challenges his father's principles. What he does, and in one sense successfully, is bringing the confrontation to the utmost point, sacrificing his life and thereby demolishing his father. The logic of force is merciless: Creon hoped for "obedient sons" whom they can take pride from, because "if a man have sons that are no use to him, / what can one say of him but that he has bred / so many sorrows to himself, laughter to his enemies?" (699–701). Now Haemon *was* obedient but the price was devastating. No government can defend itself against self-destructing subjects.

## TO WRAP UP

Political theorists appreciate the political thoughts of the *Antigone* more than ever. In the context of how governments are born, grow and decay, or fall, the play is especially relevant for the reasons discussed earlier. It teaches us, first, that no matter how well, admirably, convincingly the rule of a government is justified, it is open to various challenges. One such challenge is the very act of justification: there is an inherent constraint in it because it has, want it or not, a transformative ambition that Rousseau expresses in his characteristically sharp, poignant, eloquent but very controversial form in *On the Social Contract* where he discusses the role of the legislator who "must deny man his own forces in order to give him forces that are alien to him and that he cannot make use of without the help of others."[26] I shall return to Rousseau and his claim; the issue is that no matter in what terms Creon justifies his rule, or how morally and rationally sound his principles are, it remains true that people may have essentially and fundamentally different conceptions of how that rule should be justified. Inadvertently perhaps, Creon's hesitation about Antigone's fate is a testimony to this, and indirectly, to the constraints of his government. Death and life remain beyond the boundaries of any government the trespassing of which is always riskier than anything else. And finally, Creon falls short of his own standards: he cannot understand his virtues; as Oedipus blinds himself as a punishment, Creon deafens himself and becomes an incapable ruler; and he loses his faith in his own principles. This is his final mistake for which he pays the greatest price.

## *MEASURE FOR MEASURE*

*Measure for Measure* is perhaps less widely known than the *Antigone* is.[27] But it has been no less meticulously studied by scholars. There is hardly a line in it that has not figured in a prominent explanatory role in one or another interpretation. The play is usually called a problem play, and it is indeed intriguing in many respects, embarrassing and provocative; a most fertile soil for political philosophical reflections. As with Sophocles' play, my purpose is not to discuss other interpretations in detail but to make use of its own problems to highlight the issue of constrained governments.

A few words about the political context of the political problem of the play are perhaps in order. In *Measure for Measure*, Shakespeare relied not only on various similar sources (medieval morality plays, contemporary dramas, short stories taken from Boccaccio, even on a version of the famous d'Orco-Borgia story told in *The Prince* by Machiavelli)[28] but took inspiration from the actual and in some ways acute issues concerning James I' rule.[29] Uneasy feelings began to emerge about the new king early in his rule, though he himself took pains to make his intentions and principles of governing clear to his subjects in his treatise *Basilikon Doron*, a remarkable idea to mark the beginning of a new monarch's rule, but certainly in the spirit of Creon and his address from the throne of Thebes. And interestingly, Vincentio, the Duke of Vienna (his name is never mentioned in the play), is a beginner, at least in the sense that James was new to England (the Duke returns to build

Vienna politically). Beginning or re-founding government is thus a historically embedded problem for and in this play.

*Measure for Measure*, like the *Antigone*, is of course about a great variety of
other topics (mercy versus justice, forgiveness versus principledness, manipulation, providence, legitimacy, Puritan versus Anglican/Catholic morality,
social issues of the day, etc.), and it is, like so many of Shakespeare's other
political plays, inconclusive as far as its messages and lessons are concerned.[30] However, there can be little doubt about the centrality of the issue
of how to establish *order and government* and how to govern well, that is,
non-tyrannically yet efficiently.[31] Creon's problem and purpose was similar
as he was a new king; however, his background and the immediate political
situation was very different. He intended to restore the old order (that dis-
solved due to a bloody civil war) based on new political and moral, secular
foundations. *Measure for Measure* presents the problem of order much more
ambiguously. Nominally, it is about the establishment of a new government
by abolishing the old one, though with a twist: Angelo's government and
the Duke's government are both "new" with respect to the old. Shakespeare
manages to stage the problem twice, and eventually to draw a comparison
between the two new and the old governments. Each government's legitimacy
is strongly related to the problem of order and disorder. The meaning of order
is, however, controversial, to say the least. For there is no consensus about
whether there is a disorder in the first place (no civil war takes place before
the departure of the Duke); and if there is, what caused it; and since we witness how Angelo's government under the banner of restoring order becomes
the center of disorder, probably not against the will of the Duke, we may very
well doubt that the distinction is as handy as it first may appear.

Thus, the relationship of government and order is an even more contested
issue. The constraints of government are in this crucial respect murkier, yet
for this reason, theoretically more in the focus. Here I shall discuss only this
issue. Other, related problems such as the characters of Angelo and the Duke
as the political leaders are no less inherent problems for the constraining
of governments and they will be discussed in chapter 3. Although political
theory will be discussed properly in the next chapter, let me anticipate it by
citing Hobbes's and Mandeville's conceptions of order and disorder because
they will help us distinguish more clearly between possible readings of the
play. Moreover, these conceptions have the additional value of their (relative)
historical proximity to Shakespeare's times.

## Two Conceptions of Disorder

Thomas Hobbes's *Leviathan* was published almost half a century later that
Shakespeare's *Measure for Measure* had been written. In one of its most

famous and memorable passages, Hobbes offers a very dim view of society without government. This is the state of war. Without certainty of there being a government that protects the weak (in effect, everybody), Hobbes stresses that

> there is no place for Industry; because the fruit thereof is uncertain; and consequently no Culture of the Earth; no Navigation, nor use of the commodities that may be imported by Sea; no commodious Building; no Instruments of moving, and removing such things as require much force; no Knowledge of the face of the Earth; no account of Time; no Arts; no Letters; no Society.[32]

The point is here not the state of war conceived of as an original position but the fear of losing the blessings of civilization and civilized life, one that is worth living for humans. What Hobbes is concerned with is not the historical emergence of political order but the menace of its possible collapse. Disorder is basically about losses, hence by establishing government, we not only secure our bare lives but also—and perhaps more importantly—our property, our commodities, and all the goods that social cooperation produces. The constant fear we have toward one another has various roots, and Hobbes himself names glory-seeking, diffidence, competition as the major causes of distrust from which general fear arises. Fear does not disappear, however, once government is established, it is merely redirected toward disorder. Even within an established society, there is a generic and general fear that in the absence of government, civilization cannot survive.

Hobbes's practical conclusion is the need to establish a government whose competence and responsibility is almost unlimited. His conception entails that a government should be constantly observing obscure and latent causes of disorder (to use Edmund Burke's term)[33] within society. Promoting the well-being or the virtuous life of individuals, waging wars for glory and other more or less traditional aims of governing are secondary, if they are legitimate at all, as the ordinary business of governing is primarily about preventing social unrest, animosities, and hostilities among individuals and, worse, their factions. If there is a value that is to be promoted and defended as such, then it is order: the rest will follow, as the aforementioned quotation implies. Therefore, anticipating a point *Measure for Measure* seems to make: to enforce a sort of an anti-laxity moral legislation may be a necessary political step to buttress the idea of order and the trust in government.

The only constraint on the government as the representative of the Leviathan is the prohibition against making laws that threaten the lives of the subjects. This constraint is as obvious as only it can be. Those wary of Hobbes's conception and its potential consequences in justifying an omnipotent government can, therefore, point out the problem of how to prevent the government from inciting fear of disorder among the individuals. Should such an atmosphere be successfully created, as was the case in England (the most infamous case in point being the Guy Fawkes "conspiracy"), where plots against and miraculous savings of the monarch was somewhat of a routine,[34] the habeas corpus gets easily suspended, political trials and summary executions may become a normal business of running the government, and the criminal law may be amended with dubious clauses of political crimes. In the end, by way of evoking fear of disorder due to the possibility of anarchy (resulting, for instance, from a plot or a coup d'état), which justifies the category of political crime, the government may find itself to be the enemy to be feared most, and hence the source of disorder itself. Order and disorder, it seems, are by no means as neatly distinguishable in the Hobbesian conception as many would suppose. And Shakespeare's play is a dramatic testimony to this, as we shall see shortly. Almost another fifty years later, Bernard de Mandeville wrote his famous fable about the bees. Judged objectively,

> no Bees had better Government, More Fickleness, or less Content. They were not Slaves to Tyranny, Nor ruled by wild Democracy; But Kings, that could not wrong, because Their Power was circumscrib'd by Laws.[35]

Despite the rule of law, there is significant discontent within society. "Corruption boils and bubbles": this is how Shakespeare's Duke summarized the morals of Vienna a century ago. From a moral point of view, Mandeville's hive fares no better yet with a peculiar consequence:

> Every Part was full of Vice, the whole Mass a Paradice; Flatter'd in Peace, and fear'd in Wars They were th'Esteem of Foreigners, And lavish of their Wealth and Lives, The Ballance of all other Hives. Such were the Blessings of that State; Their Crimes conspired to make 'em Great.[36]

Then, the citizens of the hive cry out to the gods to put out sins and crimes, and Jove grants this to them. They can go on living virtuously. But virtuous life and living is also a poor one. The extreme discontent with moral disorder causes this Paradise to collapse, at least insofar as wealth and civilized life is concerned. Paradoxical as it may be, a certain (actually, rather high) degree of moral disorder is preferable to moral perfection, unless, we may add, it leads to political disorder and eventually to civil war.

Obviously, Mandeville's approach to disorder and its relation to governing is different from that of Hobbes. Whereas preventing disorder is the government's main business for Hobbes, a Mandevillean government (in the fable, Jove/Jupiter represents a government-like agent) is best advised to tolerate some amount of social evil and care about it only if too much moral discontent and discomfort arises. Disorder should coexist with order, otherwise general poverty and a much-reduced niveau of civilization is menacing. The Mandevillean position is that a government obsessed with or overly busy with putting out sin and crime threatens civilized life. The problem is that society may be overwhelmed by moral panic for various reasons, therefore making rules and norms stricter, or enforcing them more consequently than before might happen to be a judicious policy of the government, at least as long as people do not get bored by or tired of (an over-demandingly) virtuous life. This requires a more fine-tuned way of governing than an overcautious and potentially hyper-activist Hobbesian government would go about. The Mandevillean government is supposed to refrain from acting and interfering with the private lives of individuals as long as possible, tolerating all sorts of morally bad behavior, but always in the interest of the whole. Non-intervention does not exempt the government from being responsible for order *and* orderly disorder. Again, paradoxical as it may appear to be, the Mandevillean government is in a sense more powerful (albeit less coercive and violent) as it needs to be more deeply involved in adjusting the rule of laws to the actual demands and wishes of individuals than the Hobbesian governing based on command-obedience relations.

All this makes the question of how order and disorder is related to governing, and how governments can be constrained if they are essentially tied to the problem of order even more intriguing and urgent than in the Hobbesian theory. A Mandevillean government is surely more benign, peaceful, and liberal than the apparently rigorous and austere Leviathan, yet it looks more formidable because it is supposed to be free to determine what counts as tolerable and intolerable evil.

In *Measure for Measure*, Shakespeare brings us to Vienna (obviously a fancy remote world, unrelated to the real capital), and makes us meet both Hobbes and Mandeville. The play presents us with these revoltingly inconsistent conceptions about order and disorder, and it puts both into a weird but absolutely credible and real framework of practical politics.

### Disorder in Vienna?

As was said, *Measure for Measure* is generally categorized as a problem play. What is the problem, however? A no less general interpretation is that the play is neither a comedy, nor a tragedy, nor even a tragicomedy; its heroes are all doubtful, neither respectable, nor disrespectable; it does not solve the problems it raises. In the present context, our problem is this: Is there any problem at all?

Let us review the arguments for the case that Vienna is in serious trouble. Lucio and his fellows who appear in the second scene chatter freely and joyfully about murder, theft, fornication, even religious indifference, that is, the violation of almost each prohibition of the Ten Commandments. The tenor and laxity of this talk is very revolting (especially if we think of the Puritans of Shakespeare's age). Vienna does look like a modern Sodoma and Gomorrha. Then we encounter Claudio who, en route to the prison, laments that

> this new governor / Awakes me all the enrolled penalties / Which have, like unscour'd armour, hung by the wall / So long that nineteen zodiacs have gone round / And none of them been worn; and, for a name, / Now puts the drowsy and neglected act / Freshly on me: 'tis surely for a name. (I.2.)

Next, we listen to the Duke conversing with Friar Thomas and repeating the same point:

> We have strict statutes and most biting laws. / The needful bits and curbs to headstrong weeds, / Which for this nineteen years we have let slip; / Even like an o'ergrown lion in a cave, / That goes not out to prey. (I.3.)

Thus, the prevalence of crimes and criminal behavior is partly due to neglecting them by not imposing the required penalties. There is crime, but there is no law applied: that is surely close to some state of war, but at least to a moral collapse. In the last scene, disguised as a monk, the Duke rehearses the problem with Vienna:

> My business in this state / Made me a looker on here in Vienna, / Where I have seen corruption boil and bubble / Till it o'er-run the stew; laws for all faults, / But faults so countenanced, that the strong statutes / Stand like the forfeits in a barber's shop, / As much in mock as mark. (V.1.)

The case for *moral disruption* and disorder has two main arguments. First, no one disputes the fact that in Vienna, laws (basic moral norms) are being seriously and routinely violated and Shakespeare is quick to introduce to us characters thriving on crime (prostitution, drinking, killing for bait—see Lucio's company of professional soldiers).[37] Secondly, as the Duke confesses and, again, everyone virtually agrees with him, his government has contributed to this disorder by not enforcing the laws properly. A comparison between Thebes and Vienna is also instructive: what was consigned to the world outside of the city, especially the institutions of the instincts, has entered and threatened to devour it. Much as in Thebes, there are things that must be kept outside of the city walls for reasons of purity: there, purity of principles, here, purity of morals.[38] Both are supremely important for the legitimacy and efficiency of governing. Unless serious governmental actions are taken to enforce the law immediately, something terrible threatens.

There is another, subtler argument in favor of the view that Vienna has lost orientation—a version of disorder. This argument arises from Shakespeare's own historical experiences and the circumstances of his age, when a new Protestant-Puritan model of government was in the formation that rejected the Catholic idea of separating secular power and spiritual authority (roughly speaking). Let me first relate this argument, however, to the *Antigone* because an interesting parallel can be observed here. There the gods are a constant point of reference, and it was showed that Antigone's and Creon's political theologies are fundamentally different. Although Creon interprets his fall and fate as a divine punishment, his initial moralist-secularist interpretation of the gods' will stands in stark contrast to the traditionalist-ritualist understanding of divine authority over the city. Risking some degree of anachronism, but following contemporary critics, Creon's secular principles of governing were by and large in accord with the Athenian approach to politics. In *Measure for Measure*, Christianity is the natural religion, the moral authority of the Ten Commandments is not questioned (though routinely violated), nor is anybody persecuted for his or her religious or political theological views. However, whereas Isabella represents the Antigonean-traditionalist (here: Catholic) religiosity (she is a novice, desiring to join the most severe order, a form of dying for the world), the Duke's position is deeply ambiguous. On the one hand, he makes ample of use of traditional clerical authority (free access to prisoners as a confessor, to cloisters, as a monk enjoying immunities of diplomats). On the other hand, precisely from the traditional point of view, he abuses clerical powers and privileges. The sanctification and sacralization of the temporal power amounts to the abolition of important constraints and consequently, to the subversion of an old, much-criticized but intelligible order with clearly distinguishable forms (offices and institutions).[39] The Duke begins to use (abuse) religious authority for his own purposes as if Creon had tried to integrate Teiresias's authority into his government. He hears confessions but gives immoral advice (the bed-trick); he acts as a spiritual consultant to the death-bidden Claudio but in a way that is worlds apart from the Christian approach (both the Catholic and the Puritan one) and very close to a Stoic/Machiavellian spirituality. Finally, his proposal of marriage to Isabella, who is already bound by some (though not the final) religious vows, also borders on sacrilege.

Religion might be a common ground for moral norms and a strong institution, enjoying a solid social and political status and authority, yet it is no more a constraint on government. However, the emergence of an absolutist state that unifies secular and sacral powers makes the observer feel some forebodings, some kind of a danger, the roots of later disorder. On the face of it, the Duke successfully integrates these powers and creates a new order, which is, however, based on his personal charisma rather than on the coherence and evidential meanings of his principles. The inner tensions (moral standards compromised for manipulative reasons, Christian spirituality versus Machiavellian Stoicism, priestly and royal functions merged) look more threatening and menacing than the moral disorder with which play began. In other words, whereas the Hobbesian government may solve the problem of moral disorder, by its authoritarian policies, for the time being merely inconvenient and perhaps weird, it sows the seeds of a general discontent, or perhaps, of a moral panic or moral tyranny. The menace for the bees is awakened.

## Order in Vienna?

There are, however, arguments based on the text that support the view that Vienna is no serious trouble at all. Despite the robust textual evidence for the view that the law having been dormant for years in Vienna, crime and corruption have become the norm, there are different views and attitudes hidden in the text. In the very first scene, we see the Duke and his acting deputy, Escalus. The Duke does not talk about crime and disorder at all. On the contrary, he praises Escalus for his intimate knowledge of "The nature of our people, / Our city's institutions and the terms" and goes on to stress that

> for common justice, you're as pregnant in / As art and practise hath enriched any / That we remember. / There is our commission, / From which we would not have you warp. (I.1.)

He then tells Escalus that he has appointed Angelo to represent him as his plenipotentiary, again, without any reference to a serious social or legal crisis. Turning to Angelo he says: "your scope is as mine own / So to enforce or qualify the laws / As to your soul seems good." In other words, Angelo has to power to "qualify" the laws according to his judgment and wisdom.

Later, again in the monk's habit, the Duke converses with Escalus who enquires him about his travels in the world. Are there any interesting news?

> None, but that there is so great a fever on goodness, that the dissolution of it must cure it: novelty is only in request; and it is as dangerous to be aged in any kind of course, as it is virtuous to be constant in any undertaking. There is scarce truth enough alive to make societies secure; but security enough to make fellowships accursed: much upon this riddle runs the wisdom of the world. This news is old enough, yet it is every day's news (III.2.).

On the first reading, this is a rather enigmatic statement. How can the dissolution of goodness cure it? Fever can heal but death cannot. Wilson Knight has this interpretation: "our whole system of conventional ethics should be destroyed and rebuilt."[40] Yet it is an impossible task because what is new and what is old, what should and what should not be changed, cannot be clearly demarcated from one another. Governments should be reborn to make laws more efficient (biting, as it were), in other words, something must change but only if the purpose remains the same. But this is a poor advice, or, indeed, a riddle. Practical governing is always a risky business because much too often the blind lead the blind. Rulers are not different from the ruled, their knowledge is as limited as *theirs*, the outcome is miserable. "This riddle holds the key to the wisdom of the world (probably, both the false wisdom of the unenlightened, and the true wisdom of the great teachers)" (given earlier). If this is secret and ultimate truth in the play, then it is remarkably similar to Machiavelli's Stoicism, especially his last observations in *The Prince*.[41] In any case, the Duke's judgment is in a conspicuous contrast to the same monk's later invective against the bad morals he has seen in Vienna. (To this, the same Escalus responds with an anger similar to Creon's: "Slander to the state! Away with him to prison!" V.1.)

Finally, there is a whole scene in the play, which, in turn, casts doubt on the validity of a disorder-interpretation. In that, surprisingly long scene, which is clearly a parallel and precursor to the final, similarly long scene that might be titled "The Duke's Judgment," Angelo and Escalus hear the case brought to them by Elbow, the constable, who accuses Pompey of promoting prostitution. Once it turns out the Elbow's wife is also implicated in that, Escalus realizes that the case is highly complicated, and that justice (and the law) has no chance to clear it up. Significantly, by this point, Angelo has already departed: he had no patience with the proceedings. Shakespeare organizes the dramaturgy in such a way that we can now study the old style governing without the distorting presence of the new ruler. Escalus then rules: "Truly, officer, because he [Pompey] hath some offenses in him that thou wouldst discover if thou couldst, let him continue in his courses till thou know'st what they are" (II.1.). And Elbow, with his highly limited intelligence, thanks him for the instructions. At the end of the hearings, everybody is dismissed, with ample warnings that things have changed in Vienna and that the law does not tolerate any more what the government has tolerated so far.

In this scene, thus, we observe Escalus as a true governor/judge who does not mete out punishments, only warnings, and who does not solve the case at all for he understands that there is no solution that would make anybody happier (if Elbow's wife turns out to have unfaithful to her husband, the officer or constable, justice would require her punishment, yet this would also be a shame to her husband). This might sound like cynicism (and a wicked one for that, as Elbow turns to Pompey saying: "Thou art to continue now, thou varlet, thou art to continue!" II.1.) but no less as wisdom, the wise judgment that can be made only with patience, attentiveness, even compassion and pity for the constable whose intellectual powers are far below those of Pompey.

One of the implications of this scene for the problem of order/disorder is that vice and virtue, crime and its persecution are bound together in the way that any law or government is not able to separate them properly. As if Shakespeare would want to remind us of Jesus's parable in Matthew 13: "The servants asked him, 'Do you want us to go and pull them [the weeds] up?' 'No,' he answered, 'because while you are pulling the weeds, you may uproot the wheat with them. Let both grow together until the harvest' " (28–30). Moral disorder is some ways orderly, that is, to be tolerated for want of the better alternative, and its persecution may cause more trouble than it would solve. However, without principles, without law there are no crimes; if the law is made dormant, the strong and unjust will prevail; exceptions, however necessary and popular they may be, make for an unpredictable, disoriented, and arbitrary government. Only a strong leader may create temporary peace. But his power is based on his personal authority or charisma, in the trust that his decisions, however arbitrary and incoherent they are, do serve the public good. Much as in the case of the Hobbesian government, drawing the red line between order and disorder remains within the Mandevillean government's competence—to the dismay and worry of those who want to see it constrained.

It seems, then, that neither the Hobbesian nor the Mandevillean conception of order and disorder can successfully and convincingly demarcate the two concepts, providing a theoretically safe ground for distinguishing between what belongs to the government's competence and what does not, for the maintenance of order and the avoidance of disorder. However, putting this problem into the center, *Measure for Measure* gives us the necessary practical clues to how to discover if something is going wrong. In other words, theory may be helpful in making us aware of the problem, and the play (among others) may be helpful in treating the problem within the given historical and political context prudentially, intelligently, and efficiently. Let us see how.

## Shakespeare and Hobbes

For Hobbes's theory to be working, disorder must be an imminent threat, a clear and present danger, of which everyone is aware and afraid. In *Measure for Measure*, there is no clear consensus on this. Institutions are functioning relatively well, from cloisters to prisons. These institutions are, however, peripherical. Add to them the brothel as yet another institution on the fringes of normal life, and the result is a rather uncomfortable atmosphere.[42] There is no civil war or other signs of social unrest. However, as many commentators have noted, *Measure for Measure* stands out in Shakespeare's oeuvre for the centrality of sexuality. It is, however, not only the predomination of unlawful sexual relations in the play that strikes the observer but the absence of any familial relations except for Julia and Claudio (sister-brother). (Elbow's wife is, unfortunately, a prostitute.)[43] Thus, a Hobbesian ruler may suspect that there is a threat to the social order, not imminent perhaps but fundamental. Preventing it from becoming apparent and acute is, thus, the chief responsibility of the Duke.[44]

What he must first do is to reinforce the institutions of trust, in the first place, the most natural one, the family.[45] In the final scene, the Duke arranges a number of lawful marriages, some of which are already consummated, with the next generation to be born soon, and this seems to be his main concern, overriding his duty to be a good judge whose is committed to justice, broadly interpreted, rather than to political order. Marriage and family are, of course, not romantic personal relations but social institutions that are, in absence of other such institutions (e.g., the church, or civil and economic organizations and other autonomous bodies familiar to modern societies), essential to build and sustain more impersonal ties among members of society.[46]

But before coming to arrange for marriages, he must reinforce, reinvigorate the social contract. This is not an easy task when the populace does not directly sense the threat of the state of war. Hence, the first step is to increase moral panic: the Duke's inveighing words on corruption boiling and bubbling everywhere form an essential rhetorical tool to prepare the city for founding his new rule;[47] and Escalus's reaction to these words (believed to be uttered by Friar Thomas): "Slander to the state! / Away with him to prison!" is no less foundational in a negative sense. For the two essential ideas meet: absolute disorder and the very idea of the state.

The second step is, thus, invoking the state (or the government) to suppress moral disorder. Since, however, the Duke cannot refound his state without removing himself from it in the first place, he needs a new person either to do so or to prepare for the new foundation. Thus, in the first scene, we see him appoint Angelo as his deputy, instead of Escalus whose involvement in the previous government is now an impediment. And indeed: once appointed, Angelo is quick to take action. Mrs. Overdone and Pompey are the first victims: Mrs. Overdone: "But shall all houses of resort in the suburbs be pulled down?" Pompey: "To the ground, mistress." Mrs. Overdone: "Why, here is a change in the commonwealth!" (I.2.). In fact, however, this is more than a change. Houses of resort have no place within the commonwealth. The new governor commands to destroy the houses of moral destruction; the "change in the commonwealth" must start from "the ground."

Should Angelo have not fallen, the argument may go, the Duke may have had some problems with his legitimacy since everyone would have hoped for a more lenient government to return.[48] But Angelo failed (and Duke indicates that he was very much aware of such a turn, knowing Angelo's character, probably calculating with that), inadvertently confirming the view that moral disorder may corrupt even the highest authority, therefore a catastrophe was barely avoided. Thus, we have disorder everywhere, including the highest authority becoming the public enemy first as a private person.

We may go on speculating endlessly whether the Duke's intention was anything more but to merely reinforce his personal rule, give to it a new legitimacy-impulse; or perhaps he was about to teach Angelo a lesson or make him more virtuous; or that he simply wanted to get rid of his potential rival (if Angelo succeeds in enforcing the laws, the Duke may ease them and make him a scapegoat—this is the underlying Borgia-d'Orco story; if Angelo fails, as he does, then he becomes obviously unfit for any government position in the future). Such readings look upon politics and governments in exclusively personal terms. We shall discuss these aspects later on, the lesson to be drawn here is the foundational one. The Duke and his government disappeared; Angelo's new government has fallen; Friar Thomas (the disguised Duke) pronounces a state of war situation—and Lucio, the slandering character, with words that are unintendedly illustrative of the savage and wild reality of this situation, points to the solution in the most dramatic and cathartic moment of the play when he pulls off the friar's hood:

> Come, sir; come, sir; come, sir; foh, sir! Why, you / bald-pated, lying rascal, you must be hooded, must / you? Show your knave's visage, with a pox to you! / show your sheep-biting face, and be hanged an hour! /Will't not off? (V.1.)

To which the Duke responds: "Thou art the first knave that e'er madest a duke" (ibid). A political catharsis indeed, where the government is born out of nothing, with a new Duke emerging as a relief to the intolerably confused and confounded state of affairs where the greatest injustices have already been committed and even the best ones (Escalus) are close to fall victim to them. Is there a serious disorder threatening Vienna with a state of war? Shakespeare makes here an affirmative case very probable. Yes, order and disorder are descriptions that definitely make sense. Yet what he adds, and this testifies to his political philosophical genius, is that this threat is a possible source of political manipulation.[49]

Is there any chance of constraining such a government? The two steps suggest two types of answer. The first was marriage and family as natural ties to establish and reinvigorate *social trust*. However, the Duke as a natural person (in contradistinction to his artificial personality, as Hobbes later explains) must be part of this social net, he must be a discernible person who can be personally trusted. Hence his marriage to Isabella will be a freely chosen but effective restriction on his politics. The second step is related to this: if the Duke's strategy was to incite fear and panic of *moral* disorder, then his new government will be bound by moral standards. Angelo's moral fall was spectacular, yet it taught a lesson to everyone else (perhaps very much to the taste of Puritan morality[50]), namely, that morality can be central to politics. It can effectively control it once the state of war was identified with corruption.

Suppose, however, that the sort of disorder is not of a moral kind but, as was argued, a sort of a disorientation, a conflation and merging of what was traditionally kept apart and distinguished. For Hobbes and in his conception, no such problem can arise. The Leviathan is the unification of all individuals (the multitude, as Hobbes puts it), and in virtue of the social contract, they relinquish all their rights except for the right to life. In this context, it is important to observe how life and death are being handled by the Duke. He pardons the sole murderer (Bernardine), denies the wish of Angelo to be punished by death, tries to persuade Claudio to accept death stoically, and plays with Isabella in making her believe that her brother has been executed. These inchoate policies and decisions (critics point out James I's similarly unpredictable and embarrassing style of pardoning and playing such games, hence the historical context matters a lot) can hardly square with a Hobbesian state and what we expect it to do or not to do. Though no one is killed or executed (the single death in the play occurs due to disease, the deceased prisoner's head, however, is severed and used in a later stage, adding to the morbid atmosphere greatly), death lingers on in every scene, and the source of lethal threat is always the government. In this world, there is no remedy against it, and we may easily imagine a later plot emerging against the Duke and his capricious and willful rule. His decisions may be motivated by forging social peace by pardoning and not enforcing justice (once again), yet this does not seem to put a clear end to the turmoil and confusion he himself caused. Thus, again paradoxically, the Hobbesian conception remains unfulfilled. Constraining the government might be necessary, yet exactly in the way Angelo proclaimed to do it: by abolishing pardons and leniency. Death penalty as part of the lawful order must remain in force, on the condition that everyone knows when and why it is applied. Hence, the implicit Hobbesian argument for constraining the government is *consistence*—an implicit expectation that is not very far away from the principle of *law and order*.

## Shakespeare and Mandeville

Earlier, I assembled the following arguments supporting the view that there was no serious disorder in Vienna. First, Angelo is given full power over the state without any instructions to enforce laws and norms that had been supposedly "dormant" for long time. Second, the disguised Duke reveals to Escalus the "riddle" that "runs the wisdom of the world," namely, that things must change simply because people long for change (at the heart of this riddle, the second part of the old Roman counsel—circenses—hides). Third, Escalus's hearing the case of Pompey and his company suggests a normal management of social conflicts. If we accept these arguments as at least a possible and coherent reading of how a different sort of discourse or rhetoric in *Measure for Measure* hides an otherwise orderly Vienna, then the story fits quite well with the Mandevillean scenario where "reality" and "perception" part company. But this happens on the government's side rather than within the populace. If we ignore the possibility of a manipulative maneuver (this was considered above), a government may be genuinely convinced that a deep disorder is threatening the commonwealth, blocking of which needs preventive and immediate action. What this action, in fact, a series of policies involve, is to introduce measures and institutions, strictly enforced and strengthened, that promise to vamp out crime and immorality. Shakespeare, however, shows us some inconvenient political theoretical implications.

To put it bluntly: a government obsessive with enforcing high moral standards and striving for an abstract and perfect order becomes a source of disorder in society. Mandeville argues that the greatest problem of eliminating disorder caused by crime and immorality is the unintended reduction of the niveau of wealth and civilized life. Shakespeare, however, does not want to tell us a tale about a society heading toward widespread destitution and ascetic poverty. What he does tell us is the effect of pure (or Puritan?) morality on Angelo's character and action. This is similar to Mandeville's point, as the idea of unintended and paradoxical consequences of the complete victory of virtue over vice in society is essentially the same. The unsurpassable virtuousness of Angelo is replaced by the most heinous villainism imaginable, his becoming an almost disproportional criminal. He wants to rape Isabella, abuses his authority, lies to her, and wishes to see Claudio die for no obvious reason (perhaps enjoyment? bloodthirstiness? cruelty?). This is virtue being completely substituted by vice, a fundamentally disorderly behavior replacing a tolerable disorder.[51] An obsessive, even hysterical concern with moral principles or virtues causes real moral panic. But unlike in the former scenario where moral panic (disorder) was to be ended by the formation of the Duke's new government, here it is Angelo's policy that makes the government go mad, as in the French Terror, forcing society into a form of order that looks rational but utterly uncomfortable and, once again referring to Edmund Burke's assessment of the revolutionary government, in fact absolutely irrational. Shakespeare adumbrates much of this as he shows us here how a government based on virtue (after or being busy with extinguishing vice) may sink into utter moral wickedness.[52]

Why does this happen? Again, the analogy between Creon and Angelo is instructive and striking (though Creon is far less a criminal but no less a tyrant). Both rulers start as apparently right-minded, principled, (public) good-willing leaders and end up with becoming tyrants. We have seen how Creon stumbled, and we must now watch the fate of Angelo's government. Much as Creon's subjects, including Antigone, had no counter-principles against the rule publicly based on sound moral principles, Angelo's subjects have no arguments against him. Isabella's appeal is based on mercy and pardon, to which Angelo has the very same response Creon made to Haemon, namely, that no government can rule and survive on the basis of exceptions. Angelo wants the law's hand act with clarity and unambiguously. What the government does is nothing but execute the law. Angelo's rule is, literally speaking, a Rousseauian ideal where the executive power is absolutely subjected to the law, and the government is not an autonomous agency. But this has an unintended consequence, at least in Shakespeare's narrative.[53]

It allows the ruler to identify himself with the law and the law with virtue writ large (or a single moral principle such as justice): "It is the law, not I condemn your brother" (II.2.). Such equations help any government to perpetrate the most immoral acts because the argumentation is comfortably circular: the law justifies morality, morality justifies the law; the law rather than the government "acts" and so on. The law is infallible because it is identical with morality. But infallibility is a mark of divinity, and for the Mandevillean scenario to work, there must be a common conviction in the commonwealth that there must be a final and perfect authority with divine powers. Contemporary secular society is wont to be skeptical of providence but all the more prone to idolize its own secular institutions and constitution. These institutions, however, resting on perfect moral foundations, can be tools to impose a single will upon the commonwealth. Uncomfortable as it may be for the defenders of the principle of the rule of law, it may be as unconstrained and inhuman as the most directly immoral but personal tyranny. The total victory of virtue (of justice) over vice may make for an unconstrained government because no flaws, no mistakes, no imperfections are permitted, not even imagined. Thus, some sort of disorder is necessary to confirm our suspicion that the government is imperfect, much as we are, which, in turn, gives us some sort of a relief that moral perfection being unattainable, we are not required to pretend to be perfect, either.[54]

And this is, so it seems, a robust lesson of the play. Although the grandiose and deadly serious Hobbesian rebirth of the Leviathan is a possible reading, as we saw in the previous section, the comical tone of Mandeville is unmistakable. The Duke's philosophy of change, of life and death, and of morals has it that things must be changed simply because people demand change for its own sake. He understands this. He is not worried about his government, his rule, and his legitimacy, he only wanted to stage something novel to his subjects, which necessarily contains some *measure* of disorder—not the tragic but the comic kind. He talks about both the dangers and the virtue of constancy. It is dangerous not to change anything, but it is no less dangerous for the ruler to change with the changes. Moral panic is dangerous but what about a moral spectacle in which no one is shown to be perfect?

The closing scene (the whole Act V) is, again, a grand hearing, ending with the judgments and verdicts of the Duke. What happens here has been one of the major issues of the commenting literature. No doubt, justice plays a major role here. Angelo and Lucio receive their punishments, Mariana gets "her" Angelo, Lucio's child gets a lawful father, Claudio's and Julietta's child lawful parents, and if we consider Isabella guilty for taking part in the dirty bed-trick, she is also duly punished with the news that her brother is dead. However, these rulings of justice are obviously more than what the law entails. On the one hand, legalizing sexuality by the institution of marriage, giving a proper place to children in society, as well as punishing the villain for his outrageous crimes are clearly within the written law. On the other hand, both Angelo's and Lucio's punishments consist in forced marriage and public shame, rather than prison (though Lucio must go to prison) or corporal discipline; Bernardine, the murderer is pardoned; and the Duke's marriage proposal to Isabella makes almost no sense here, before the "court," except in a political sense (marriage becoming the foundation of the commonwealth). These inconsistencies may not be all humorous but at least promise a government that does not pretend to be perfect and infallible. Order is created or reestablished but it does not satisfy everyone. There is no Paradise emerging but no Hell, either.[55] Vienna is freed from Angelo's perfect and perfectly disordered government, yet Escalus's weak and ineffective governing is also over.

*Measure for Measure* shows not only that there is no ideal government, but that nor should there be. Only non-ideal decisions are available, and this non-ideal or non-utopian (by no means dystopian!) nature of governing serves as its internal constraints. Contrary to the Duke's honest or dishonest pretensions of acting as Providence does, Shakespeare leaves us with odd feelings about any government wishing to produce a perfect judgment and arrangement of social relations. There is always room for moral improvement both in terms of characters and principles, yet even the best final decision that goes well beyond pure legality is still fallible, imperfect, and harmonious. The fallibility, imperfection, and disharmony make even the best government more or less difficult to tolerate, and therein lies the constraint.

## TO WRAP UP

*Measure for Measure* puts the problem of order and disorder into the center. It forces us, and in its historical context, the Jacobite government, to reflect on the issue of how order and disorder can be recognized, in what sense is it a "real" or a "perceived" problem, and how the government is supposed and able to do about it. We know that Hobbes and Mandeville had very different views on what counts as disorder. For Hobbes, disorder is an evident reality and the government's responsibility is to prevent it. However, Shakespeare's drama shows that governments have a formidable inventory of instruments by help of which they can make the threat of disorder credible. Mandeville's insight is that disorder, and the fear of it, often takes the form of moral panic. His government is in practice considerably more liberal and tolerant than that of Hobbes, so it seems at least; however, the possibility of moral panic is more prevalent and imminent than most people would think. Therefore, the Mandevillean government, again, as Shakespeare's play shows, can be more interventionist and oppressive than the Hobbesian one.

Shakespeare himself does not, of course, offer a theory of constraining governments and governing. He does, however, bring us to the core of the matter. And he does hint at certain clues of how a Hobbesian and how a Mandevillean government can be constrained. For no matter how benevolent the governmental attempts to create or maintain order and prevent or overcome disorder are, the very problem of how to make sense of order and disorder remains unsolved and most probably unsolvable. To constrain a Hobbesian government, Shakespeare suggests first the idea of trust that both sides desperately need, and which requires transparency and social honesty: hence the importance of marriage and clear interpersonal bounds. Secondly, the inconsistent behavior of the Duke is a negative argument: after having watched the play, we are forced to rethink what went wrong, and what gives us misgivings about the stability and reliability of the new order. To constrain a Mandevillean government, Shakespeare suggests that we are right in having second thoughts about the inconsistent behavior of the Duke: no government is infallible, hence we should not expect too much of it. Therefore, alleviating or mitigating moral panic is not the government's responsibility, on the contrary: we have reason to be watchful of any agent, for and foremost, the government that promises a heavenly designed and executed order to us.

## NOTES

1. For a classic overview of the "uses of literature" for political studies, see Maureen Whitebrook, "Politics and Literature?" *Politics* 1 (1995): 55–62. These uses

include illustration, criticism, and education. There are, however, even more directly political genres such as utopian novels. Two collected volumes are also highly informative: John Horton and Andrea T. Baumeister (eds.), *Literature and Political Imagination* (London, New York: Routledge, 1996); Deborah Philips and Katy Shaw (eds.), *Literary Politics. The Politics of Literature and the Literature of Politics* (New York: Palgrave, Macmillan, 2013), 15–25, 18–19. See also Kyle Scott, *The Limits of Politics. Making the Case for Literature in Political Analysis* (New York, London: Lexington Books, 2016). Even more recently, we have an encyclopedia-like summary: Booker, Keith (ed.), *Literature and Politics Today. The Political Nature of Modern Fiction, Poetry, and Drama* (Santa Barbara, Denver, Oxford: Greenwood, 2015). In teaching political science, the use of literature has a long tradition, though systematic attempts to teach political science via literary works are still rare. An exception is Douglas A. Van Belle, *A Novel Approach to Politics. Introducing Political Science through Books, Movies and Popular Culture* (Los Angeles, etc.: Sage Publ. 2016) [4th edition]. Besides literature, other arts have also received attention by political theorists or historians of political ideas, for instance, Mitchel Cohen, *The Politics of Opera: A History from Monteverdi to Mozart* (Princeton: Princeton University Press, 2017).

2. For an interpretation of Plato's Republic as (partly) a comic text, see David Robjant, "What Use is Literature to Political Philosophy? Or the Funny Thing about Socrates's Nose." *Philosophy and Literature* 2 (2015): 322–37. What may appear as an impossible idea, even Rawls's *A Theory of Justice* has been read as a dramatic text: Iain Mackenzie and Robert Porter, "Dramatization as Method in Political Theory." *Contemporary Political Theory* 4 (2011): 482–501.

3. The edition used throughout this book is this: Sophocles, *The Complete Greek Tragedies I*, ed. by D. Grene and R. Lattimore, translated by David Grene (Chicago, London: The Chicago University Press, 1991). References are to lines and not to pages, given in the main text after the quotation.

4. On his reading, see Hannes Charen, "Hegel Reading 'Antigone.' " *Monatshefte* 4 (2011): 504–16.

5. Many contemporary *political* readings pay more attention to Creon and his cause, yet the focus remains mostly on Antigone. It is through her that some social and political consequences are discussed. See Jean-Pierre Vernant, Pierre Vidal-Naquet, *Myth and Tragedy in Ancient Greece* (New York: Zone Books, 1990); Judith Butler, *Antigone's Claim: Kinship between Life & Death* (New York: Columbia University Press, 2000); Jonathan Strauss, *Private Lives, Public Deaths. Antigone and the Invention of Individuality* (New York: Fordham University Press, 2013); Bonnie Honig, *Antigone, Interrupted* (Cambridge: Cambridge University Press, 2013). Honig's political reading of Antigone is connected to the recent interest within contemporary political theory in the concept of the "political." In an earlier paper, she argued against the formerly prevailing moralistic-humanist interpretation of the *Antigone*, an advanced "an agonistic humanism that sees in mortality, suffering, sound, and vulnerability resources for some form of enacted universality, but also sees these as no less various in their significations than are the diverse languages that unite and divide us. Moreover, agonistic humanism is not centered on mortality

and suffering; it draws as well on natality and pleasure, power not just powerlessness, desire not just principle, in quest of a politics that is not reducible to an ethics nor founded on finitude. The agonism in this humanism means it even insists on attenuating rather than resecuring the human/animal distinction on which other humanisms are focused." In "Antigone's Two Laws: Greek Tragedy and the Politics of Humanism." *New Literary History* 1 (2010): 1–33; 4. Slavoj Žižek's rendering of Antigone follows a similarly political line: *Antigone* (Bloomsbury, 2016). Honig sums up the recent political interest in the play, and the character of Antigone as a political figure: "For Lacanians, she is the revolutionary suicide, a heroic subject of conscious death; for some political or feminist theorists, an antistatist advocate for the private realm's virtues (Jean Bethke-Elshtain); for others, a heroine of the public (Mary G. Dietz, Costas Douzinas). For Butler, Antigone models kinship structures yet to come; but for Lee Edelman, Antigone exhibits a valuable antipathy to child-centered kinship as such. This is the contested terrain into which the reading tendered here ventures not unwarily, for Antigone's passion is something about which her devotees are quite passionate" (ibid., 18).

6. In *Oedipus at Colonus*, when visiting Oedipus and demanding his return to the outskirts of Thebes so that his body may be buried there, Creon appears to be a person wholly dedicated to the good of Thebes. He does not hesitate to blackmail and coerce Oedipus by attempting to kidnap Antigone. He is a politician through and through, making use of force when necessary, but not excessively.

7. Bonnie Honig calls Creon's speech "Periclean" especially in view of the central metaphor (the "ship of the state"). "Antigone's Laments, Creon's Grief: Mourning, Membership, and the Politics of Exception." *Political Theory* 1 (2009): 5–43. "Creon begins in statesmanlike voice . . . . If he becomes tyrannical over time, that may signal a defect of character; or it may suggest perspicacity: He sees that his struggle with Antigone is about more than a burial and a body" (9).

8. Vernant-Naquet, *Myth and Tragedy in Ancient Greece*, 41.

9. Honig, *Antigone's Laments*, 6, 9. She also critiques Judith Butler's interpretation (in her *Antigone's Claim*), which considers Antigone as representing a "democratic-political" alternative.

10. Strauss, *Private Lives, Public Deaths*, 1.

11. Laurel J. Apfel, *The Advent of Pluralism. Diversity and Conflict in the Age of Sophocles* (Oxford: Oxford University Press, 2011). Apfel also argues that Antigone is a "monist" who ignores the city (though he admits that the burial of Polyneices can be a "famous" and "heroic" act). Creon suffers a defeat in his oikos but still represents the interests of city.

12. Strauss, *Private Life*, 40.

13. Analyzing the last drama, and virtually taking stock with the whole trilogy, Peter Ahrensdorf argues for the democratic-political theme prevailing over the old aristocratic-religious views. See "Blind Faith and Enlightenment Statesmanship in Oedipus at Colonus." *The Review of Politics* 70 (2008): 165–89.

14. Honig, *Antigone's Laments*, 28.

15. Agnes Horvath and Arpad Szakolczai, *The Political Sociology and Anthropology of Evil: Tricksterology* (London: Routledge, 2020).

16. Defenders of Antigone and her action who claim that what she does is nothing but what common sense dictates and therefore she represents the "normal" and natural way of thinking about the deceased ones tend to forget that Antigone herself was anything but "normal." "There is, it would seem, something monstrous about Antigone"—Tina Chanter begins her essay on Antigone ("Antigone's Political Legacies: Abjection in Defiance of Mourning." In S. E. Wilmer and A. Žukauskaitė (eds.) *Interrogating Antigone in Postmodern Philosophy and Criticism* (Oxford: Oxford University Press, 2010), 19–47, 47.

17. On funeral and mourning practices in ancient Athens, see Jennifer E. Ballengee, "Mourning the Public Body in Sophocles' Antigone." *Colloquy* 11 (2006): 31–59; and Cynthia B. Patterson, "The Place and Practice of Burial in Sophocles' Athens." *Helios* Supplement (2006): 9–48.

18. A. Žukauskaitė discusses Antigone's character in terms of Agamben's concept of the homo sacer. This is a political theological concept, at the heart of which is a deep ambiguity: the homo sacer is both sacred and untouchable, yet for this reason also outside of the community and an object of contempt. Antigone is in this sense both sacred and profane. She does not belong to the normal world anymore (and she is aware of this), has no place here, and in that sense, she cannot be said to represent a rival version of political founding. She is a damned soul. Thus, she has no political conception comparable to Creon's. However, for this very reason she is reduced to "pure life," as it were, to an asocial type of existence, which, in turn, is the very foundation of politics and political life. Paradoxically, Antigone as an outcast, as an asocial being is as important for founding a new, non-religious city as are Creon's principles. The two match each other as the new, but tragic citizens of a new age. Audrone Žukauskaitė, "Biopolitics: Antigone's Claim." In S. E. Wilmer and A. Žukauskaitė (eds.) *Interrogating Antigone in Postmodern Philosophy and Criticism* (Oxford: Oxford University Press, 2010), 67–81. The same Agambenian argument is discussed by Cecilia Sjoholm, "Naked Life; Arendt and the Exile at Colonus." Ibid., 48–66.

19. Jennet Kirkpatrick, "The Prudent Dissident: Unheroic Resistance in Sophocles' Antigone." *The Review of Politics* 3 (2011): 401–24.

20. J. Strauss: "The scapegoat represented a paradox in the definition the state, a necessary but inherently unsatisfying line between inside and outside. Similarly, the corpse, as we have seen, played a phantasmatic intermediary role that was crucial to distinguishing between life and death, between sentience and inert matter—as well as between the "unconscious" of the animal, the family, and woman, on the one hand, and the "consciousness" of the state on the other." *Private Life*, 71.

21. Rush Rehm, "Sophocles' Antigone and Family Values." *Helios* Supplement (2006): 187–218; 199.

22. Other translations are less existentialist, so to speak; but they also refer to some irrevocable loss and personal destruction.

23. *The Fragility of Goodness* (Cambridge: Cambridge University Press, 1986), 80.

24. Reed, Valeri, "Bringing Antigone Home." *Comparative Literature Studies* 3 (2008): 316–40; 320. [Greek letters are transcribed.]

25. Ibid., 338.

26. Rousseau, Jean-Jacques, "On the Social Contract." In Donald A. Cress (trans.) *The Basic Political Writings* (Indianapolis/Cambridge: Hackett Publ. Comp. 1987): 141–227, 163.

27. The text is available in the public domain: http://shakespeare.mit.edu/index.html. For copyright concerns, I shall refer to the text by Act/Scene numbers within the main text. Readers interested in a critical edition may turn to *Measure for Measure. The New Cambridge Shakespeare*, ed. Brian Gibbons (Cambridge: Cambridge University Press, 1991).

28. For comments on this see Zdravko Planinc, "Shakespeare's Critique of Machiavellian Force, Fraud, and Spectacle in Measure for Measure." *Humanitas* 1–2 (2010): 144–68; Jessica Apolloni, "Local Communities and Central Power in Shakespeare's Transnational Law." *Studies in Philology* 1 (2017): 124–47.

29. Carolyn E. Brown, "Duke Vincentio of Measure for Measure and King James I. of England: 'The Poorest Princes in Christendom.' " *Clio* 1 (1996): 51–78.

30. For Shakespeare's political interpretations, see John E. Alvis and Thomas J. West (eds.), *Shakespeare As Political Thinker* (Wilmington, Delaware: ISI Books, 2000); David Armitage, Conal Condren and Andrew Fitzmaurice, "Introduction." In *Shakespeare and Early Modern Political Thought* (Cambridge: Cambridge University Press, 2009), 1–22.

31. Planinc (op.cit.): "In stark contrast [to morality play-interpretations], the contention is also made that the problems raised in *Measure for Measure* are the problems of political philosophy. The play has Shakespeare's most explicitly political beginning—the Duke's first words, 'Of government, the properties to unfold . . . ' (1.1.3)—and it continues to study government right through to its concluding political spectacle. And yet it is seldom read as political philosophy" (146). Of course, it would be an exaggeration to expect Shakespeare to advance an exoteric political philosophy (to use Leo Strauss's term), but his greatest non-historical tragedies, from *Hamlet*, *King Lear*, as well as his purely fantasy plays, from *Measure for Measure* to *The Tempest*, form highly suitable stuff for a political philosophy or theory class.

32. Thomas Hobbes, *Leviathan*. Introduced by C. B. MacPherson (New York: Penguin Books, 1977).

33. "In states there are often some obscure and almost latent causes, things which appear at first view of little moment, on which a very great part of its prosperity or adversity may most essentially depend. The science of government being therefore so practical in itself, and intended for such practical purposes, a matter which requires experience." Burke's further point is that such experience belongs to the governing elite, rather than to a single person *Reflections on the Revolution in France*, ed. L. G. Mitchell (Oxford: Oxford University Press, 1993), 61.

34. See Jonathan Dollimore, "Transgressions and Surveillance in Measure for Measure." In J. Dollimore and A. Sinfield (eds.) *Political Shakespeare: New Essays in Cultural Materialism* (Manchester: Manchester University Press, 1985), 72–87.

35. *The Fable of the Bees or Private Vices, Publick Benefits*, Vol. 1. With a Commentary Critical, Historical, and Explanatory by F.B. Kaye (Indianapolis: Liberty Fund, 1988), 66.

36. Ibid., 69.

37. Jeffrey R. Wilson writes that "in Measure for Measure, the desire for law, virtue and justice surfaces as crime, villainy and sexual abuse. As such, Shakespeare's Measure for Measure can shine some light on the abuses of power that can result from putting an ethically compromised officer who desperately wants to maintain order on the ground in a crime-ridden community and relying upon the individual discretion and judgement of that officer." " 'When Evil Deeds Have Their Permissive Pass': Broken Windows in William Shakespeare's Measure for Measure." *Law and Humanities* 2 (2017): 160–83, 176.

38. B. Gibbons explains: "In the suburbs a livelihood is made from what the city excludes, suppresses and exudes, but the suburbs witness also to the evils produced by the city. These things are openly apparent in the suburbs of the city just as they are in the sub-plot of this play, where disease, poverty and degradation are obvious and contempt for the law is outspoken, but the conditions in which the inhabitants have to survive are also shown to be harsh: having no money, being thrown out of work, catching disease, being arrested, these are the repeated and feared experiences of their daily lives. Lies and scandal and rumour, theft and deceit and illegitimacy, contaminate relations between them, but they devise nevertheless outside the law a kind of crooked simulacrum of the official system which seems to produce a crude normality, and a means to survival." "Introduction." In Brian Gibbons (ed.) *Measure for Measure. The New Cambridge Shakespeare* (Cambridge: Cambridge University Press, 1991), 1–68, 23.

39. Jessica Apolloni (*Local Communities and Central Power*) argues that "by merging religious and legal power, the Duke alone teaches his citizens how to conduct themselves and understand the consequences of crime. Accordingly, the Duke is able to enact further power over his subjects than in his typical role as a prince, and his perceived connections to the community only allow for further control" (140). The play "exemplifies theater's role in imagining English common law and the new conflicting relationships occurring within the English legal system—such as the divides between ecclesiastical and secular legal authority, monarchical and parliamentary power, as well as local officials and centralized legal positions" (144). For a historical-contextual view, see Debora Kuller Shuger, *Political Theologies in Shakespeare's England. The Sacred and the State in Measure for Measure* (New York: Palgrave MacMillan, 2001). Jonathan Goossen summarizes the view that the Duke is an emerging new model, replacing the old two-sword model of state and government: "By sharing English radical reformers' strong disregard for the nature of political and religious office and the traditional division between the functions of church and state, the Duke actually bases his governance on the same principles as did they and Angelo. Though a kinder, gentler one, he is a philosophical and theological Puritan nonetheless, attempting to deal with the personal spiritual issues of his subjects by means of the state's public law" (218). "'Tis set down so in heaven, but not in earth': Reconsidering Political Theology in Shakespeare's *Measure for Measure*." *Christianity and Literature* 2 (2012): 217–39, 218.

40. *The Wheel of Fire. Interpretations of Shakespearean Tragedy* (London, New York, 1930), 89.

41. "No man is found so prudent as to able to adapt himself to [the change of times], either because he cannot deviate from that to which his nature disposes him,

or else because having always prospered by walking in one path, he cannot persuade himself that it is well to leave it." Niccolo Machiavelli, *The Prince and the Discourses* (New York: The Modern Library, 1950), 93.

42. Michel Foucault's idea of power unmasking itself precisely in such places suggests itself. See Dollimore (1985). Gibbons also stresses the polarization of social life, agreeing also with Pompey's remark that in the end, prison and "house of resort" become indistinguishable from one another. Cf. *Introduction*, 24.

43. Harriet Hawkins, Measure for Measure. *Harvester New Critical Introductions to Shakespeare*. (Brighton, UK: The Harvester Press, 1987).

44. For a Hobbesian reading of several plays written by Shakespearean, see Andrew Moore, *Shakespeare between Machiavelli and Hobbes. Dead Body Politics* (Lanham: Lexington Books, 2016). Moore concludes that *Measure for Measure* raises doubts about the Duke's competence as a Machiavellian prince.

45. "Marriage and the family are the conventional institutions by which the city attempts to resolve the tension we see in the exchanges between Angelo and Isabella. Sexual passion is potentially a powerful source of social disorder and therefore needs restraint. Ordinarily, the city achieves this restraint not through harsh punishments but rather by channeling that passion into marriage. In doing so, it also obtains an important benefit: it protects the institution responsible for raising the next generation of citizens. Marriage and the family provide a restraint on sexual passion that makes coercive legal restraint less necessary, while also providing fundamental benefits to the political order" (Apolloni, *Local Communities and Central Power*, 197). The locus classicus for Shakespeare's political understanding of marriage is in Allan Bloom and Harry V. Jaffa, *Shakespeare's Politics* (Chicago, London: Chicago University Press, 1974).

46. "Understanding marriage's political significance, therefore, is key to unraveling the play's political teaching. By carefully framing marriage within Pauline language of sin and grace—and in particular by using the image of death and rebirth through baptism—Shakespeare offers a theological as well as a political image of a kind of self-government capable of easing the city's legal dilemmas and reconciling justice with mercy." Peter C. Meilaender: "Marriage and the Law: Politics and Theology in Measure for Measure." *Perspectives on Political Science* 4 (2012): 195–200, 195.

47. Gibbons assumes that Shakespeare's audience was probably in agreement with the idea that bastards, being in an essential way outcast from society, should be integrated into it, and that the Duke's harsh policy were considered beneficial and in the public interest. Cf. *Introduction*, 78.

48. It is interesting that the Duke's invective against Vienna (his own city) comes after Angelo has already taken serious steps to enforce the law. The reference to corruption is perhaps already directed against him there.

49. For a morally optimistic reading, see Krystal Marsh, "Reconstructing the Morality Play and Redeeming the Polity in William Shakespeare's Measure for Measure." *Journal of the Wooden O* 13(1) (2013): 81–95. She considers the drama a modernized morality play: "The Duke reconciles society by mercifully employing the law. As Angelo's example demonstrates, the problem with the law in Vienna is that

it can be used as an instrument of moral corruption. In order to reform the law, the Duke is forced to begin at the heart of the problem, namely, with morality itself" (94). J. Goossen also argues for a grand moral restoration taking place at the denouement, though he calls this a political theological solution: "Where [Isabella] there rejected Angelo's scriptural equation of Claudio's sin with murder, she here rejects the Duke's scriptural reflexive justice, arguing for Angelo's pardon on the grounds that spiritual sin cannot be judged by the state. She learns selfless compassion; he, perhaps, that traditional political theology can also judge compassionately. Isabella's distinction between the public obligations of a magistrate and the private duty of an individual Christian offers an alternative to Angelo's harshness and the Duke's ineffectiveness. The results of their administration are indeed radically different, but both arise from misapplying spiritual principle to temporal law in a way that ignores past centuries' interpretations of those principles. Philosophically, both are radical Protestants." Goossen, *"'Tis Set Down So in Heaven, But Not in Earth'."* 236–37.

50. Was Shakespeare's intention to mock Puritans by presenting a Puritanical ruler's fall or to confirm the no less profound Puritan idea of our essential sinfulness? Commentators have devoted considerable attention to these questions. Goossen (see previous footnote) argued that Shakespeare's conclusion is a confirmation of Puritan morality. Michael Sugrue argues for a Catholic and anti-Puritan reading of the play: "Measure for Measure: The Bible Contra Puritanical Christianity." *Praesidium* 4 (2008), formerly available at www.literatevalues.org/prae-8.4.htm#measure. Huston Diehl, on the contrary, opts for a Protestant reading: " 'Infinite Space': Representation and Reformation in Measure for Measure." *Shakespeare Quarterly* 4 (1998): 393–410. Robert B. Bennett's reading is neither-nor: *Romance and Reformation: The Erasmian Spirit of Shakespeare's Measure for Measure* (Newark: University of Delaware Press, 2000). M. R. Rowe reads Shakespeare as an Aristotelian thinker: "The Dissolution of Goodness: 'Measure for Measure' and Classical Ethics." *International Journal of the Classical Tradition* 1 (1998): 20–46.

51. Later we learn that Angelo was less than virtuous in his declining marriage to Marianna. Yet he seems to be genuinely surprised by the force of vice overcoming him, which means that he may have been honestly struggling for virtuousness.

52. "The case of Claudio and Juliet, of better social rank, illustrates the wider significance of this issue, while the cases of Angelo—and, even more strikingly, Isabella—illustrate the difficult terms in which the play confronts an audience with the issue, showing that extreme abstention from appetite, too, brings its own forms of corruption, distortion and abnormality—an almost perverse paradox. The paradoxical structure of the play's design begins to emerge very early, when it is shown how the dominant claims of instinctive nature in the lower ranks make them able to nourish a sympathy for the blighted youthful hopes of Claudio and Juliet, and this sympathy reveals that the lower ranks have a better grasp of common justice and humanity in this case than the educated Angelo does. According to Angelo's severe interpretation of the letter of the law, the spirit of love is mortally sinful." Gibbons, *Introduction*, 25.

53. Shakespeare seems to be making a psychological point as well (though we should remember that Angelo as many other characters are most probably variations of medieval morality play figures; yet the playwright's psychological insight is much

deeper). Absolute power can be a poison, or a drug that has devastating consequences on any moral character. Call it hubris, or anything else, the sad truth is that the kneeling Isabella, perhaps overplaying her sexuality a bit (instigated by Lucio), confronting the unconstrained local freedom protected by the safety that absolute political and legal power can grant, represents the united power of vice (in the form of temptation) and virtue (represented by the purity of her case and her innocence). Human nature is such that moral perfection can be source of wickedness, a provocation, of resistance, of cynicism, broadening the psychological horizon toward theology (of grace and sin, of salvation and damnation), and that should be, again, a warning about an obsession with achieving moral perfection in matters of governing and ruling. Cf. Wilson, *When Evil Deeds Have Their Permissive Pass*, 169.

54. Goossen (*'Tis Set Down So in Heaven, But Not in Earth*) argues that the medieval view on government was more balanced, sober, and moderate than the Puritan vision. He thinks that even the Duke's efforts were motivated largely by this vision as he was so preoccupied with the personal salvation of many of his subjects.

55. Gibbons concludes that the play leaves the comical expectations unsatisfied, the reconciliation scene is strained, and that the feeling of a struggle for survival predominates it. *Introduction*, 26.

*Chapter 2*

# The Idea of Constraining Government and Political Theory

## POLITICAL THEORY AS A CONSTRAINT

*Antigone* and *Measure for Measure* help us explore the problem of constraining governing from various angles. Neither Sophocles nor Shakespeare are political theorists by profession, though both lived in an age when philosophers turned to the problem of governing with increased interest. As I argued, such literary works are at the crossroads of theory and popular imagination, of the practice and intuition. Sophocles wrote for the Athenian agora, Shakespeare wrote for the royal court (at least *Measure for Measure*), in other words, to those involved in and affected by the philosophy, practice, style, and manners of government. Both authors put the question of how to rule or govern a city (a polis, a commonwealth) well into the forefront. Both take it for granted that the audience who is subjected to a real-time government has an idea of it and of what it is like to be obedient and disobedient to rulers, to follow or reject laws and orders. Tyranny is evil in both plays, and its emergence is a disputed but central issue for both. More pertinently to the topic of this chapter, they—and actually, we—are able to make a distinction between what is good and bad, right or wrong; between life and death, governed by principles and virtues on the one hand, and sheer will and vices on the other hand; between order and disorder, and justice and injustice. They all share a somewhat opaque but firm conviction that there is such a thing as the public good. And they are informed about the basic moral norms. It is also evident in both the *Antigone* and *Measure for Measure* that the business of governing entails the enforcement of these norms.

We see the fall and collapse of Creon's rule and later Angelo's government (perhaps also the old ducal government as well). Each story tells something about the transgression of certain limits. Thus, we may say that however unspecified the meaning of the common or public good is, and however it is dependent on there being a government to promote or protect it, governing involves an *idea of the limitation of government.* I have tried to explore the various ways this idea emerges in the two dramas: there are *descriptions* of events and characters; these descriptions give rise to *explanations* of what went wrong with the project and business of governing; thereby a loosely formed conception of what is wrong, what is evil, and what is being expressed; which then establishes a *norm* of constraining what governments should do.

This process of description, explanation, and norm-formation is highly stylized, and is itself a product of reflection. But for such a reflection can begin, there must be a conversing, discoursing community, though of course not necessarily a real discussion group, and not even a dialogue between living persons, in which descriptions are confronted, explanations debated, and norms promulgated. Such discourses may take place within various, formal and informal structures, including canons and vocabularies that connect past stories, concepts, images with those of the present, or make the past part of the present. Political theory is part of this discourse. It may be asked whether it is substantially distinct from what may be called "political thinking."

Creon and Angelo do political thinking. Real politicians—orators, kings, advisors—may do political thinking. Sophocles and Shakespeare, too. This means that all of them use highly abstract political concepts competently, address political questions or problems, and may even develop their own theories of government (like James I). But they either have a clear stake in politics, or have different, unphilosophical interests as well (theatrical success, dramaturgical effects, etc.). Political theorists or philosophers, however, at least insofar as they are doing political theory or philosophy, are generally supposed to do it *impartially* (not having a stake in the power games) or for the sake of *truth.* It goes without saying that the qualification "insofar as" is crucial once it comes to evaluating individual theories or philosophical views. One does not need to accept Marxism to see that there are no absolutely pure theories, disengaged from reality (Marxism holding that "reality" is somehow "material") or from a particular political "context." Plato was worried about philosophy and its survival in democracy (Socrates's death being the political end of philosophy). Aristotle's moderate optimism was in conformity with the relatively conflict-free and peaceful political environment he enjoyed. Hobbes was said to cite the somber and portentous circumstances of his birth, namely, that his mother began labor when she heard the news of the Armada sailing toward England and concluded that "I and fear were born twins." Hume's more serene and less dramatic political thinking is certainly influenced by his relatively uneventful life and the prosperity England enjoyed those times. Notwithstanding the importance of such influences, however, theories and philosophical systems have their own lives, and it is very natural today to treat all these philosophers and theorists as contributors to a grand debate about classical or canonical problems of politics, which has been supposed to remain more or less separated from politics and governing as a practical activity.

However, this relative autonomy and distinctness of political theory and its separation from politics and political thinking in general has been challenged. In the next section, I wish to reflect on this challenge by asking the question of what it means, in the first place, to do political theory or political theorizing. Is it true that political theorizing is, after all, merely a form of political thinking, and thus, of doing politics? For if it is, let me repeat, then the thesis that political theory is a constraint on governing collapses into the trivial proposition that governments are run by people having different political views, and those criticizing governments also have different political views, and this causes conflicts and disagreements, which make governing more difficult. This is hardly interesting.

Impartiality and truth-seeking appear to be important and reliable marks of political theory as being distinct from political thinking. Descriptions, explanations, and normative statements can be subjected to these measures. However, the very history of political theory or philosophy pursued with adherence to these measures has demonstrated sufficiently that political theory can never be apolitical. It is not necessary to accept Leo Strauss's theses on esoteric teachings of political philosophers to see that Socrates's challenge to Thrasymachus ended with Socrates's philosophical victory but with Thrasymachus's political victory, and that this may have had far-reaching consequences for Plato and many later political philosophers' thinking. The very existence of political theory, let us make it clear, has itself become, and remained, a constraint on governing, sometimes a partially enabling one (where political theory turns into a guiding ideology of a regime, which, however, must be committed to it), sometimes an effectively blocking one (enabling individuals to reflect on their respective government's policies and actions, and, minimally, ask questions about them). The central argument of this chapter will be exactly this meta-argument: I am going to show that the very activity of political theorizing constitutes a constraint to governing.

To do so, four traditions in political theorizing will be discussed in some detail. Each of them has a conception, at least a few hints at how governments are constituted and should be run, and each theory *dismisses* the idea of a moderate-constrained government. The point is that notwithstanding the dismissing (though not always outrightly rejecting) the idea, theirs being a *political* conception entails the implicit acceptance of a constrained government. Hobbes's theory was already cited and will be discussed from this new angle. The Leader State and the Society as a substitute for government will be analyzed after it: both are rather off from the present agenda of political theory, yet in view of the rise of authoritarianism, their significance seems to be growing. More popular is Rawls's conception of justice as the governing principle of the political community. I will call it the Watchmaker State and argue that it represents another virtual rejection of the idea of constraining the government.

There is an ongoing debate among political theorists on the role of political theory, which is highly relevant to the thesis about the inherently constraining nature of political theory in relation of governing. It centers around the issue of whether the descriptive and the normative aspects of political theory can be separated. Let me first reflect on this discussion.

## Descriptivism versus Normativism

A strongly defended position is that political theory consists in trying to contribute to our knowledge of politics and governing by producing good and useful *descriptions* of it. Political theory is different from political thinking because theorizing is a politically "passive activity," consisting in writing, recording, chronicling of the deeds of political actors, analyzing events, reflecting on the thoughts of other thinkers, and so on. Whenever it does more, namely, begins to evaluate, prescribe, give guidance, it immerses in real politics and ceases to be theory, though does not cease to be "thinking."

Raymond Geuss, for instance, argues for such a view. According to it, politics is in the first place about finiteness, vulnerability, power, interdependence, scarcity of resources, and making decisions about timing and action. The business of political theory is to cover and account for these relationships. However, Geuss is aware of the importance of evaluations, the evaluative behavior of the participants in politics. People routinely and often vigorously evaluate one another, both in positive and negative terms. Therefore, a "realist" (good and useful) political theory must take into account the evaluative dimension of politics as well. Since our evaluations have many dimensions and standards, political theory can only record this evaluative pluralism and perhaps construct classifications and categories. But political theory is often invited and its instruments—categories, ideas, descriptions—are used in politics. Political theory then offers guidance for political action and *that* fact is no less part of reality. To use a recent example: populism is one of the most fashionable topics of scientific conferences. It is a theoretically contested concept, yet one that is extensively used in political debates as well. This constitutes a perennial temptation and danger to political theory, yet also a chance to demarcate itself from political thinking. These three tasks of political theory—that is, understanding, evaluation, and orientation, as Geuss summarizes them—are based on the truth-requirement that, so it seems, is constitutive of any theory and philosophy.[1]

Michael Freeden seems to hold the same position, though he formulates it from the negative pole:

> The specific claim that the features of political concepts and arguments are particularly unsuited to the political language of finality [his concept of the political] pertains to the three forms of failure in political thinking on which I focus: flaws of temporal durability, of the definiteness and robustness of decision making (the ending of contestation) and of control over the political space which a political theory penetrates (universalization and the thorough embracing of particular cases).[2]

The first type failure is by and large the problem of utopia: political theory gives visions, makes promises, and predicts the future, but fails to deliver it:

> Paradoxically, utopian and anarchist discourses are frequently inspired by what *they* see as current political failures, and their thought patterns are conscious or unconscious diversionary strategies to transcend the awfulness of those experienced failures while presenting themselves as genuine desires for (lasting) human and social improvement. . . . But in insisting on full success, such theories set themselves up for inevitable failure.[3]

Similarly, "ethicists," though they are not utopians, hope to constraint future by erecting moral bulwarks against morally undesirable actions. Of course, such hopes are mostly unfounded. The second type of failure is, basically, entailed by the intrinsic openness and unpredictability of politics: certain debates cannot be resolved. For instance, the metaphysical or non-metaphysical origin and actual content of human rights is essentially contested. And thirdly, no (political) theory can be specific enough to guide action. Thus, the failures of political thinking are inherent to it, yet realizing this is an argument for the superiority of the descriptive account of political theory over the normative rival account of it.

John Horton's view is different. As other realists, he rejects the "moralist" understanding of political theory because of its descriptive deficiencies. However, he complains that since moralists fail to give good descriptions of politics, their own moral ideals and principles remain within the confines of political theory, within the academia and a narrow circle of theorists. Without a sound account of political action and power, moralism (especially liberal moralism revolving around problems of justice and equality) remains silent on crucial political questions, including the problem of a transition to the desired political institutions and schemes. Does it follow then that realism, understood as a political theory that aims at offering better descriptions of politics than moralism, should be favored because it is a more efficient or successful type of political thinking? Perhaps yes, because Horton thinks that even if moralism were a more efficient political theory, then it would still be "no more than another voice in political debate and argument; one that is without any special claim to normative authority."[4] But in fact, Horton thinks, there is little trace of political theory influencing actual politics (at least in the United Kingdom). It would seem to follow that moralism is just less efficient than realism. However, Horton seems to ignore this consequence (which may or may not be true realistically, that is, descriptively) and returns to the baseline "realist" position according to which

> it is not really the business of political theory to be offering guidance or advice to politicians, political activists or even citizens in general. Rather, what we should learn from a realist orientation is that the activity of politics is for those practically engaged in it, whereas political theory, by contrast, should not be engaged in an ideological competition, but be primarily about trying to understand, to make sense of politics. This will involve some element of evaluation, as such a political theory is not "merely descriptive."[5]

Such a political theory

> will also eschew prescription in the straightforward sense that it will not have being action-guiding as one of its principal aspirations. Instead, it will aim, at trying to understand the fundamental concepts of political discourse and argument and at elucidating the structures of different ways of thinking about politics.[6]

So-called moralists have noted this inconsistency. Maynard and Worsnip, for instance, took issue with both Geuss's and Horton's account (they criticize the whole "realist school"),[7] contending that political philosophy is a normal part of political thinking and thus of politics. The moralist project is simply one of the many political issues of the day. Normative or moralist political theory has no less rights to assert itself as political theory or political philosophy than the realist/descriptivist school, and, contrary to what Horton thinks, it has proved to be quite a powerful project. From Rousseau to Marx, from Nietzsche to Lenin, we have a bewilderingly wide variety of normative projects having found their ways to politics and successfully changing real politics (for better or worse: that is a different question). Geuss himself admits this: he does not hesitate to cite Lenin who claimed that what made Marxism successful was its truth, *therefore* it is right to implement its political program which prescribes the partisan politics of favoring the proletariat over other social classes.

> This means that any kind of comprehensive understanding of politics will also have to treat the politics of theoretisation, including the politics of whatever theory is itself at the given time being presented for scrutiny as a candidate for acceptance.[8]

Even past the grand utopian visions of Marx, Lenin, or Mao, despite not being quoted by many politicians by name, Rawlsian or Dworkinian ideas about justice and equality have arguably exerted considerable influence on policy-making or judicial decisions. Thus, normative political theory is not at all far from reality. Nor can it be: our moral dilemmas and judgments are part and parcel of our political activities. Notwithstanding the abstract and speculative nature of some normative political theories, Maynard and Worsnip claim that these theories are in fact responses to real political problems. Political theory should not be afraid of engaging in normative speculations.

> By connecting sociological, historical, economic and institutional analysis, political theorists can engage in serious study at either the highly applied level or, no less interestingly, in an attempt to construct more general theories of political judgement, agency, and conduct relevant to multiple real world political contexts.[9]

Normativism so conceived is arguably a narrower project in political theory than any grand theory of politics as a system, as a human activity (or a special condition, to recall Hannah Arendt's phrase). However, realist/descriptivist critics would possible retort to this view that normativism is usually or tendentiously not a diagnostic, and not even a casuist-therapeutic project. Rather, normative political theorists usually endorse and advance a particular moral agenda.[10] As a matter of fact, Geuss himself, who is generally revered as one of the most influential thinkers of contemporary realism, does not seem to be very much worried about such an agenda. To the list of tasks of political theory that he expounds, he adds the normative or ideological function: if ideology as a term "has any real use at all, then it would seem that a political theory or political philosophy could be related to a given ideology in at least two distinct ways."[11] One way is to combat ideology as an illusion. Descriptive political theory has the philosophical duty to unmask power, to tell why and how ideology is necessary or useful to gain and retain power. The other way, on the contrary, is in which political theory or philosophy "itself played an ideological role in society in that it fostered certain common ideological illusions."[12] This is still political theory insofar as truth is not denied or falsified but subtly directed, inflected, and put into contexts in which moral and political implications change. Perhaps Geuss should have been more generous with ideologies, especially in view of the moral honesty and sincerity of many political theorists who stood up for a more activist political agenda, based on what they considered to be the true account of politics and not "merely" an ideology (i.e., a deliberately manipulative, illusionary belief). Normativists may, however, insist that normative political theory is different from political ideology in the sense Maynard and Worsnip explained earlier and that political ideology is part of political thinking, and in that, part of doing politics.

Descriptivism and normativism are certainly sensible positions within political theory. Each is able to handle both the *Antigone* and *Measure for Measure*, our standard "real" examples. For instance, analyzing the *Antigone*, a *descriptive theory* may point out the realities of power in Athens/Thebes, the constitutional framework in which these cities lived. It will have to admit, however, that no description can be valid without admitting the real political force of many normative and conceptual ideas about legitimacy, lawmaking authority, tyranny, good governance, public good, and so on: in fact, the tragedy would be unintelligible without taking the moral conflict seriously. A *normativist theory* may focus on the moral principles that guide Creon's politics, and the moral mistakes he makes (not necessarily doing something immoral but misunderstanding, say, the values of goodness and badness), and perhaps conclude that Creon would have had to be more prudent, less obsessive with his principles, more attentive to the city's moral convictions.[13] A more robust moralism (Kantianism: respect the absolute dignity of human beings; utilitarianism: whatever seems to produce the greatest happiness to the most, should be promoted—the actual outcome is clearly inferior to that) would have been perhaps more difficult, though not impossible, to derive from the play. (Who knows, for instance, how happiness is to be further enhanced beyond the proper burial of Polyneices's body: perhaps Antigone should be promoted to be an ombudsperson—something that happened later in Rome when the office of the people's tribune was created.) However, these ideas invariably lead the normativist to the conclusion that prudence is a (political) virtue that cannot be institutionalized or routinized, hence it is always and inherently mingled with power considerations; and that choosing between Kantianism and utilitarianism, for instance, is a political choice, which means that it is embedded in the various descriptions of the "political reality."

Much the same is true for Shakespeare's play. Here again, the realities of power (manipulation, equivocation, second thoughts, hidden intentions, unexpected reactions) should be amended with the realities of normative expectations, commitments, and principles (Isabella's religious vows,

Angelo's views on the rule of law, the conflict between justice and mercy). The policy of strengthening the law and enforcing the norms is both a realist project in either a Hobbesian or a Mandevillean interpretation (the social contract must be renewed; preventing moral panic due to the corruption of the government is a realist aim), and it may please a Puritan moralist as well. It seems therefore that descriptivist political theory cannot hermetically close itself, and that normative political theory is almost self-evidently part of political thinking and by extension, of politics.

In spite of the problems of a full separation of political theory from the business of politics, *doing political theory* or political theorizing remains an activity with special goals and standards, and minimally a form of *doing politics*. It is perhaps better to leave the terrain of battle between descriptivism/realism and normativism/moralism and integrate them into a single and meaningful alternative, which better captures the political nature of political theory. This I term here "conceptualism."

## Conceptualism

Raymond Geuss himself writes that the "fourth task that political philosophy might perform is one of making a constructive contribution to politics by conceptual invention or innovation."[14] He adds that the

> archetypical case I have in mind here is the early modern invention of the concept of "the state" as an abstract structure of power and authority distinct both from the population and from the prince, aristocracy, or ruling class, which successfully enforces a monopoly of legitimate violence within a certain territory.[15]

Further, he emphasizes that the construction of a concept is different from constructing an object or an experiment, or finding a technical term for a newly discovered natural law or species or phenomenon. In social sciences, and especially in political theory, conceptual innovation does not occur in a normatively neutral context.

> Characteristically, the concept "the state" is introduced *together with* a theory about the nature and the source of authority which the abstract entity that is so named is supposed to have. In the early modern period this was usually some version of the social contract theory [italics in the original].[16]

Citing some classical authorities from the canon of political thought, Sheldon Wolin makes a similar point:

When Hobbes allowed that his readers would be "staggered" by his theory, he was not merely stating the obvious fact that his views concerning religion, authority, rights, and human nature were incompatible with traditional religious and political notions, but the more profound point that unless his readers were prepared to revise or discard those notions, they would not be able to grasp the full meaning of the theory and the theory itself could not become an effective force in the world. The same general assumptions had been made by Plato in his challenge to traditional Greek values and to the democratic ethos of Athens, and by Augustine in his effort to demolish classical notions of history, politics, virtue and religion.[17]

Wolin's point is stronger than Geuss's one, in that he allows for revolutionary notions and the evolving conceptions that fly in the face of prevalent ideas. Nevertheless, even such conceptions must be intelligible descriptively and normatively, which is best ensured by the power of concepts. It is then that they can be considered as relevant responses to the problems identifiable by others as well. But should we also think that conceptual innovation and political theory are so strongly interconnected?

Taking now *Measure for Measure* for example, we find a whole array of political concepts. The play begins almost literally with a reference to "government," followed by the Duke's remarks about the "nature of our people" and the "institutions of the city." Later we find Mrs. Overdone's exclamation about the "change in the commonwealth," Claudio's likening of Angelo's rule to a horse rider, where the horse is the "body public," and countless invocations of law, power, authority, justice, or mercy. Of course, concepts such "state" or "social contract" or "consent" or "republic" are absent here, but the play can be easily transposed into a modern setting, including the conceptual framework and context in which we use these concepts extensively. Shakespeare's political conceptual apparatus is refined, he uses it with ease, describing and framing positions and connecting them with the individual characters consistently. We may never know whether an uneducated woman in his age would have ever uttered the word "commonwealth." Shakespeare's recurrent character of the comic constable (here Elbow) who desperately tries but is never capable of using abstract technical-bureaucratic concepts competently may be there for purely dramaturgical-comical reasons, and we know little about how illiterate people of that age used abstract political (and moral, theological, legal) concepts. Most probably, such concepts were, and have ever been, intertwined less with political theories and more with the language of the imagination, and of metaphors and allegories that are themselves derivatives of nonpolitical narratives, myths, and visions.[18] It is a commonplace today that, for instance, political theory has borrowed many concepts and, more importantly, contexts from political theology. For instance, the doctrine about the church as the Body of Christ is an important precursor to the organic doctrine of the political body, which is both a doctrine in a theoretical sense, and a powerful, because easily comprehensible, metaphor. Claudio's (or Shakespeare's) metaphor of Angelo riding the body public is also very poignant and expressive of a deep (but rather helpless) animosity against the ruler of the commonwealth. The Duke's behavior itself is a grand metaphor of a new sort of power or authority emerging, though Shakespeare does not invent a concept for that, the silent formation of the Leviathan is clearly sensible in the play and through his figure. Thus, conceptual innovation in politics and political thinking has more than one source.

Most probably, neither Wolin, nor Geuss would deny this. What conceptualism as a concept itself can highlight for political theory is that beyond the values of impartiality and truth-seeking, and the personal commitments to these values, some further theoretical-logical virtues are also necessary for political theory to qualify as such. For instance, it needs to possess some degree of coherence, at least in the sense of a coherent terminology and conceptual apparatus; a systematic logic (similar to law or theology); and, more importantly, mental discipline, moderation, and self-restraint. Wolin's caveat about metaphors is applicable to conceptualism in general:

> Ever since Plato, theorists have recognized the fruitfulness of metaphorical thinking, but they have also come to realize that at certain crucial points a metaphor may become misleading, primarily because the metaphor has a thrust of its own which leads to grotesque implications for the object or events which it is supposed to illuminate.[19]

Thus, political theorists need a sort of self-referential consciousness. By this, I mean the awareness of the source of the force of their concepts. The descriptive strength of a concept may arise from its political power, and its normative authority may be a result of a specific (often distortive) description of social and political reality. The likening of governing to steering a ship, the leader to the captain, may have a self-evident tinge about it, yet these analogies are already politically loaded. Famously, Carl Schmitt defined political theology as a development produced by the secularization of theological concepts, which entails that we (believers and non-believers alike) use concepts that inherited their authority from sacral-religious sources. Being conscious of these possibilities is, however, tantamount to being in charge of them, at least to some extent. And this implies that political theory, by its very existence, constitutes a constraint to governing.

Political theory may not be able to separate as neatly as it wishes the descriptive, the explanatory, and the normative aspects of politics and political thinking, since its own concepts carry all these aspects. But it is able to reflect on this fact, it is able to use these distinctions, and, eventually, it is able to misuse them. Misusing it makes political theory dangerous, yet again, political theory has its means to explore these faults. This is precisely what I wish to do in the second part of this chapter. That is, I shall try to demonstrate how conceptions in political theory that went the farthest on the route toward eliminating any constraints on governing, and this they did partly because of their conceptual innovations, invariably re-institute those constraints in virtue of their theorizing.

## FOUR CONCEPTIONS OF POLITICAL THEORY

### The State

For its ambition, scope, depth, and impact, the *Leviathan* stands out in the history of political thought. Hobbes's purpose was indeed breathtakingly grand: to solve the problem of stable and efficient governing once and for all, by integrating the field of politics, which included what we may today call the world of all social interactions and institutions into "science," together with "natural philosophy."[20] It would be superfluous to try to revise the gigantic Hobbes-literature. I restrict myself to cite some recent works that specifically draw the attention to the conceptual innovation in Hobbes's theory. Of particular importance are his constructions and explanations of concepts such "personhood," "consent," "covenant," "sovereign," and, of course, the "Leviathan," the "mortal god," which is clearly more than an abstract concept, it is a powerful image of a powerful agent.

   At first sight, it is striking how the materialist Hobbes was so successful in influencing our imagination. For this, conceptual innovations have begun to live their own lives, in various ways. Adam Lindsay discusses the concept of *constituent power*, so important to modern constitutionalism, which entails an assumption of there being somebody "having" or "possessing" and "exerting" this power. He writes that this concept "serves one tool among the many fictional components of our political language that contribute to the rich, layered thought-practices that comprise and pattern political thinking."[21] He notes that since Hobbes was a materialist, he had to reject such non-material objects or subjects. Constituent power is, therefore, not a free-floating essence but "a normative justification for obedience."[22] Nonetheless, Hobbes knew well that our imaginative needs are very much real and have a tremendous impact on our behavior. He therefore developed his argumentation toward a more metaphorical language. In that, the concept of personhood *and* the image of a person take the primary roles. Obeying a person is more efficient, so to speak, more human, than obeying or observing a contract (for its own sake). To switch the logic: it is easier to observe a contract when it is a "must," that is, when and if we consider it an obligation, a duty, because obedience conjures up the image of a more direct, primitive, and efficient agent to whom we are subjected. This does not refute, Lindsay asserts, the truth of materialism. The authority and efficient power of the state (the artificial person, or the sovereign power personified) rests on its normative justification, which is based on the power of the concept of the state.

> The state itself existed only in the imagination of citizens whose individual practices allowed responsibility to the attributed from the sovereign to the state and continued to exist only so long as they continued to buy into that fiction.[23]

There is, however, a problem with the idea of personification, the creation of artificial personhood. To see this, Quentin Skinner's concise interpretation of the argument seems to be helpful.[24] He inserts this interpretation into a broader political theoretical landscape, implying also that Hobbes's conceptual innovations were not absolutely context-free: indeed, as I argued, Shakespeare's idea of the commonwealth being represented by the Duke anticipates something of the image of the emerging absolutist state. Thus, Skinner argues that Hobbes rejected both a republican fiction of a constituent and free-floating collective power and an absolutist, self-engendering notion of power. The basic idea is, from this point of view, the amalgamation of both positions. For Hobbes, construes two political persons: the state that is the personified collective of individuals, and the sovereign who is the person representing the state. This person may be carried or instantiated by a natural person (especially visibly in monarchies). Put in a nutshell:

> The act of covenanting may thus be said to engender two persons who had no previous existence in the state of nature. One is the artificial person to whom we grant authority to speak and act in our name. The name of this person, as we already know, is the sovereign. The other is the person whom we bring into being when we acquire a single will and voice by way of authorising a man or assembly to serve as our representative. The name of this further person, Hobbes next proclaims in an epoch-making moment, is the Common-wealth or State.[25]

The two-person theory of the state and sovereign preserves the consensual, or least consent-based creation of the state, a sort of autonomous existence, which does not amount to "free floating" but remains distinct from the sovereign whose identity is revealed by the agent (monarch, assembly) who is able to speak and act on our behalf. The Leviathan comes later to be identified as the state, whereas the government (who is the sovereign power to make and enact laws) is distinct from it.

Skinner concludes with some remarks on the normative implications of the Hobbesian double-person theory:

> If we reflect on what I have been calling the absolutist and populist [republican] theories, it is hard to avoid the conclusion that they are nowadays of exclusively historical interest. If we turn, however, to the fictional theory, we come upon a way of thinking that ought never to have been set aside. As a number of legal and political theorists have begun to urge, we can scarcely hope to talk coherently about the nature of public power without making some reference to the idea of the state as a fictional or moral person distinct from both rulers and ruled. According to the fictional theory, the conduct of government is morally acceptable if and only if it serves to promote the safety and welfare of the person of the state, and in consequence the common good or public interest of the people as a whole.[26]

Thus, the "fictional theory" of the state, in contrast to what may be called the institutionalized concept of the state (which virtually identifies the state with the government), helps us control the government and make a judgment of its legitimacy. Once we understand that the government does not own the state, that the state belongs as much to the people as it does to the sovereign, once this idea takes its root (again, perhaps) in the conceptual world, and what is more important, takes a more visible shape in the imagination of citizens, so Skinner, they will be better equipped against the abuses of governmental power.

Since my aim is not exegetical, the correctness of the double-person interpretation of Hobbes is of secondary importance. The distinction between the sovereign in the form of an artificial person represented, perhaps embodied, by a natural person, and the Leviathan as the shape or image of the state may not be as conveniently and easily imaginable as the conceptual analysis may suggest. Notwithstanding the normative urgency to reclaim at least part of the collective agent, in the form of a personified state, it is hard to see both how it can become a persuasive argument (the distinction appears to be impractical, overly sophisticated), and how it could actually serve the defense of citizens' (relative) autonomy and independence. For what we are asked to imagine may be two distinct persons or agents, but *both* completely outside of our control. Moreover, if we take another look at what Skinner suggests in the previous quotation, it may easily strike us as embarrassing, perhaps even astonishing: "the conduct of government is morally acceptable if and only if it serves to promote the safety and welfare of the person of the state, and in consequence the common good or public interest of the people as a whole." It is hard to imagine how the government should or could tend to the safety and welfare of the "person of the state" and how from this the common good or the public of the people is supposed to ensue. Governments, no matter how enlightened and constitutional they are, have indeed—at least in the popular imagination—a very special relationship to the state. They may in fact tend to "its" needs, though in reality, it amounts often to nothing else but protecting and serving the interests of the state bureaucracy. Alternatively, governments may freely and sovereignly make use the legal powers and authority of the state to implement absolutist, freedom-constraining, highly biased, and so on legislation. Therefore, if there is a strong conceptual bulwark against the government being identified with, rather than separated from, the state, then it is arguably the idea of constraining the government-cum-the-state, keeping their joint forces at bay.

However, Hobbes's theory as a political theory using the conceptual method creatively contains another, more useful though a bit less explicit, distinction. Put very briefly, this is inferable from his conception of the commonwealth or the state as a political theoretical construction. The idea is that the state as represented and personified by the sovereign (again, it is a safe bet to suppose that most people do not think of the state as a personification of the "multitude") commands us to suppress our political inclinations for conflict and disagreement, hence, and crudely put, this is a *prevention*, in fact, a *prohibition of politics*. At the same time, and unintentionally, following this command presupposes a consciously exerted self-rule as well. We are not required to agree with the government and its policies, only remain silent. But we should recall Creon's case: silence, if effectively enforced, makes his government omnipotent yet at the same time weak; his rule wild but fallible. The reason is that people are, inadvertently, encouraged to reflect on their views all day, and make their decisions about what is permitted and what is not in the public sphere. As St. Paul writes, without the law, there is no sin, and without a prohibition, there is no thinking about how to observe it. But this is tantamount to bringing politics back in, if only in a distorted, disfigured, and uneducated form.

The received view is that Hobbes's aim was to constrain politics, inasmuch as politics is a terrain of disagreement, pluralism, agonism, and conflict. As is well-known, Hobbes's main concern was civil war, serious disorder, arising from the conflicts among citizens. Robin Douglass argues that "for Hobbes, the pursuit of peace (and what it entails) solves the fundamental problem of politics, rather than simply being the precondition for further political disputes to be negotiated."[27] The argument is made against one type of realist reading of Hobbes in which politics is an autonomous field. No such autonomy is tolerable, however, since it threatens peace and order. Another type of realism, on the contrary, claims that peace and order being essentially non-moral conditions of social cooperation and co-existence, it is politics (or the political truth) that precedes morality (or any moral principle of the good or the right). Douglass points out that one does not need to accept the realist-moralist conceptual framework. It does not matter too much whether "peace and order" is called a political or a moral principle (having either the logical or theoretical precedence over the other). The decisive step is to preclude, prevent, or prohibit (administratively, or by ways of education) any serious disagreement, pregnant of actual hostilities, among citizens: it is indifferent whether citizens themselves justify this step in moral or political terms. Hobbes makes concessions to both directions: he does not exclude either the possibility of justifying obedience in terms of natural law (a moral sort of justification), though he is indeed skeptical about its convincing force, or the purely rationalist-utilitarian type of justification (so popular in contemporary rational choice theory).[28] In either way, disagreement, pluralism, and conflict are potentially harmful to peace and order, and must be curtailed, possibly tolerated only as long as their disruptive potential remains low.

To see and decide whether and when these conflicts jeopardize the public interest of maintaining peace order is in principle an exclusive prerogative of the government created precisely for this purpose. If, however, conflicts and serious disagreements belong to the essence of politics, then such decisions amount to a prevention or prohibition of politics. However, Hobbes no less explicitly proclaims that this argument is an open one. Everybody is invited to share it. This invitation to a deliberative and willful (albeit fear-motivated) choice is addressed to all individuals in the state of nature. They all are supposed to see that this is the only choice, namely, the only reasonable choice to make. But making a choice logically presupposes of at least two alternatives, the deliberation over which is itself a non-trivial process. Hobbes may call it pure theory, a lonely reflection on how to justify obedience. Yet if it amounts to denying or rejecting, for instance, the commands of conscience, which may prescribe an utmost dedication to the promotion or defense of certain principles, then it implicates a constant conflict, the suppression of which is dependent on the power that any individual can exert over himself or herself. The individualism of the Hobbesian political theory cuts in both ways: on the one hand, it explains and justifies the state; on the other hand, unintentionally perhaps, it creates the reasoning and justification-seeking citizens.

In one sense, this is not particularly news.[29] It may be read as a reformulation of the point made by Skinner, among others, which claims that Hobbes wished to steer clear of both the republican and the absolutist extremes. However, in another sense, it does look to be an important lesson to realize how state, government, *and* politics are being jointly constituted, despite their apparent mutual exclusiveness. To repeat: the state-constituting act of consent consists of the decision of every individual taken individually but at the same time to give up their individual powers of governing themselves. There is, thus, an original idea of self-governance, of independence, of autonomy enjoyed in the state of nature, which is, therefore, in a robust sense a political "state of affairs." But the state-constituting act is a negative one, by definition, because it is an act of relinquishing the right to enjoy political freedom. The reason why individuals choose to abandon their absolute freedom of action is that they are fully aware that they—and all the others—are very much willing to enjoy it, at the expense of the next and the rest. The *desire* to have power over others is indeed all-effective and constantly active urge and motive is the *reason* for curtailing it. This is the principal function and main business of the government: to fight against the power of individuals, and in this fight, the state as an apparatus, with all its procedures and institutions, is the crucial agent. What happens or what has happened since Hobbes's day is, in some ways contrary to Skinner's view, that the state has gradually become a persuasive image by which the political task of the government to suppress conflicts by suppressing the power of individuals has become more easily accomplishable. Moreover, the concept and image of the state has turned out to be a highly useful tool for obfuscating the political nature and origin of the government. Even in the totalitarian Soviet Union (and other Communist countries), both the real and the nominal political rule of the Communist Party was overwritten by references to the state, especially in relation to the law and order functions (the NKVD/KGB was a *state* organ, firms were *state owned*, etc.) Hence, according to this theory, the state is there to prevent politics, for the very political purpose of suppressing power, which is the main political responsibility of the government. The state is a negative political (or a "politically negative") concept, but this negativity does not delete its political nature, inadvertently, it is constantly evoked.

In the previous chapter, *Measure for Measure* served as a particularly apt illustration of social disorder and order. It was argued that the *image* of disorder was essential to establish the new ducal government. It is worth remembering that the words of the disguised Duke about corruption and the complete dissolution of law and order in Vienna: these are emphatically uttered, even harangued in the widest possible public arena, practically, to the citizenry of the state.[30] But we do not hear these words having a positive echo. Escalus and Lucio find them revolting, anarchist, state-slandering, and the Duke masked as a friar is proclaimed to be a public enemy, himself the cause of disorder. Yet again, by Lucio's demasking of him, and creating the new Duke, the audience witnesses a wonder, a miracle, a slanderer to the state becoming the sovereign, and the state personified. In and by itself, this justifies the description offered before since it would be an unthinkable thought that the state was founded on nothing else but a trick, an image, indeed, a mirage. And yet unthinkable as the idea is, the trick remains a trick, and though the Duke immediately turns to his normal business of sentencing, pardoning, condemning, and ordering, his subjects will ever remember of the beginning of his government, and the lesson that was taught to them about the possibility of anarchy and tyranny "crouching at their door." Thereby, however, they are awakened to the necessity and logic of ruling, to the truth that law and government have their origins, that their fate is forever intertwined with, but distinct from, the government.

Returning to contemporary vocabulary: by laying out the conception of social contract, political theory performs a political action. It puts the problem of anarchy and government to the center of political thinking. Both the political elite and the citizenry are directed to these issues in their political thinking and imagination. The state appears to be the neutral here, the only area from which political thinking is removed. It is meant to be a non-political concept, again, contrary to Skinner's suggestion, it appears to have been very successful on precisely that account: citizens trust (as much as they do) the state for its being unpolitical, whereas the inherently political governments trust the state for its being non-political. Yet again: it is this unpolitical and nonpolitical nature of the state that makes it a politically interesting subject. Citizens have an interest in, and are therefore called to, reflecting on the impartiality and neutrality of the state, and its unpolitical essence, which entails that they expect the government to respect these values and the only terrain of the commonwealth (in this theory) where politics is truly prohibited. The Hobbesian (broadly speaking, Hobbes-inspired) political theory, perhaps a tradition, invents a form of a state whose essence is its negative political power or negative political charge, as it were. In that, however, consists the political nature of this type of political theory. It seeks a justification of obedience without political partisanship, and thus it contributes to the formation of a political community. And history has shown that it is indeed possible, much against the presumptions and conclusions of the theory, to personify the people, to democratize the Leviathan, to conceive sovereignty as popular, and finally, to make governments serve democracy.

### The Leader

Many political philosophers have been fascinated with the figure of the political leader. However, despite the urgings of Plato to find a philosopher-king, or Aristotle to find the most excellent citizen in whom virtue dwells and shines forth more than in anybody else, he is naturally entitled to become king; and despite the ensuing tradition of searching for the best textbook on how to educate kings and what to teach them (with Machiavelli joining the line), political theory after Hobbes has been largely preoccupied with institutions, principles, and abstract deductions. The discovery and reinstitution of the leader as an *imaginable concept* occurred and evolved in a rather unexpected way. The story begins with the rise of the absolutist state and the no less absolutist thinking of Rousseau. Then the core idea crossed the borders and came to fruition in the philosophy of the state as the rule of Reason in German Idealism. From this tradition, various conceptions flowed, and the one I wish to discuss here led to the Führerprinzip. The idea is that "the" government is replaced by the leader, whose will directly creates the laws and whose orders are to be executed by the state bureaucracy without hesitation. In fact, laws and orders are not substantially distinct, the differences are merely formal. The justification of this idea is that only the unconstrained will of the leader is an authentic expression of the unconstrained will of the people. Paradoxically then, the desire for freedom leads to the greatest unfreedom, supported by one of the greatest tour de force of political theory.

Admittedly, we are far from the age when political theorists wrote whole monographs on the topic, and modern leadership research is only remotely connected to this tradition. But history may repeat itself, and although contemporary political theorists may consider themselves immune to the mysticism that flowed from this thinking, such ideas have their lure. The Führerprinzip looks obsolete but the spell of charismatic leaders and leadership is on doubtlessly spreading today across countries that boast of their enlightened political traditions. Understanding the logic and structure of this thinking is therefore not without lessons, especially because whatever the future will bring upon modern democratic political societies, the point will be, again, that despite the absolutist conclusions, and despite its own aspirations, the theory itself constitutes an important constrain on and of the government.

One of the most outstanding, consistent, and pathbreaking thinkers of this tradition is arguably J. G. Fichte. His political thought has been largely forgotten. But it has influenced this approach hugely.[31] His ideas appear in Hegel's dialectical philosophy, in Marx's conception of the waning of the state, and in Carl Schmitt's (and others') conception of the Führerprinzip (Fichte used the term "Zwingherr," a bizarre creation of his).[32] The way he solved the problem of justifying the government was strongly interrelated with his general philosophy, part of which was a continuation of Kant's universal rationalism and its connecting to Rousseau's conception of the general will. As so many of his age and his (young) generation, he expected the political and historical victory of freedom under Reason. Being confronted with the Napoleonic turn, the cessation of the French universalism and its "degeneration" into an oppressive power, however, Fichte's early political optimism vanished. His thinking underwent a sort of "Hobbesian change," the conflictual nature of human history began to preoccupy his philosophy. He never relinquished the basic tenets of his political views but clearly grew more pessimistic.[33]

Characterizing his own historical epoch full of conflicts, Fichte chooses a curious term: the state of complete or completed sinfulness. It is not exactly a version of the state of war but it is not very different from it, either. He claims that after the formal and material abolition of absolutisms in Europe that rested on authority and coercion (though always, historically speaking, led by Reason by the influence of the select few), the age of complete chaos ushered in, in which doubt replaces knowledge, fantasy replaces action. It is not, however, a senseless and reversible sort of state of war, provided a consensual and political solution is agreed upon as in Hobbes's theory. On the contrary, the abolition of the old absolutisms was a historical necessity, and the state of completed sinfulness is also a historical precondition of the final and ultimate victory of Reason. There is no way of returning to an acceptance of the state or government as a result of coercion, or forced consent (as in Hobbes), but neither is a Rousseauian democratic republic feasible or desirable, with voting, participation in the legislation, and the executive being merely a function of the general will. What Fichte envisions as a way of overcoming the conflicts that are apparently rooted in the individualist, skeptic, and romantic convictions and views that people can accept and tolerate is a rationalist (i.e., reason-based) state. No one believes anything but what he or she finds worthy of belief: this is a fully rational, yet a purely negative way of using our faculty of Reason (hence the term "sinfulness"). What is necessary and inevitable is a positive (later in Hegel: dialectic) turn, namely toward understanding that Reason can be the only authority that everyone can accept. Therefore, Fichte continues, obedience to the state is contingent upon whether it is reasonably constructed and whether its laws are in accord with the principles of Reason.

Fichte's speculative and individualist philosophy follows basically the same logic.[34] To achieve maturity, the human consciousness emerges as a result of a series of conflicts. Conflicts are necessary for realizing the limits of consciousness. These limits are of various nature, the most important being the realization of there being other, similarly rational and free beings. The realization of this (in fact, of *them*, thereby of *my* limits) leads to recognition of equal rights, which leads to respect, and mutual respect results in the greatest degree of human freedom possible. The philosophical realization of this process is reasoning (i.e., the Procession of Reason through History—fully expounded in Hegel's philosophy), and its political realization is the emergence of the Reason-guided or perfectly rational state. In such a setting, individuals enjoy the maximum degree of freedom by embracing the authority of Reason. In Fichte's own words, the state penetrates the individuals completely and inwardly.[35] Obedience ceases to be obeying orders and becomes an automatic adjustment to the laws of the state.

Who is the author of the laws? It is not easy to tell this within the confines of this conception. As I indicated, in one of his more political writings (which are usually long historical commentaries), Fichte introduces the figure of the Zwingherr, who is the best among the best, who is able to take the necessary decision and bear the burden of conscience consciously, and in whom Reason achieves its highest peak that history momentarily allows.[36] It seems that for Fichte, the full and perfect rule of Reason would not need the state (hence its raison d'être is its own destruction), but achieving this is a long process that requires decisions and external coercion (hence the reference to "Zwang"). Being the most rational person, this figure replaces everyone else in politics. The state, then, is almost literally embodied in him, whose views and decisions, representing Reason, cannot be questioned or challenged. Political thinking is reduced to the leader but at the same time it is inflated gigantically. Contrary to the Hobbesian conception in which politics is understood as a world of conflicts resulting from the pluralism of views, here in the state governed by Reason politics is not prohibited but comprised in the leader, and, consequently, all politics is absorbed by the state. The state is not a legal-artificial person as in Hobbes's theory but a sovereign whose actions and decisions are ipso facto political. Paraphrasing Carl Schmitt's dictum— "the sovereign is he who decides on the exception"—we may say that "the sovereign cannot decide but on exceptions." Political action and sovereign action, state and leadership become identical, or at least indistinguishable, especially for the general public.

Repugnant as such ideas may seem today in light of the later developments in the totalitarian regimes of the twentieth century (German Idealism was clearly instrumental to the state-mysticism of the Nazi ideology and the party mysticism of the Communist ideology), it is just for this political success that Fichte (who is, let me repeat, as an illustrative thinker here) is worthy of discussion. Is there anything in this political theory that can be exploited in a defense of a constrained government?

The pan-political nature of such a state embodied in an absolutist-political sovereign leader magnifies the problem of obedience and its justification. It is *loyalty* toward the leader that becomes the single main political motive, at least until Reason becomes the only authority, inhabiting every citizen. On the reverse side, evoking, sustaining, and securing loyalty becomes the main issue for the leader himself. And here is where troubles begin to emerge for the theory.

First, loyalty is an ambiguous virtue because it is highly personal. Recall Creon's concern over his son's political loyalty being compromised by his loyalty to Antigone, and, in a negative sense, Creon's own supposed loyalty toward his kins, including Antigone, that he thinks he must deny. Creon thinks loyalty can be corrupted by disloyalty, or by betrayal, which is rank immorality. Hence, he becomes obsessed with securing his son's loyalty to him, and with assuring everyone that he is merely loyal—absolutely loyal— to his country. "Anyone thinking / another man more a friend than his own country, / I rate him nowhere" (202–204). Evidently, he considers himself to be the greatest friend of his country, through whom everyone else's friendship—read: loyalty—is put to test. But he himself subjected his own government to principles of justice, impartiality, and generally, of morality. However, picking up loyalty and proclaiming it the supreme, nay, the only virtue that counts for governing is obviously a cause of moral confusion for him and everyone else. It simply is not the case that personal loyalty can trump every other moral value and principle. On the contrary, overblown loyalty has ever been a source of moral corruption and much evil. Meine Treue ist meine Ehre—this is a fundamentally suspicious proposition. The result is that this political conception inadvertently makes us alert to the possible abuses of governing based on personal loyalty, and make us seek for guarantees against such abuses.

Secondly, the pan-political state or its leader must spend a lot on securing loyalty. The feudal regimes survived on exactly this principle but did not have the ideal theory of the leader yet. The ideal theory does not, however, admit or calculate with the enormous costs of overseeing loyalty ties, so familiar to medieval kings and princes. Further, such leaders are forced to seek conflicts to test their subjects' loyalty. Spending on loyalty (monitoring, rewarding, supervising, and testing) is itself a serious constraint on the putatively absolute political freedom of the leader.

The Duke of *Measure for Measure* is (again, to a degree mirroring James I.'s behavior) an observer of his own rule. He tests his subjects' loyalty by enquiring, gently interrogating them, and he is confronted with, even confused by the ambiguous responses by Lucio, and the contradiction between how Escalus, his true servant, and Lucio assess his personality. (Escalus describes him a temperate and reserved character yet Lucio makes allusions to the Duke's secret adventures, and Friar Thomas's untold question the response is "No, holy father; throw away that thought; / Believe not that the dribbling dart of love / Can pierce a complete bosom" [I.2.]—which implies that the good friar had his presumptions about the true desire of the Duke.) The results of his personally conducted surveys are not unequivocal. He does make a grandiose attempt to renew loyalty ties in the final scene, but first, these are natural ties among his subjects and political ones connecting them to him; and secondly, the conflicts between loyalty and justice, and rewarding and punishing are very conspicuous, which underlines the problem of how to reconcile loyalty with other virtues and principles. And precisely due to these problems, the ending of the play conveys an atmosphere of uneasiness, pretensions, and consequently, a troubled future.

The lesson is easily generalizable. The ideal state thought of as being constituted within the person of a leader is a concept that can be very conveniently put to practical use, namely, it makes the state easily imaginable. However, the theory produces an unintended constraint on the freedom of absolute government as it makes personal loyalty a center of politics. No doubt, strong loyalty ties may release an incredible amount of energy and reduce the costs of enforcing cooperation (armies are good examples of the benefits of mutual and leader-directed loyalty); yet they also tend to reduce freedom and reasonableness, the benefits of free creative action, and, in a longer run, the performance of the state. Finally, and obviously, such an over-personalized government that puts loyalty first to everything else provokes distaste, disagreement, and disloyalty—and the emergence of alternative and rival loyalties, creating the logic of us-and-them, thereby constraining their effective sphere of action. This may take considerable time as modern, personalist dictatorships show, yet the effects and symptoms begin to appear in the earliest phase.

## The Society

State or party mysticism culminating the adoration of the supreme leader appear to be outdated political theoretical conceptions in Western democracies, though they may have considerable influence over and in non-Western polities, and this is crucial in understanding them, and it is very much possible that other, more fashionable conceptions such as leader democracy or populist democracy, or perhaps some other theoretical constructions liable to personification display similar conceptualist characteristics. It is possible, however, to launch a theoretical expedition into the opposite direction, that is, where neither the impersonal state, nor the personified state, or the leader as such is identified as the concept through which all constraints on governing are eliminated. The guiding idea is simple: to absorb the government within society.

At first reading, this may appear to be the core concept of anarchism. Historically, anarchism did have or still has versions parallel to this idea, yet if anarchism is understood as being fundamentally at variance with any governing, except anti-governing, then it would be not fair and accurate to call the conception of society absorbing governing an anarchist one. On the contrary, the idea leads to a robust conception of central governing, yet with the justification of its flowing directly from the relevant social forces.

Moderate versions of the conception that governing should be somehow subjected to such direct social control include various ideologies. Historically, corporatism stands perhaps in the pole position. It had its rightist versions such as the Catholic teaching, especially popular, and officially supported by the Magisterium in the 1930s. Its leftist versions include the neo-corporatism of the 1960s and 1970s, although, especially in Austria, both the Christian Democratic and the Social Democratic political parties found this system attractive and operated it consensually. Even the post 1968-era in the Eastern Soviet bloc, especially in Yugoslavia, Czechoslovakia, and Hungary saw mostly theoretical (in the Yugoslav case, also practical), attempts to reform the more and more obsolete-looking party-state model according to such a "socialization" of governing (of course, "corporatism" was a banned label). State-owned companies were thought of as particularly suitable organizations to begin with such experiments, but the conception mostly remained highly abstract and a vile kind of wishful thinking. At the beginning of the transition, neo-corporatism looked to some theorists to be a viable way of reform, but such conceptions quickly lost their attraction, and mainstream liberal-constitutional democracies were established. Lastly, and more recently, in Anglo-Saxon countries, conceptions of communitarianism can be cited as versions of the central idea. Again, no serious communitarian thinker proposes to abandon political governments, but the strengthening of communities and their roles in governing the political community, the invitation of various social forces to solving many political problems *is* a political conception.

Since my aim is not a rehearsal of the history of ideas, but an analytical and conceptual exploration of why and how conceptions of governing that do away with its constraints run into difficulties and re-admit, unintentionally and as a result of their speculations, those very constraints, I propose to examine this once again in one of its more extreme form. To repeat: the core idea is the rejection of individualism both empirically and theoretically, and subsequently, the founding of the state in and on the primordial communities of the society. The thinker I am discussing here is the Austrian legal theorist, Othmar Spann. Although he is even more forgotten than Fichte, he was very influential in the interwar period, especially in the German-speaking world. In any case, his theory of the state conceived along these lines is a very detailed one.[37] The rejection of individualism is not particularly interesting insofar as it is grounded in the "discovery" of the *Gemeinschaft* as opposed to the individualist *Gesellschaft* in the German social and sociological theories. The criticism of individualism has found strong support in leftist and rightist political movements and ideologies, as the brief overview in the preceding paragraph showed.

However, the empirical truth of the inherently social nature of human beings does not engender self-evident political truths, not to speak about a theory of government. Hobbes, for one, wholeheartedly agreed with the axiom, namely, that we are social beings, but he derived from this his thesis of the state of war, rather than a conception of harmonious order. Spann, based on his sociologically more commonsensical assumptions about the inherently communal nature of pre-political life, dismisses such derivations, yet he is confronted with the problem on the next stage. Instead of personal individualism, the problem is the emerging communal individualism. How are the conflicts between different communities (we may call them collective identities today) be treated, reconciled with one another, in absence of a Leviathan? His answer lies in his assumption that the various communities realize that they are members of "the whole." Spann makes much of the concept of "wholeness" in precisely the sense we need: this is the conceptual innovation (not only his, but an entire array of similar-minded thinkers), which also invokes further images of organism, of the body, of the "diversity united," and so on. This suggests a social theory already in its political mode of operation. It may not work today as it did a century ago, but it was efficient, persuasive, and influential in its day.[38]

Much as loyalty is an implicit political motive in the Fichtean theory of the state, harmonious order is the hidden political core motive, on which the workability and efficiency of this theory hinges. The state is no longer a core concept. Rather, the community-based society is proposed to be an adequate solution to the problem of conflicts and disorder, provided that the required sense of harmony and order is pervasive. Mainstream Nazi ideology, itself an amalgamation of all sorts, now outlandish-sounding and absolutely unacceptable fantasies about race, blood, soil, and the like, did not work with such concepts. According to it, there is no harmonious order in nature, only struggles for domination and life. It is easy to see why Spann's theory, though he was himself enthusiastic about the National Socialist movement, was not to become its official ideology: the Führerprinzip, the utmost personification of the state, which fights its life and death battle with other states (supposedly based on other races), is hardly reconcilable with the idea of a society in its manifoldness, and with its replacing the state, the government, and its leader. Spann and other like-minded theorists of the whole sought a solution to their problem of how to maintain the unity of the whole, of society, without falling back either on the concept of an omnipotent and neutral state, or on the concept of Reason residing in the supreme leader. The idea Spann proposes is, thus, that the intellectual elite intuitively understands and expresses the meaning of harmonious order, from which a general sense of order ensues and a form to the state is given.

It remains very obscure how this actually happens. Formally, there is a political caste, entrusted with governing, yet we know that the fundamental responsibility of any conventional government, namely, of dealing with, or better, of preventing all conflicts, rests with the intellectual elite. However, Plato was the first to realize in his ambiguous story of the Cave that such an elite, or a philosopher, is also unable to cope with these conflicts, and govern in the conventional sense. For a philosopher is interested in truth, in the order of ideas, and governing for him has at most an instrumental value: it is one way of a learning about herself and thereby about the truth.

Everyone else may wonder why that would be a public good, and how that leads to better navigation of the ship. As was argued earlier, although it is true that hubris, the pretension of wisdom, causes disaster, but it is no less true that an unceasing questioning, reflections, and pursuit of the ultimate truth can have no less catastrophic consequences. The Duke, much like Prospero in *The Tempest*, is interested in things other than the business of governing. Upon the disguised Duke's question about the person of himself, Escalus responds that the Duke "above all other strifes, contended / especially to know himself" (III.2.). Prospero, a later version of the Duke, got punished for his inattentiveness to politics, due to his immersion in his studies (in exile, on one possible reading, there he learned, thanks to Ariel and Caliban, how to govern efficiently, and returned to Naples triumphantly). The Duke is perhaps sensing a similar problem, the weakness of his rule. These dangers arise from the intellectualism of their governments. Knowledge and philosophy, search for and enjoyment of truth, spiritual and other lofty aims and concepts, pleasing and exciting that may be to philosophers, artists, scholars and scientists do not guarantee a good rule, and cannot be meaningfully represented as governing, except for the fantasy of such an elite having a vision of harmony, which they can reveal to the public that may stand in awe but more probably at a loss.

Having visions, however arresting and enjoyable, amounts to being incapable of governing. By an argumentum e contrario, however, it follows that although the intellectual elite is incapable of governing, its very activity is a constraint to any governing. The vision about a harmonious society without government (or with a political class as one corporation among many others) becomes itself a problem for governments in the conventional sense. A philosopher or a class of intellectuals worthy of this name incessantly pursues of knowledge. It may feel itself compelled to ask questions and to challenge the extant norms, the adopted laws, the decrees of the government, and thereby to confuse, to embarrass others, as Socrates did. Alternatively, it may merely hold up its visions of harmony and order, offering it as a solution to all troubles and disagreements. In both cases, however, they represent an authority outside of the government, which it may want to crush or incorporate into itself, but which ever remains an alien force.

## The Watchmaker

John Rawls's theory of justice as fairness is well-known.[39] As one of the cornerstones of postwar liberal theorizing on politics, it is widely regarded as a conception that protects individual rights against the government, the abuses of state power, and the menace of totalitarian ideologies. It grounds justice in the inalienable rights of individuals, embraces the Kantian conception of human dignity, and, at least nominally, dismisses the utilitarian principles of modern governing. On the face of it, the original Rawlsian theory is as far as it can be from any sympathies toward unconstrained governing.[40]

Early objections to the original theory raise various points with respect to its assumptions of human nature, and its understanding of the concepts of justice, fairness, and consensus, among others.[41] More pertinent to the concerns of this book have been so-called realist criticisms that have a different problem with the original theory. This problem is its putative and putatively oppressive moralism.[42] This entails that the first political question, as Bernard Williams labeled it, should be answered by way of finding the ultimate and most fundamental principles of social cooperation acceptable to everyone. Whether these principles are "moral" or "political" has become a matter of debate: Williams thinks they are moral,[43] others think otherwise;[44] it is possible perhaps that a sort of a "neutral normativity" is at issue.[45] The major point of controversy is clearly the deductive method: from an abstract and hypothetical situation, working with a few empirical assumptions (e.g., rationalism, constrained egoism, and risk-avoidance) about human nature (understood at least as common knowledge: people need not be such but assume this of one another), two principles of justice are inferred. Defenders of Rawls point out that abstraction actually enhances applicability, thus, the theory allows plenty of room for taking into account the various intricacies of reality, and historical and political embeddedness.[46] Critics maintain, however, that the analytical rigor, the closed system-like argumentation, and theoretically "binding" conclusions of the theory are undeniable as well as incompatible with real politics and realist governing. Indeed, it is especially alarming, so the criticism may go, that these principles of justice are being applied to the political sphere intolerantly and with an authoritative voice. Institutions that fall short of these principles must be reformed: no wonder that many commentators found this pronouncement a moral conclusion-turned-into-a-political-command.

The more specific doctrine about the government that Rawls's original theory involves makes this authoritarian tone even stronger. First, writing about the constitution of the just and well-ordered society, he wants to

> consider political justice, that is, the justice of the constitution, and to sketch the meaning of equal liberty for this part of the basic structure. . . . First, the constitution is to be a just procedure satisfying the requirements of equal liberty; and second, it is to be framed so that of all the feasible just arrangements, it is the one more likely than any other to result in a just and effective system of legislation. The justice of the constitution is to be assessed under both headings in the light of what circumstances permit.[47]

There is an unmistakably normative tone in the argument, which is that constitution-making is subject to the principles of justice, first, to secure equality in providing basic goods (including non-material and political rights) to each individual; and second, to make-up a system of legislation that is in conformity with the requirements of justice. The first principle does not seem to be a moralistic one, or if it is, it serves as a hard constraint on the political system, including the government. It may bother hardcore realists, but it is a traditional idea of protecting individuals against tyrannical government reformulated and re-packed. Critics of Rawls usually have a problem with the second principle, which appears to be too specific and virtually oppressive. Its precedence over any other political consideration can be regarded as a constraint on free deliberations, giving a political advantage to the political theorist, as it were, to predetermine the acceptable outcomes. Rawls continues explaining:

> The intuitive idea is to split the theory of justice into two parts. The first or ideal part assumes strict compliance and works out the principles that characterize a well-ordered society under favorable circumstances. . . . My main concern is with this part of the theory. Nonideal theory, the second part, is worked out after an ideal conception of justice has been chosen; only then do the parties ask which principles to adopt under less happy conditions . . . . Viewing the theory of justice as a whole, the ideal part presents a conception of a just society that we are to achieve if we can.[48]

The swinging between the reference to "we" who "are to achieve" the ideal structure and the passive mode of speaking ("existing institutions are to be judged in the light of this conception") where "this" is an ambiguous term (meaning both the present theory and the non-specified "ideal theory") blurs the real agent here, but it is not very difficult to infer that the political theorist, having the necessary and sufficient methodology at his or her disposal, is in the best position to do this job.[49] And once the theorist has finished his or her task, the implementation may begin, much as in the deistic conception of the providence with the Watchmaker God who finishes His work on the last day of creation, after which the laws of nature will take care of making and keeping the world go around.

> The social system is to be designed so that the resulting distribution is just however things turn out. To achieve this end it is necessary to set the social and economic process within the surroundings of suitable political and legal institutions. Without an appropriate scheme of these background institutions the outcome of the distributive process will not be just.[50]

Rawls has more specific ideas as well about how these political legal institutions should be organized. He recommends a design of government that consists of four branches: the allocation, the stabilization, the transfer, and the distribution branches. The details can be ignored here. What is clear is that these branches are not thought of as checks and balances, different sorts of power, constituting a scheme of balance and harmony for the sake of, say, freedom, by preventing a monolithic, absolutist, tyrannical government from emerging, as Montesquieu argued. What is at stake is a just scheme of the distribution of goods. Therefore, these branches are basically derivative functions of the government understood as a grand structure that includes all the traditional branches. In effect, the scheme overwrites the traditional idea of the separation of powers that seeks to justify each branch in terms of a specific *political* task. The four-branch system is imposed upon legislation, execution, and the judiciary, and the potential conflicts between the traditional and the new system are not discussed at all. The emerging conception of government is justified by and found legitimate for its efficiency in implementing the principles of justice that have been enshrined in the constitution. The principles of justice should virtually work as natural laws, under the indirect but efficient and constant control of the Watchmaker, that is, the representative individual in the original position, or its representative, the political theorist.

As I indicated, there are many defenders of Rawls as a not-so-moralist political philosopher. They usually point either to the "later Rawls" and his works, or to the countless cautionary and qualifying remarks in A *Theory of Justice*, or to some of its key concepts such as overlapping consensus (read: no single conception of the good life prevails); well-ordered society (read: stability is a major value); reflective equilibrium (read: deliberations are inherently open); and justice as fairness (read: justice so conceived is broader than its traditional meaning).[51] His critics, however, recite and repeat the core of the conception, which is a deductive approach, highly specified principles of the justice, and a government whose main job is the implementation of these principles as consistently and efficiently as possible. If this latter interpretation is defensible, and the quotations given earlier suggest that it is, then we have a version of ideal political theory, which aims at exploring the mechanism of a workable society. "Mechanism" is not a word that Rawls anywhere uses, nor is the "Watchmaker" such a word, but much as Deism was a theological-political conception or perhaps a tradition, or a perspective of life whose philosophical background was hardly widely known in its age, yet more and more people lived their lives according to it, so the welfare-state conception, or perhaps a tradition already, of which Rawls's theory is arguably the most outstanding and influential political philosophical justification, does suggest metaphors that suit the core idea well. And this idea is widely shared. There is the passive mode of speaking on government and politics (see the quotations given earlier: this mode of writing is not indicative of a scholarly method, of philosophical impartiality, nor is it merely the dry style of scientific treatises, rather, it is politically suggestive of a non-present agent); there is the obsession with justice reduced to but also widened by welfare legislation and wealth re-distribution (again, with the government as the visible agent of an invisible mover); and there is the institutionalization of politics and governing, with "institutions" working as the "nuts and bolts" of a big machine run by some mortal providence.

No such conceptions and concepts were available to either Sophocles or Shakespeare. The welfare state is truly a new invention, which (perhaps apart from images of pastoral power as Foucault calls it and from the gentle, yet formidable parental-paternal power Tocqueville finds in it) lacks the arresting power or attractiveness of the images discussed so far. Rawls's treatise is as remote as a dry philosophical conception can be from the world of fairy tales. However, no one else but Plato taught us that philosophy must rely on tales, and especially political philosophy, if it is meant to be political, will be told and understood as a tale about common life. Therein lies the problem. The untold but implied tale about the Watchmaker becomes a metaphor, a story difficult to believe. As Deism is no more fashionable because its theological lure is basically extinct, people begin to believe in something else, or in nothing at all. Many share views close pantheism, a belief in supernatural forces, or nature or similar things that may resemble Deism but, most probably, without its most important feature, namely, Reason or reasonableness. This is not the place to assess modern religious sense, or religiosity in contemporary secular societies in detail, but it seems a safe assumption to think that notwithstanding our scientific knowledge and our undeniable collective power over nature, the optimism of the sort transhumanism advances (which is also close to a quasi-religious creed) many people have retained many views grown out of religious practice and theological thinking that include, among others, historical projections and musings about progress or regress (with some apocalypse waiting for us at the end); awareness of evil; and beliefs related to determinism and indeterminism, to the source of the self and moral responsibility, to the benevolence and malevolence of external forces, and so on. Political Deism with the unpainted Watchmaker image aims at purging these beliefs (Hobbes, Machiavelli, Rousseau—these atheists and Deists were firmly convinced that religion cannot be ignored). This is a vain effort and this vanity resulting in futility is the constraint that we are seeking for. How does this work?

I contend it does so in three ways. First, the purgative efforts lead to much moralization, and regardless of the conceptual sophistry and accuracy of Rawls's writings, the Rawlsian tradition has already become a target of realism, at least and so far mainly in political theory, with the well-known anti-moralism agenda and arguments (some of which have been cited here). In some sense, much as the Rationalism and Deism of the Enlightenment provoked Romanticism and its cult of the emotions and its rehabilitation of

the Irrational, showing the limits of Reason not by way of Cartesian speculation (i.e., from inside) but in a form of an individualist and existentialist
revolution, realism in political theory has some characteristics of a counter-
revolution. Generally, what realism stresses are the personal, agonistic, and
historically predetermined aspects of politics. If the Watchmaker is a fair
and credible (not caricaturist) image of the Rawlsian tradition, then perhaps
the time-honored metaphor of the Captain or Navigator steering the ship
on rough waters with a limited number of instruments is an appropriate
counter-image.[52] Anyhow, strong images of government provoke no less
strong opposing images, which make it difficult to govern under the pretext
of consensus.

Secondly, the prohibitive aspect of the theory, that is, the presupposition
that justice must come first and everything else is permitted to enter deliberation after that, has another provocative and consequently, a resisting effect.
The resistance aims at abolishing the presumed barrier and even if the other
side does not *see* the barrier, this resistance *creates* it. In other words, anti-
Rawlsians insist that there is an implicit but hard constraint on free deliberation. Now Rawlsians and other ideal theory proponents would perhaps never
think of it as a prohibition, they have no power over those who think otherwise. Thus, the political issue to be talked about is no more justice and the
just distribution of goods, and the government whose business is to set up the
most suitable institutions for this; rather, the political issue is the prohibition,
the agenda-forming idealism, and this unwanted talk and discourse inevitably
shakes the basis of any Rawlsian government.[53]

And thirdly, the Watchmaker image with the implication of benevolence,
the goodness of the instrument and its governing laws, and the almost automatic corrections of the mechanism (say, the constitution) ignore the evident
and common experience that governing is to a great extent about power
games, about clashes of interests and views, about orders, even commands
and obedience, and about exclusion and inclusion, using force for both. This
is, again, a commonplace objection, often made by realists of all sorts.[54] The
point here is that if a political theory that claims to be able to lay down the
foundations of a constitution once and for all, and does not say anything
about the possible dangers of pluralism and power, then it risks losing its
credibility. As an ideal theory, it may be perfectly construed and have considerable attraction and many followers; others, however, who need not be
Thrasymacheans at all, may find it incomplete, imperfect, and incredible.
Whatever the true meaning of Einstein's oft-quoted proposition of his disbe-
lief in a God who "plays dice with the Universe" is, a God who does so nonetheless, is surely more personal, interesting, and inspiring. The Watchmaker
Government that supervises the operation of just institutions of society (that,
unfortunately, have a propensity to go wrong quite often) is an uninteresting

agent; at least as long as someone does not discover that control over super-vision, or controlling the supervising agent might be an excellent idea to gain power. But this is no secret: hence politics keeps returning, and as the Hobbesian state was shown to be an instrument, a filter or a shield by which the political government wants (albeit in vain) to prevent power and politics emanating from the citizens to enter, the Rawlsian government is itself the depoliticized instrument, which unwillingly invites the power-hungry politi-cal animals. To what extent and how or should they be contained? This is the constraint-constituting problem, then, which the theory produces.

## SUMMARY

The main thesis of this chapter was that political theory, which is as old as the classic Greek tragedy, was born and has grown with it, itself constitutes important and effective (though of course never insurmountable) constraints for governing. To see the argument clearly, it was necessary to reflect on the nature of (doing) political theory first. In contemporary political theory, the debate between realism and moralism has highlighted the underlying dilem-mas. What I have called here the descriptivist view of political theory aims at exploring politics and give the most realist descriptions of it possible, yet for its being realist enough, it must take into account the normativist approach as well, since normativism is often a hard player in real politics as well. Normativism, in turn, cannot ignore the realities of power and conflict to promote values and moral principles, hence it must rely on descriptive accounts. Both approaches can contribute to the idea of making sense, as well as of justifying, the constrained government, and for this very reason, both of them have their own ways of becoming parts (in some cases, players) of the political game.

Admitting the merits of both descriptivism and normativism, I suggested that the approach called conceptualism serves better the purpose of build-ing a more accessible and broader bridge connecting ordinary or common political thinking and political theory. Conceptualism seeks concept-images or image-concepts, which help us imagine, more than conceptualize and theorize, governments. The challenge is to show that the most powerful images of the government without (effective and political) constraints that political theory has developed, confirmed, and elaborated (for philosophi-cal purposes, formulated in often highly sophisticated arguments) vindicate, despite their overwhelming force and power, their own constraints. First, I discussed the Leviathan, the imprint of the modern state, and argued that its political neutrality or unpolitical nature is an indirect invitation to consider the limitations of politics and political governing. Second, I argued that the figure of the leader as a representative, often embodiment, of the government imposes on everyone the test of personal loyalty, which, in turn, constitutes the limitations of such personalized forms and systems of government. Third, I considered the idea of society in substitution for the government. In its full-fledged form, it is apparently a bit obsolete now but in many hardly detectable channels, it seems to be returning to our imagination. Overarching and emotionally overwhelming as it was and is, its indifference to the harsh realities of conflicts and the plurality of interests and values may make people concerned with and alert to the capabilities of the government in handling this plurality and world of conflicts. What emerges is the idea of the administrative government, with its vaguely drawn yet very real limitations. Finally, the Watchmaker image behind of a well-designed and functioning, justice-obsessed society may work, again, as a provocative device to make people look for other idols, for more autonomy and freedom in political thinking and innovation, and for the real games of politics.

## NOTES

1. Raymond Geuss, *Philosophy and Real Politics* (Princeton: Princeton University Press, 2008).
2. Michael Freeden, "Failures of Political Thinking." *Political Studies* 1 (2009): 141–64, 145.
3. Ibid., 149.
4. John Horton, "What Might it Mean for Political Theory to Be More 'Realistic'?" *Philosophia* 1 (2017): 487–501, 9. In his view, realism makes two broad claims: first, that liberal moralism misconstrues political reality (descriptive inadequacy) and that it is normatively irrelevant (utopian). The first claim merely underlines the importance of power, agonism, vices, contingency, and so on in politics. The second claim is that "appearances and all claims to the contrary, liberal moralism can provide us with little normative guidance about how we should act in the real world" (5). This is partly related to the first question: since liberal moralism is said to have no theory about political action, it remains silent on many political questions, including the transition to the desired just institutions.
5. Ibid., 11.
6. Ibid., 13.
7. Jonathan L. Maynard and Alex Worsnip, "The Realist Narrative about 'Ethics-First' Political Philosophy." (2015) downloaded from: https://www.academia.edu/20790102/Politics_Ethics_and_Power_Making_sense_of_the_realist_challenge_to_political_moralism_through_Raymond_Geuss_Philosophy_and_Real_Politics?auto=download
8. Geuss, *Philosophy and Real Politics*, 29. Not every project was so successful, Geuss adds: "The centerpiece of the [liberal] argument was the idea of a strict limitation of government. *If* government was sufficiently limited, the thought ran, it would

not matter who was in a position to operate the state apparatus, and who was subject to it. Utopian speculation, of course, is free and in some sense highly desirable, but if this liberal suggestion was intended to imply that such a free from of political organization was actually *realizable* under nineteenth-, twentieth-, or twenty-first-century economic conditions, that was certainly an illusion" (24–25). This is a dubious claim, it seems to me.

9. Maynard and Worsnip, *The Realist Narrative*, 17.

10. It seems more and more probable that John Rawls's *A Theory of Justice* is a source of much confusion within the moralist-realist debate. It begins with a very provocative claim about the necessity of revising social institutions according to principles of justice. This squares hardly with a therapeutic normative project, which would simply propose to take the actual moral needs of a society seriously, which is more in tune with Bernard Williams's idea of the Basic Legitimation Demand that he introduced and explained in his posthumously published essay "Realism and Moralism in Political Theory." In G. Hawthorn (ed.) *The Beginning Was The Deed. Realism and Moralism in Political Argument* (Princeton, NJ.: Princeton University Press, 2005), 1–17. Further, Rawls does make metaethical (but normative) choices at crucial points, for instance, he accepts Kantian ethics and rejects Utilitarianism. However, his principles of justice comprise Kantian and utilitarian intuitions alike, and give room for moral-causal deliberations (who are the worst-off in a society at a given time?), and he develops his ideas of overlapping consensus, well-orderedness, pluralism of conceptions of the good life that suggest a more neutral approach, closer to the neutral or impartial normativism that Maynard and Worsnip endorse. In any case, it seems to me that Rawls and his theory is most probably not the best or ideal target of realists. Nonetheless, he himself is responsible for having misled many of his critics. A detailed analysis is, however, an off-topic here.

11. Geuss, *Philosophy and Real Politics*, 53.

12. Ibid.

13. Martha C. Nussbaum (*The Fragility of Goodness*) concludes that the "play is about Creon's failure. It ends with his abandonment of this strategy [elevating the good of the city to the ultimate standard of good and bad] and his recognition of a more complicated deliberative world" (60). Not all human relations are of civic nature, the concerns of family may override the idea of the single ship to be subjected to the orders of a single person. Creon's collapse is due to his pain over the loss of his son: the very same passion that moved Antigone.

14. *Philosophy and Real Politics*, 42.

15. Ibid., 44.

16. Ibid., 45.

17. Wolin, *Political Theory as a Vocation*, 1075.

18. Modern scholarship is now discovering the importance of imagination in classic political conceptions, including the Hobbesian theory. Kye Anderson Barker argues that not only fear and similar emotions but also awe and wonder are central to Hobbes: "Of Wonder: Thomas Hobbes' Political Appropriation of Thaumauzein." *Political Theory* 3 (2017): 362–84. Without acknowledging the feeling of wonder or curiosity, there is no philosophy in the first place, and even less political theory.

Sixteenth-century philosophers, notwithstanding their rejection of Aristotelian philosophy, agreed about the central importance of passions such as wonder. It is commonplace today that political theory and political theology have many parallels, and the parallelisms arise to a great part from the common imaginative source. "The theological form of wonder is *controlled* by [*sic*] Hobbes and becomes a tool of the sovereign power. Although the sovereign power cannot perform miracles, since that power belongs only to the divine, it can define what may and may not be considered a miracle. The sovereign cannot create this type of wonder, but it can eliminate it" (375). This is "a matter of using a conceptual framework from ancient philosophy to build a certain apparatus of the state, one which alters the emotional makeup of the citizenry" (ibid). Carl Schmitt would have probably disagreed with the view that earthly sovereigns are unable to create miracles. Of course, the meaning of "miracle" is itself ambiguous, inasmuch as a miracle seems to presuppose some readiness or openness toward the miracle-maker. Anyway, unbelievers are often unconvinced by miracles, insofar as they presume that whatever they see, hear, and experience *must* have a natural cause and explanation. Wonder is elicited, thus, only if people are somehow predisposed to it. How this works in politics and governing is a highly interesting political psychological question.

19. *Political theory as a vocation*, 1076.

20. Paul Sagar, "Of Mushrooms and Method: History and the Family in Hobbes's Science of Politics." *European Journal of Political Theory* 14 (2015): 98–117.

21. Adam Lindsay, " 'Pretenders of a Vile and Unmanly Disposition': Thomas Hobbes on the Fiction of Constituent Power." *Political Theory* 1 (2018): 1–25, 2.

22. Ibid., 13.

23. Sagar, *Of Mushrooms and Method*, 15. Besides the concepts of personhood and the state, "consent" has become another important image (though perhaps less visualizable), as Robin Douglass argues. The notion of consent "seems to occupy a prominent place in the popular imagination, at least in liberal democracies." He agrees with the view that Hobbes was very much aware of the crucial importance of our imagination for solving the problem of governing: "The concern with how people understand their relationship with the state was at the forefront of Hobbes's thinking. Although it is not for what he is most famous, he placed great emphasis on the role of opinion in governing human affairs." "Hobbes and Political Realism." *European Journal of Political Theory* 1 (2016): 1–20, 14.

24. Quentin Skinner, "A Genealogy of the Modern State." *Proceedings of the British Academy* 162 (2008): 325–70.

25. Ibid., 345.

26. Ibid., 361–62.

27. Douglass, *Hobbes and Political Realism*, 6.

28. The by-now classic treatise is David Gauthier's *The Logic of Leviathan: The Moral and Political Theory of Thomas Hobbes* (Oxford: Clarendon Press, 1969).

29. For an overview and discussion of the views that consider Hobbes's theory anti-absolutist ("rebellious"), see Patricia Sheridan, "Resisting the Scaffold: Self-Preservation and the Limits of Obligation in Hobbes' *Leviathan*." *Hobbes Studies* 24 (2011): 137–57. She is closer to the opposite view that does not allow much room

for political deliberations over one's obligations toward the state. Nonetheless, the individualist foundations of the state are not questioned.

30. Michael Feola, "The Body Politic: Bodily Spectacle and Democratic Agency." *Political Theory* 1 (2017): 1–21.

31. Douglas Moggach, "Freedom and Perfection: German Debates on the State in the Eighteenth Century." *Canadian Journal of Political Science* 4 (2009): 1003–23.

32. The "Zwingherr" is a word composed of two parts: Zwang means coercion (zwingen: to coerce), Herr means lord or master. More about this see in David James, "The Political Theology of Fichte's Staatslehre: Immanence and Transcendence." *British Journal for the History of Philosophy* 6 (2016): 1157–75.

33. "Fichte's political ideal is, in the first place, a welfare state. Superficially, it has much in common with the absolutistic state of his time. Although he repudiates the despotism of the absolutistic regime, with its concern for the happiness, the property, the health, the beliefs, the virtues, and the eternal salvation of its subjects, he extends the function of the state to include the regulation of all practical affairs of life. Yet he remains a liberal republican with regard to the purpose of the state, which is to free man for his essential duty, the use of reason." F. W. Kaufmann, "Fichte and National Socialism." *The American Political Science Review* 3 (1942): 460–70, 461–62. The closed commercial state is a Zwangsstaat, a coercive state, which imposes enormous restrictions upon individual rights and individual freedom. Yet Fichte maintains in all his writings that freedom is the purpose of life, and he never ceases to attack the oppressive government of the absolutistic rulers. The resolution of this paradox is to be found in his conception of man, not as an individual, but as an integral part of human society, and of national community in particular. For a recent overview of Fichte's changing political philosophy, see Hector O. A. Igor, "Morality and State in the Fichtean Political Philosophy." *Araucaria* 1 (2019): 79–90.

34. J. G. Fichte, *Foundations of Natural Right* (Cambridge: Cambridge University Press, 2000), esp. par 1–4.

35. *Characteristics of the Present Age* (Gloucester: DoDo Press, 2009).

36. "To the question of 'Who has the right to be the overlord'—the answer is now closer: the highest human reason; since however this can never exist, it has to be him who has the highest human reason of his age and his people" (444, my translation). J. G. Fichte, *Werke IV. Zur Rechts und Sittenlehre II*, ed. H.G. Fichte (Berlin: W. de Gruyter, 1971).

37. Othmar Spann, *Der wahre Staat* (Leipzig: Quelle, 1921). Especially relevant are pages 197–210. There is little scholarship on Spann: Anthony Carty, "Alfred Verdross and Othmar Spann: German Romantic Nationalism, National Socialism and International Law." *European Journal of International Law* 1 (1995): 78–97. Lucian Tudor, "Othmar Spann: A Catholic Radical Traditionalist." Accessed February 14, 2020. at https://archive.org/stream/EssaysByLucianTudor/OthmarSpann-ACatho licRadicalTraditionalist_djvu.txt. It is questionable, especially in the light of the encyclicals of Popes Leo XIII and Pius XI that Spann's theory was indeed within the Catholic tradition.

38. The idea of "wholeness" seems to resurface in current ecological and environmentalist thinking, especially in the context of the political debates around

climate change. The human race is thought to be part of a larger "whole" and has limited "rights" in it, which implies that the "corpus" and its members are intrinsically tied together. Sure, this thinking does not lead—yet—to the idea of a global *political* wholeness, but the imaginative holism is, again, unmistakably back on the table.

39. John Rawls, *A Theory of Justice* (Cambridge, MA: Harvard University Press, 1971).

40. To repeat: individual authors are cited here for the purposes of demonstrating how a particular type of political theory can emerge. In his later works, Rawls modified and restated many of his arguments, accepting and incorporating many objections and criticisms, some of which are used here to construct the Watchmaker metaphor. Most notably, he began to emphasize the political and contextual contingency of the validity of his theory, at the expense of its moral universalism.

41. John Kekes, *Against Liberalism* (Ithaca, London: Cornell University Press, 1997). The book usefully summarizes the objections made against Rawls's modification of the concept of justice (transforming it into fairness).

42. Bonnie Honig, *Political Theory and the Displacement of Politics* (Ithaca, NY: Cornell University Press, 1993); Jeremy Waldron, *Law and Disagreement* (Oxford: Oxford University Press, 1999).

43. Williams, *Realism and Moralism in Political Theory*.

44. Even William A. Galston, himself a realist, observes that Rawls sometimes denied that political philosophy is applied moral philosophy: see "Realism in Political Theory." *European Journal of Political Theory* 4 (2010): 385–411, 388. Indeed, Rawls begins the restatement of his conception of justice political philosophy is there to help handle "divisive political conflict and . . . to settle the problem of order." See *Justice as Fairness: A Restatement*, ed. E. Kelly (Cambridge, MA: Harvard University Press, 2001), 1. Robert Jubb, too, thinks that especially the later Rawls comes close to a Williamsonian version of political realism: "Playing Kant at the Court of King Arthur." *Political Studies* 4 (2015): 919–34.

45. Eva Erman and Niklas Möller argue that "we should refrain from conceiving of the moral and the political as entirely separate spheres, which realist expressions like 'prior to' and 'external to' might delude us into believing." See "Political Legitimacy in the Real Normative World: The Priority of Morality and the Autonomy of the Political." *British Journal of Political Science* 1 (2015): 215–33.

46. Nicholas Tampio, "A Defense of Political Constructivism." *Contemporary Political Theory* 3 (2012): 305–23. Alan Thomas, "Rawls and Political Realism: Realistic Utopianism or Judgement in Bad Faith?" *European Journal of Political Theory* 1 (2015): 1–21. Thomas argues that realists tend to ignore Rawls's more flexible theoretical notions such as that of the reflective equilibrium or misinterpret others such as the overlapping consensus (which is not a sort of agreement). No specific conception of the good life can prevail over the rest. Notwithstanding these arguments in defense of a more practical Rawls, he suggested that his principles of justices were implementable throughout his whole theory of the state and its organs.

47. *A Theory of Justice*, 194.

48. Ibid., 216.

49. "Rawls' critics argue . . . that (1) he eliminates plural perspectives and selves, and therefore the theory articulates the reasoning of a single, rational deliberator, and that (2) his 'contract' is of a cognitive rather than voluntarist sort." Deborah Baumgold, "Hobbesian Absolutism and the Paradox of Modern Contractarianism." *European Journal of Political Theory* 8 (2009): 207–28, 221. Insofar as the "rational deliberator" is, according to the assumptions of the theory, every individual, Rawls's theory falls back on the Hobbesian idea where consent is a prerequisite of the social contract being constituted in the first place. This means, as was argued earlier, that everyone is expected to discipline oneself, and in that sense create his or her own political self, besides that Leviathan. (This double-constituting act is a main feature of Rousseau's theory of the social contract.) This introspective-self-disciplining political activity has, as was also argued, the unintended consequence of separating the sovereign from its constituents. See more on this Bonnie Honig, "Rawls on Politics and Punishment." *Political Research Quarterly* 46 (1993): 99–125. However, supervising the state and the government presupposes an active and vigilant constitutive power, an active Watchmaker ever ready to repair the watch. This cannot be everyone's job. Rawls has a different conclusion.

50. *A Theory of Justice*, 243.

51. Assessing Rawls's moralism and Williams's realism, Alan Thomas points out that "abstraction, here, does not imply emptiness: a schematic view is abstract, but not for that reason unclear in the institutional forms it has to take" (*Rawls and political realism*, 9). As Hegel "specifies" Kant and his abstract moral theory, Rawls's political principles are capable of being put to practical use.

52. Of course, other images are also available. The classic one is the Prince. Here is a particularly colorful description: "Consider the prince in his cabinet. From thence flow the commands which coordinate the efforts of the magistrates and captains, of citizens and soldiers, of provinces and armies, by land and sea. It is the image of God, who directs all nature from his throne in the highest heaven. . . . You see order, justice, and peace throughout the realm. These are the natural effects of the authority of the prince. Nothing is more majestic than all-embracing goodness: and there is no greater debasement of majesty than the misery of the people caused by some prince" (J.-B. Bossuet, *Politics Drawn from the Very Words of Holy Scripture*, tr. P. Riley (Cambridge: Cambridge University Press, 1999), 161–62). Bossuet's Prince is truly an unmoving, passive agent from whom authority emanates (the sacred nature of power); however, he alludes to misery "caused by" "some prince" as well, though "causing" does not necessarily entail activism. Such absolutist-passivist images are hardly attractive today, yet some contemporary theorists boldly experiment with the image if the democratic (and very much proactive) prince. I shall discuss H. Mansfield *Taming the Prince* later; an even more up-to-date version is arguably Tilo Schabert's book on François Mitterrand: Ein klassischer Fürst. François Mitterrand im Spiegel einer vergleichenden Regierungslehre. In B. Sauzay, R. von Thadden (eds) *Mitterrand und die Deutschen* (Göttingen: Wallstein, 1998): 78–106.

53. The bitter debates between proponents and opponents of "public correctness" are a testimony to the political importance of the debate over debate, the polemic over polemics. There are no politically innocent meanings.

54. Andrew Mason, "Rawlsian Theory and the Circumstances of Politics." *Political Theory* 5 (2010): 658–83. Mason cites Jeremy Waldron who already objected to the Rawlsian conception that it does not render "justice to" pluralism adequately. Mason himself recommends "inclusivity" instead of Rawlsian principles of justice.

## Chapter 3

# Shame and Moderation

## *The Internal Constraint*

### POLITICAL VIRTÚ AND GOVERNING

Political theory at its best helps us conceptualize the government so that an image of it may be formed that has an enduring influence over political thinking. I have tried to demonstrate that even the most extreme versions, that is, those that tend to lead us toward an image of government, which rules us in some totalistic (by no means necessarily a totalitarian) ways, by the very act of giving a conceptual form and image to it, become an element of the wall constructed to surround, indeed, encircle, the government. Of course, speaking the professional parlance of political theory is a skill of the very few. And even though political thinking is a broader category, and these images influence the way common people think of politics and especially of the government as being "out there," such conceptual and imaginative influences remain mostly unreflective (though not ineffectual). When it comes to a more reflective and politically conscious thinking about government, it takes a more personalized form.

Thus, the normal and reflective way of thinking about the government considers it as a constantly operating machine, the bureaucracy or state administration, but with discernible persons, professional politicians and bureaucrats running it. The almost obligatory metaphor, cited in the previous chapter as well, is the ship. Indeed, it brings out the point more poignantly: on the bridge, discernible persons are in service with the captain in command and in charge of navigation. The metaphor suggests that governing is always a personal business. This has far-reaching political and moral consequences for how to handle the problem of containing the government. If political theory is somewhat like speculating about navigation while being on sea (nautical astronomy was a highly mathematized and increasingly standardized "knowledge" that captains learned from textbooks written on land from the sixteenth century), then navigating the ship on open waters is very much a practical knowledge and experience, to the point that captains had more powers over passengers and crew member than kings over their subjects back at home. Creon, we remember, explicitly refers to the metaphor and cites it as a decisive argument in his address from the throne. Isabella relentlessly implores Angelo to pardon her brother, doing her best to personalize the issue. She succeeds, though with the horrible realization that Angelo's character does not contain internal constraints, he is ready to tread upon anything he held sacrosanct before. If governing is commonly likened to navigating the ship (as a rule, on rough waters), then notwithstanding all constitutional and institutional constraints, political leaders responsible for governing have virtually unlimited powers; all that remains to hope for is the internal, personal constraints the captain or navigator may have. Are such hopes entirely dependent on the contingent qualities of the leader or are there any qualities and features of the "job," or of simply being the leader, that suggest some inevitable constraints of personal governing?

In the realist literature/tradition, the interest in the political leader as such—the leader as a role, almost an institution—has a long history. The consensus seems to be that it is possible to develop and defend a "realist ideal type" leader. This means that, following mainly Machiavelli's "research track," the ancient/classic/Medieval ideal leader theory (if there was such a thing) presented us with a misleading picture of the "good" leader. Since real politics is different from ideal politics, a suitable conception of realist ideal type is necessary. In an early paper, Bernard Williams argued that there are profession-related activities of politics, hence vague as they are, the successful going about these activities requires distinct qualities. There is, first, an interest in being and remaining in office, selfish as it is, but certainly more pertinent to the profession than, for instance, in a businessman's career. But creativity, a preparedness to take difficult (immoral) actions, is also necessary and well-known feature of politics, though Williams does not think that all immoral actions are justifiable in terms of the public good, but are still acceptable.[1] Another, perhaps more optimistic, version is offered by Edward Hall. He discusses "integrity" as a possible standard for the realist ideal type politician.[2] The problem with integrity as a summary character trait is, of course, that the commitments integrity presupposes can be willful and evil; and that insisting on them at all costs may simply cause the politician (and his projects) to fail. Compromise is necessary, and not every compromise jeopardizes a politician's integrity. It is difficult to tell, of course, which compromises are hazardous. Hall writes that "at a minimum, political integrity . . . requires principled public-spiritedness"[3] and the exclusion of a purely predatory behavior. Thus, the lesson is that "political integrity requires politicians to stand for their deepest political commitments, while being flexible enough, and cognisant enough of their proper role, to recognise when concession, or perhaps even the renouncement, of certain commitments is called-for."[4]

Mark Philp has devoted an entire book to the topic of *Political Conduct*.[5] He discussed Machiavelli at length and argues that the Renaissance thinker "provides the grounds for a sense of political virtue, which is neither moralism nor wholly an account of the skills needed in the struggle for dominance."[6] In other words, we are in search of a "realist ideal type" politician. It is ideal inasmuch as such a politician herself has an ideal. Machiavelli names greatness or glory as such. Glory is a complex and comprehensive value as it provides guidance not only for the present but also for the future. In that sense, glory helps the politician avoid or at least control the urge of satisfying immediate self-interest. To attain glory, virtú is necessary. Virtú is more than "a collection of skills or technical abilities"[7] but not identical with moral virtuousness. Since, Philp argues, politics and governing is about finding the proper answers to the actual challenges (the storms) and consolidating rule (keep the ship in good order and navigable), virtú presupposes an exclusion of certain inadequate, unsuitable (perhaps even "harmful") moral virtues such as gentleness, benevolence, or friendship.

As a matter of fact, in this respect governing is not terribly different from other vocations and professions. Navigators or captains of real ships have their own codes of virtues in which compassion or gentleness may also play a very minor role. However, after discussing political virtú within the MacIntyrean conception of virtue ethics, Philp concludes that "politics [is] an activity that is in part constitutive of the social order" but adds that as such it is

> partly outside that order. The creative agency of the prince is incompletely framed by existing norms and practices, to the extent that, while many of those who have some sense of the demands of political rule will be able to understand the prince's achievements (or failure), they may only do so after the fact.[8]

Philp then explains that normal politics (the everyday business of governing) may be more or less within the competence—and, we should add, imaginative-evaluative competence—of citizens but there is a larger picture, a deeper understanding of what is at stake when it comes to governing for the future, with a far-reaching and all-encompassing vision. If Philp is right, then the metaphor of the ship and the captain are indeed misleading, since the practice of navigation is fairly intelligible to everyone on board. What may strike us is the consensus that seems to be emerging between Plato and Machiavelli in a dark corner. The prophets of virtue (as a lofty ideal) and virtú (which involves being able to do morally wrong acts) seem to agree that although virtue and virtú in fact exclude to a great part one another, governing as a profession and activity is really behind the comprehension and evaluative competence of ordinary people.

This is, however, controversial. Many people (including myself) may not have the slightest idea how, for instance, a composer's mind works, but the composer herself may not have the understanding of how and why certain (quite a few) people *cannot* understand things that are evident to her. Nonetheless, composing music is something that can be taught, practiced, and made for a living, and in that sense, it is not something entirely mysterious or mystical. Very many people are devoted consumers of this or that kind of music and are able to tell whether or not they like what they listen to. The analogy holds for a wide variety of activities. We are competent consumers of various goods, including the public good or goods, and actually, the business of governing is probably one of the least obscure activity that we are aware of. It may very well be that even if governing has something mysterious about it (charisma, authority, the sense and taste of power, the atmosphere of history, whatever), the outcome—order, unity, peace—is nonetheless a good that everyone enjoys and is able to evaluate. Therefore, it is not beyond, even in exceptional cases and times, what ordinary people can, at least partly, understand, appreciate, evaluate, and even respect. Moreover, if we do not think that governing is a very special, arcane activity, then we can drop the idea that a realist ideal type, again, as developed by and held up as a measure by the political theorist, is the internal constraint of governing as done by recognizable persons. Thus, in agreement with this realist approach, I presume that governing is a discernible profession with characteristic sorts of activities, and with identifiable persons doing it. But I also assume that notwithstanding its special characteristics, politicians/leaders are also subject to the most general forms of evaluation that ordinary people are capable of.

These evaluations pertain to the character of the person. Having a good reputation is essential to most of us, and therefore we are interested in having a good character. "Goodness" remains unspecified here but since "governing" is assumed to be a discernible activity, it is not very difficult to find out what character traits are most in demand, of course, partly depending on the historical and political context. Much of our personality is predetermined; however, it is a general expectation that people, especially those who claim to have leadership qualities, have considerable control over parts of their character. For sake of convenience, I shall call these parts "moral character" and the control center the moral self.

After discussing moral character and moral self, I shall argue that losing the reputation of having a good character in this sense is arguably the greatest danger facing a politician (or any other professional), which is manifested in experiencing shame. Shame operates as an internal constraint, or at least as a red light (literally: think of the blushing), which indicates control problems over the moral self. To learn how to strengthen control requires moderation. It is a virtue that features prominently in many treatises on governing (think of the idea of moderate governing), yet it is usually cited as a virtue whose usefulness and goodness is somehow self-evident. It is not. However, it can be shown to grow out of shame and become an effective, though of course never absolute or unsurmountable, constraint of governing. Both the *Antigone* and *Measure for Measure* provide us with highly useful insights into the mechanism and importance of shame in and for governing.

## THE MORAL CHARACTER AND THE MORAL SELF

Within the realist tradition of ontology, our knowledge about this world is knowledge of properties and relations.[9] If this vocabulary is applied to moral knowledge, then we can conveniently distinguish between moral properties or qualities such as *values/disvalues* (kindness, goodness, etc. and their opposites) and moral relations that find their philosophical homes in ethical theories (e.g., the basic *consequentialist* relation being "is conducive to," namely, to a lesser or greater good/bad; a prominent *deontic* relation being "is forbidden to").[10] Of special interest are the *virtues*. It is a sensible proposition that one is filled with love or benevolence (or their opposites), or "possesses" these virtues, but in reality, such propositions are incomplete: love presupposes something to love, thus love is (primarily, perhaps always) a relation ("loves" or "is loved by"). Less evidently but other virtues have the same character, which is explained by the fact that virtues arise out of practice, which requires a context with objects (usually other human or at least sentient beings). Virtues are relations insofar as for them to be instantiated (and appear as properties), action is required. Looking upon a random photo of an unfamiliar person, we can tell hardly anything about her moral qualities. Whether or not she is kind, for instance, acts of kindness must be verifiably attributable to her, which involve her and at least one other person (or a sentient being), establishing a natural relation between them. But if such acts are truly hers, then we are right in calling her a kind person. Hence, even if there is such a thing as the property of kindness, it can be predicated of an individual only in virtue of her performing kind acts. Of course, there can be other moral properties equally predicable of her, including good and bad ones (besides being kind, she may be lazy or forgetful, but also attentive or diligent), but every one of them in virtue of the corresponding and justifying actions.

I do not pretend to have given a philosophically undisputable description of how we know moral truths about moral selves or characters, but I assume that this account is sufficiently commonsensical and familiar. Why do we need predications that may not be ontologically correct (i.e. relations appearing as properties)? We need them because it is by help of such utterances that we are able to talk about one another, moreover, develop further relations to one another. If I know that she is a kind person, I shall behave myself accordingly. Someone prone to gossiping is a bad idea to talk to loosely. A timid person is best left behind when boldness is required. Most of us know to whom we can turn for a personal loan, and moral expectations matter a lot in making our choice. Of course, in a sufficiently complex society with various institutions and offices, moral reckoning and putting great efforts into learning about the moral character of officials, clerks, all sorts of bureaucrats can be spared because of the very existence of non-moral, routinized, automatized, and standardized patterns of behavior. Also, we are inclined to think that the necessity of moral calculations is morally undesirable in these relations: we do not wish to depend on the benevolence, kindness, compassion, empathy, friendliness, and so on, of the doctor, the professor, the plumber, or the car repairman. There may be moral attributes of these offices that we count on (we generally expect honesty, truthfulness, and professionalism, some general benevolence), but it is more the office and less the person that we think (or pretend to think) has a moral character. Notwithstanding these cases, the moral character of an office is different from the moral character of a person. It is, thus, socially rational and morally inevitable that we use evaluative propositions that make us to others and others to us morally recognizable. It is in this way that our moral and non-moral reactions and anticipations are adjusted to the moral character of the other person.

How do we learn what kind of a moral person we are, or how our moral character looks like? The answer is that the moral truth about us is to a great extent derived from the *descriptions* of our character.[11] During our lives, we are usually confronted with various descriptions of our characters, mostly rudimentary and fragmental ones (e.g., when our behavior is being characterized in a given situation, or when we have done something praiseworthy or blameworthy, according to observers and the affected persons). Many of these descriptions are purposively one-sided (as in a laudation, or in a HR evaluation), some are more comprehensive than others (e.g., a psychological test, or—heaven forbid—a judge's verdict that attempts to mete out the most appropriate punishment to a person), and some are incompatible with one another (different persons may think differently about us, and their evaluations are dependent on their fallible judgments, biases, and their own character flaws). It is also possible to observe ourselves from an impartial point of view, especially when we deal with our reactions, reactive attitudes, and emotions (whether we are generous or parsimonious, passionate or dispassionate, easy-going or reserved, etc.). Naturally, our self-descriptions are also partly a function of our characters. For instance, it is difficult to make sense of one's "knowing" that she is a humble person, since we are inclined to think that "knowing" certain things may be incompatible with "having" or "possessing" them. Again, a timid person may think of himself as a cautious character and hold a brave person to be reckless. Notwithstanding such complications, and the many possibilities of misunderstandings, distortions, and outright lies, there is simply no other way of learning about our moral characters but describing them, both by way of introspection and by way of listening to others.

One may wonder whether these various and diverse descriptions can ever be integrated in such a manner as our political images of the Leviathan, the Organic Body, the Society or the Whole, the People or the Leader (as, say, a superego in perfect control of the subjects/passions/instincts) as such can arguably be. Great painters such as Titian, Velazquez, or Rembrandt are famous for their skills to paint moral portraits, that is, images that make the moral character of their subjects visible and in that way perceptible to the senses. Of course, once it comes to decode what we see and translate it to words, another series of descriptions follow, more focused and concise perhaps than without the image, yet rarely unanimous and final. Rembrandt, for one, never ceased to study himself via his self-portraits, suggesting that his own moral character remained to him an object of interest, in other words, an object with aspects and dimensions providing him with a perennially interesting theme. Absent such portraits and painting talents, most of us look into the mirror, or take selfies, hoping that we can discover something about our inner selves, including our moral character, not only about the environment. The problem is how to integrate these various photos: Is there a single final description of our moral character? Moral philosophy, especially its virtue ethics tradition, ever since Plato and Aristotle, has struggled to find an affirmative answer. Aristotle was especially concerned with how to integrate the virtues under the conception of the good life, or eudaimonia. Is there such a thing as "the" virtuous character? Or "the" virtuous life? What do we mean by a "good character" or a "strong character"? Or a fox-like/lion-like character, to recall Machiavelli's metaphors? Especially since the Romantic era, the ideas of "autonomy," "originality," "authenticity," and "self-fulfillment" have been influential in shaping our moral imagination. The various efforts to find the gravitational center of the moral character seem, however, to be frustrated by the simple problem that the more specific (and thus authentic, truthful, objective, impartial, precise, etc.) we want to be about ourselves, the more and more descriptions we need, causing us to lose orientation. There seems to be a vicious circle being formed in our moral explorations. In searching for our moral center, the moral self, we need as much information as possible, but the more information we have, the deeper it sinks under them, the more difficult it becomes to give a name to it, to give a picture of it: the most we can do is to conclude that on the balance, someone is a good person, is a strong character, leads a fairly autonomous life. But *these* descriptions are very vague and uninteresting.

What remains as a point of interest is, then, neither the name nor the final image but the fact that we are constantly, though of course to various degrees, interested in our moral character; we are sensitive to the descriptions we are offered about ourselves; and our moral actions (actions with some moral aspect) are influenced and informed by the lessons we draw from these descriptions. "Being interested" presupposes a subject with a concern about herself, and this is what is called here the *moral self*. Thus, the moral character is not the final "truth" about us—about our "selves." There is something deeper and more personal than the character and its descriptions, at least in our moral and social tradition. Being morally recognizable means more than the sum of all available descriptions of a character, there is a further assumption that the moral character is at least partly under the control of the moral self.[12]

It is in virtue and by help of the moral self that we are able to evaluate ourselves and others, and to reflect on the plurality of the descriptions. If we are interested in our moral character, then there is a deeper subject that/who is interested in it. Further, only when our moral self is operative, can we demarcate the moral character from other descriptions that tell about ourselves a non-moral story. For instance, the idea of there being various "temperaments" and "moods" is no less ancient than the idea of the moral character. Rembrandt's paintings tell us as much about the psyche as about the moral character. However, whereas a temperament or a mood is somehow given to us, a moral character is in an essential sense an "object" in the hands of the moral self, or of the self whenever it is acting morally, or it is using its moral authority. Consequently, the moral character is constituted by descriptions that have a morally evaluative component.[13]

The upshot of this section is this: generally, we are interested in our moral character, conceived as an object of descriptions over which we are supposed to have considerable degree of control. The concept of the moral self is meant to capture this fact. We learn about our moral character from these various, though often contradictory descriptions that contain a normative (or morally evaluative) aspect. We may or may not strive for a comprehensive or final description, a stamp as it were (a moral saint, a hero, or a villain, a traitor); therefore, it seems more practical and realistic not to insist on the assumption that everyone has such an ambition. But it does not follow that without such ambitions most people are unconcerned with their moral character: nor could we be unconcerned with it because it belongs to the routine of our days that we evaluate others and process moral information on various persons, and we are very much aware that we are constantly subject to such evaluations and information processes.

## ENABLING CONSTRAINTS OF THE SELF: SHAME

The descriptions we have at our disposal about our moral character makes us recognizable as moral agents. Though a few exceptions may be allowed, we are usually deeply interested in making the good impressions on others, to suggest authentically or persuasively that we possess the required moral character or characters traits in a given situation. (Let us not forget that the term "moral character" is very broadly used here, a "good impression" may be a calculated intimidation, behind which an image of an austere or "mercilessly just" character may hide.) Being recognizable for a "good" moral character amounts to having some favorable reputation, prestige, or fame. Fame, good reputation, honor, glory, respect, prestige, recognition are just a few notions to capture a precious family of goods related to public recognition that politicians are thought to covet and strive for. Hobbes, unlike Machiavelli, considered them to be goods desired by everybody and claimed that they are scarce. This, he concluded, is a major cause of competition and distrust, and it is responsible for the (fear of the) state of war. Much of contemporary liberal moral and political philosophy is concerned with how to grant equal respect to everybody, notwithstanding his or her moral and other merits, inadvertently admitting Hobbes's point which is, of course, nothing novel, after all. Appearing in public and securing the best possible moral descriptions for ourselves is indeed an important goal of everyone. Though Hobbes was antipathetic toward Aristotelian philosophy in general, they are largely in agreement on the hedonistic/eudemonic value of good reputation. Even in Jewish and Christian ethics, the value of glory is an intrinsic one, though fully such only for god.[14]

Losing this value can be very painful. In the world of humans, there is a special moral emotion we used to identify as a symptom of this painful event: this is shame. It may be a moral emotion over which we may exert control, and it is a perfectly sensible description of a moral character to say that he is "shameless" (not showing signs of shame we he should) or "shy" or—more specifically—"prudish" (feeling or showing shame when he should not) and so on.[15] Nonetheless, the experience and moral emotion of shame is generally a spontaneous reaction, which, however, remains relevant in the moral development of all individuals, and hardly less important in a politician's public image, which is essential in making him or her capable of governing. Shame can be appropriate, of course, in non-moral situations as well, thus it is an emotion that serves to connect morality and politics (and other areas of social life that fall outside the scope of this book) effectively, pointing out the over-laps between them. More pertinently, the triggering function of shame is not restricted to making us aware of having transgressed certain (not exclusively moral) norms. Rather, it has the deeper significance of making us aware of what is knowledge and what is non-knowledge, and of what is within and outside of our control. Thereby shame is connected with self-governance and by extension with governing others. Shame is, I contend, both one of the constitutive dimensions of politics and governing, and one of its inherent constraints, working in and by the personal side of governments.

Philosophical accounts of shame go back to Aristotle, Aristotelian Scholasticism, and the seventeenth- and eighteenth-century philosophy of moral emotions. Recapitulating this vast tradition is unnecessary. The consensus has been, unsurprisingly, that shame is essential in establishing a moral community and it is deeply formative of our personal relations. Modern explanations align with this consensus, though with an even greater emphasis on personal worth and autonomy, on esteem and respect. Rawls, for one, contends that "shame implies an especially intimate connection with our person and with those upon whom we depend to confirm the sense of our own worth."[16] Shame is aroused whenever our self-esteem is harmed, either by ourselves or by others, either voluntarily or involuntarily. No shame is felt due to interpersonal differences in terms of excellence, achievement, ambitions, skills, or talents, as long as such differences are not thought to be relevant to the social and personal status of the individual. Of special rel-evance is moral shame. This is connected to moral achievement such as the acquisition and display of virtues

> as properties that his associates want in him and that he wants in himself. To possess these excellences and to express them in his actions are among his regulative aims and are felt to be a condition of his being valued and esteemed by those with whom he cares to associate.[17]

Shame is different from guilt, Rawls explains, because guilt is essentially outward-oriented, while shame is inward-oriented. Feeling guilt, it is the other's pain that counts, feeling shame (on many occasions, shame accompa-nies guilt), it is the person's own pain that stands in the center.

More recent accounts of shame are usually variations and refinements of the basic insight, though some of them go further than explaining shame in terms of pain and loss of self-esteem (which may be deserved, hence shame may be morally desirable). Gabriele Taylor, for instance, emphasizes the difference between self-respect and self-esteem, arguing that "shame is the emotion of self-protection," that is, it is a more basic reaction than humilia-tion or feeling humiliated, which is the proper reaction to harms done to one's self-esteem. When we feel shame, we feel having been subjected, conquered, and perhaps even devastated, by an external force.[18] John Deigh agrees with her: shame "is self-protective in that it moves one to protect one's worth." He adds that "experiences of shame are expressed by acts of concealment."[19] This is an important observation because it underlines the protective role of shame: concealing one's face is erecting a symbolic wall. As a matter of fact, staring at someone whose face is burning of shame can itself be a shameful act, thus, turning away our head is a mirror image of the wall being erected. Cheshire Calhoun stresses the moral worth of shame, criticizing those think that shame has power-aspects, and it can be abused. Thus, it should be restricted, and we should be wary of feeling shame. However, Calhoun repeats what is essentially the point outlined earlier:

> Even if particular social practices of morality seem flawed from the individual's critical, normative perspective, the social practice of morality is the only moral game in town. It is only in real social worlds that I have a moral identity. Who I am, morally, is who I am interpretable and identifiable by others as being.[20]

Shame is a moral emotion through which are destined to communicate with others. Of course, it is not always justifiable or automatically justified but as a moral *emotion*, it is no less important than, say, love, which can also be unjustified, misplaced, or morally dubious.

However, shame is not merely a *moral* emotion. It has cognitive aspects as well. David Velleman offered an even more in-depth analysis of shame, very properly making use of the story of Adam and Eve in which shame is a constitutive, perhaps constructive, emotion having both moral and cognitive significance.[21] His basic argument is that the feeling of shame is aroused by a loss of control over own public personality. This may happen either due to our own action, or the action of others, or simply due to the circumstances, bad luck, or an incontrollable bodily reaction (like an involuntary attack of laughter, trembling, unstoppable coughing, etc.). A public personality is made possible, of course, by the idea of having a private personality—or a self—as well. Shame is especially interesting in this respect because it enables us even to detach ourselves from our own body. The body reacts (blushing, sweating, paling, dizzying) without asking for "our" permission, thereby helping us discover our inner self that feels literally alienated from its own representation. It that sense, shame has an alerting function, cutting toward the innermost part of the self, forcing us to reflect on the problem of who controls us. The power of the *Genesis* story hides in its being able to integrate the problems of control, will, self-knowledge, body, and limitation in an apparently simple image. Interpreting Velleman's account of the story liberally, the shame felt by Adam and Eve of their nakedness after the fall resulted from their realization of having the power to disobey, and at the same time realizing that they have no control over their own bodies. Their immediate reaction was to cover themselves, to cover their shame, namely, of no having full control over themselves, thereby making themselves as well as each other aware of their inner selves. To this, it may be added that by hiding themselves in the Garden from the Lord they wanted to do the same to Him, as they did to one another, namely, to create a space in which they were absolute rulers. Yet again, notwithstanding the new knowledge of such a space being possible, it did not make them happy but full of fear, not only of the Lord but perhaps of losing it.

What emerges out of these analyses confirms the central importance of shame as a moral emotion and more generally, as a negative experience that has a constitutive cognitive aspect as well. It is negative inasmuch as points toward a failure, sometimes but not always of a moral kind, sometimes but not always a voluntary one, which harms the public image of the person, makes her representation deficient or, in the worst case, to collapse.[22] Yet, it is constructive inasmuch as it plays a constitutive cognitive role in our moral life, making us aware of the distinction between our public self (often a certain description of our moral character) and our private (mental and moral) self. It is definitively a constraint, yet an enabling one.

Since by assumption, governing is, despite its undeniable special internal goods and aims, the skills and techniques, perhaps some other unique characteristics, an activity discernible and assessable to ordinary people, shame is no less important in and for it. Perhaps even more so than in many areas of private life, where people rightly feel to be more at liberty with violating certain norms and rules (at least those of good manners). Then and there, we read about the loss of shame in politics. Some think that shamelessness is bad, others think that it is can be a refined calculation.[23] I think that shame is very strongly related to fame and respect, shown to be absolutely important in ordinary life and the governing politicians alike, and if the analyses cited earlier are correct, shame is rooted in control, more precisely, the loss of control, and it is therefore eminently relevant to consider it an important candidate for the role of internal constraints of government.

Thus, fame, reputation, prestige, and glory do not only have a hedonistic or eudaemonist, intrinsic value-dimension. They have an instrumental dimension as well, which may be, perhaps surprisingly, more important than the intrinsic value-dimension. Paradoxically, this dimension is revealed by and in experiencing shame, that is, the loss of fame and respect, which we enjoy due to the good, favorable, supportive descriptions of our moral character. If Velleman is right, then the greatest shame arises from the event when are confronted with our inability to give a good description of our moral character because our moral self loses control over it. It may or may not be our fault, the pain is, nonetheless, ours: the revelation of our lack of control. However, this loss of control makes us aware of the fact that we *have* a moral self. The loss of control forces us to realize that there is something to control, hence shame has a constitutive role in our self-reflective moral life. Put in sharper terms, and in accordance with the Genesis, without shame there is no self-knowledge; in a society with a perfectly equal distribution of respect, self-reflection has less chance to develop and flourish.

## FROM SHAME TO MODERATION: THE CHARMIDES EPISODE

Shame is often accompanied with various bodily symptoms, and these symptoms are the primary means of communicating this emotion, which, as I have argued, reveals the innermost part of our personality. Shame is truly exceptional in this respect, though not the only one. Fear, for instance, is also highly existential and easily recognizable by its corporeal effects: it sometimes causes us to sweat and pale. All these symptoms are, thus, signs of an existential exposure, though not all are as effective as is shame in making us alert to our self in a reflective sense. Fear, for instance, puts our existence very much into the center, more than anything else perhaps, yet it does not help us reflect on our social status, its boundaries, the intricacies of our relationship to others, and so on.[24] In other words, there is always a greater potential of sheer passion and irrationality in fear than in shame, though shame can also be excessive, overwhelming, and irrational; and fear can also be a powerful standing motive in forming our character, our emotional economy, indeed, our religious and political views: again, Hobbes's conception is the best example.[25] Further complications arise once we ponder cases of "fear of shame" or "being ashamed for fear." Such intricacies can be ignored here, however. I think as an immediate reaction shame and fear have different characteristics and are distinguishable to most people. Fear makes us move, react—often aggressively—and arrests our imagination, sometimes to the point that we become unable to reflect on the situation objectively, even less on ourselves. Shame makes us passive, and incites us to withdraw and disappear, after having exposed ourselves, our inner selves against our will. We know, and know that others may also know, that especially cases of shame arising from bad luck or involuntary reactions do not correctly characterize our moral self. Feeling shame is not always a result of a confrontation with a bad or unsuccessful description of our moral character: it is revelation of the lack of control. It is therefore both very personal and very impersonal: shame always carries with something of the fall, of the fallen condition of mankind, of our collective and shared bad luck. This is why looking at someone in shame intensely makes us ashamed, too.

It is also worth keeping in mind that bodily symptoms can be misleading. Sweating as a symptom of some emotional event is not always a sign of fear, much as laughing is not always a sign of feeling superiority, which was Hobbes's opinion. However, in view of the enormous significance of our body in our communicating of what is going on within our self, its secret life, sometimes its innermost part, let me use the symptom most commonly associated with shame to further the discussion of shame toward an account of moderation, which has generally been considered to be a major moral and political virtue of political leaders and governments. Evidently, if moderation is operative, either in a personal character, or somehow as an attribute of an office, perhaps of the government as such (moderate government), then we have identified an important constraint.

How shame and moderation are related is perhaps most beautifully and memorably captured by a dialogue of Plato. As always, the event and the scene is as important as is the subsequent discussion. In the *Charmides*, Socrates confronts the youngster with Critias's question: "Please, therefore, to inform me whether you admit the truth of what Critias has been saying; have you or have you not this quality of temperance?" What happens next is in some way extraordinary:

> Charmides blushed, and the blush heightened his beauty, for modesty is becoming in youth; he then said very ingenuously, that he really could not at once answer, either yes, or no, to the question which I had asked: For, said he, if I affirm that I am not temperate, that would be a strange thing for me to say of myself, and also I should give the lie to Critias, and many others who think as he tells you, that I am temperate: but, on the other hand, if I say that I am, I shall have to praise myself, which would be ill manners; and therefore I do not know how to answer you.[26]

What is or may strike us as extraordinary is not only the dramaturgic perfection, the psychological insightfulness and the fine-grained description Plato gives us of Charmides's reaction and reply but also the graceful unity of aesthetic value (the blush heightening the beauty of the boy), moral value (his modesty and honesty), and intellectual value (his thoughtful ignorance). One may wonder whether Plato himself is aware of this unity, which in one way anticipates the philosophical significance of the topic. Plato was, of course, less of a phenomenologist and more of an analytical philosopher, thus, what follows this beautifully and meaningfully "shot" moment is a long and sometimes tedious, though in many respects useful and illuminating discussion of the meaning of sophrosyne (temperance or modesty). Let us first do therefore what Plato skipped over: to learn from the experience.

Charmides blushes. This natural emotional and physiological reaction that we conventionally associate with shame is here neither a symptom of actual shame, nor a symptom of some imminent fear of shame. Rather, it seems to have to do something with his appearance as a public person, someone who must be able to present and vindicate himself in the agora. He was not asked about the abstract meaning of temperance but about his own evaluation of possessing or not possessing it. In other words, he was publicly called to give a description of his moral character, therefore he had to present—or *represent*—his moral self in a public situation. His reaction testifies to the stake of his decision. Much depended on his reply, as his description was about to commit him to something that he might not have had, especially for not having been familiar with it sufficiently. "Blushing" in this situation is an appropriate reaction not to having done something wrong (and becoming a public fact) but to the very act of appearance, here of a distinctively moral kind, with the risk of failing, and the anticipation of shame. He had to present his moral self with its full gravity, engraved in a particularly weighty description. Will he succeed? He does not know yet—hence the blushing.

What we witness here is the full psychological force of morality as it puts a self-chosen constraint on the moral self, and at the same time we see how the moral constraint works by adding up a new positive description to his moral character. Charmides understands that his reply is not a philosophical answer but a moral action that reveals something and gives a description of his moral character. And he wants to be a temperate or moderate character, therefore he chooses *not to* tell Socrates whether he has, or thinks he has, that trait. He comes very close to but carefully and wisely avoids shame: would he tell Socrates that he is a moderate character, he would be put to shame (of course, a mild one, given his tender age and the relatively law stake of the situation which is, after all, a philosophical conversation and not, for instance, a political debate); yet if he denied that he was a moderate character, he would be identified with what might have appeared a negative character trait, at least in the given context. (He would have been praised for his honesty, of course; especially if he added that he wanted to learn modesty; there are also contexts where modesty is not thought to be praiseworthy in the first place; in this particular situation, however, declaring oneself to be immoderate borders on being ridiculous.)

Charmides does not tell Socrates whether he is temperate/modest. Yet his reply tells his audience and possibly—via the positive reactions from his audience—to him that he *is* (at least close) to having a modest character. Again, in what moderation and temperance consists in can be discussed in more neutral and philosophical terms, and this is what Socrates and Critias will do shortly after this scene, but Charmides, ingeniously indeed, but perhaps also as a result of his proper education that had implanted temperance in him already, has already anticipated the gist of the matter. Temperance or moderation is a virtue or character trait that is not amenable to the usual modes of moral description. For it points toward the moral self, the center of moral authority and decision making, and its *self-knowledge* and self-ignorance (non-knowledge). Should Charmides really think that he is a moderate person, his moderation would be somehow harmed or reduced; therefore, he would risk losing an important element of his prestige and he would be put to shame. Should he deny that he is a moderate person, he would mislead himself and others and be untruthful. But that, again, would be something shameful.

Whenever it comes to *moral reflection*, we are somehow forced to retreat into our moral self, and by this moving, we depart the world in some ways, leaving all evaluations and descriptions, and consequently, all commitments behind. What looks to be moderation is therefore also a way of moral being and living. Consequently, being conscious of one's moral self and dealing with it, reflecting on it, in some sense, governing it, one is already practicing some degree of moderation. Shame alerts us to our moral self, and moderation is a method, a way of examining, dealing with and governing it.

On a closer look, however, moderation is more than *a way* of governing ourselves. It is worth returning to the dialogue for a moment because it takes the topic of moderation to the farthest possible philosophical point: knowledge and non-knowledge.[27] Socrates first continues asking Charmides about the meaning of moderation. The boy suggests the notions of order and quietness or tranquility, but Socrates quickly dismisses this idea and directs the conversation toward the idea of goodness in which moderation must "participate." However, as it turns out, many good things are in opposition to quietness, hence moderation—let us never forget that the Greek word, *sophrosyne*, is not perfectly identical with either temperance, or moderation, or sagacity, or prudence—must be a higher virtue. Here is where knowledge enters. Critias then suggests that moderation amounts to *knowing* one's place in society, in a community, consciously constraining one's inclinations and desires to be elsewhere or otherwise—an idea that Socrates himself supports in the *Politeia* (cf 430–431). Here, however, Socrates is much less certain about the meaning of this virtue, perhaps because it suggests a perfect knowledge of the whole, which would, then, be inconsistent with the practical role and meaning of moderation. For a virtue must be something specific, a distinct quality that is meant to instruct, educate, guide, and constrain us in our activities. As far as moderation is concerned, it is desirable for protecting us against excesses, pretensions, and distortions, and thereby against risks of shame; further, it adds to the value of being good. Briefly, it helps us understand what we are capable of doing. It also helps us resist every temptation to do whatever we do not know, and hence helps us govern ourselves, not let loose the control over ourselves, whenever it is in our power. If I am, or if I pretend to be in full possession of all knowledge (the political and social order), then this virtue seems to be useless, it literally evaporates.[28] But such a knowledge is impossible, only its illusion. *Governing ourselves* on the basis of illusions is itself illusionary. Thus, moderation is not *one way* of governing ourselves. It is *the only way* to do so.

On the most abstract philosophical level, the conclusion of the dialogue is hard to endure: "Does not what you have been saying, if true, amount to this: that there must be a single science which is wholly a science of itself and of other sciences, and that the same is also the science of the absence of science?"[29] Alan Pichanick calls this the tension between the Knowledge of Ignorance and the Knowledge of the Whole, with what seems to be a rather optimistic belief in the compatibility or reconcilability of these "knowledges":

> I believe that the tension of our in-between state will remain. For this tension is exemplified in the problem of having sôphrosunê itself: Socratic sôphrosunê and Socrates's philosophical method lead to a transcendence of oneself, and such a transcendence is at odds with the notion of sôphrosunê understood as keeping to one's place and not attempting to reach the height of the gods. But yet it is because this transcendence leads to knowledge of ignorance, that it can be properly called sôphrosunê after all. For this knowledge of ignorance is not ultimately a resolution to the tension of human existence, but rather it is predicated on the recognition of this tension.[30]

On a less optimistic reading, what we are dealing with is not simply a tension but a true paradox of self-knowledge: the more we learn about ourselves and the more descriptions we gather together, the less we may know what to do with them, and the more strongly we may feel that that we know nothing, or less than necessary. How much knowledge is, then, necessary? And for what is it necessary? These Socratic questions appear here not only desperate but hopelessly and uselessly abstract. However, they are practical both perennially and in situ: Charmides's reaction was and is clear and intelligible to any mature person; and the dialogue's politico-philosophical context was anything but innocent. For Critias, the main antagonist in this dialogue, was later to become (according to a near-consensual view of scholars) the head of the Thirties, infamous for his excessive, violent and cruel—highly immodest—government.[31] Critias understands well the importance of knowing—and he wishes to know everything. True moderation would require the knowledge of non-knowledge, the art of governing not everything, or the art of knowing where government should end.[32] To achieve this virtue, self-knowledge is necessary because it teaches us how knowing non-knowledge is possible.

Only by not knowing is freedom of action possible, both in a negative and a positive sense: non-knowing entails choices as well as non-tyranny.[33]

Again, however, the more we know, or pretend to know, of our moral character, the less moderate we shall become, being packed with layers of moral descriptions that may fill us with too much self-knowledge. This may fill us with self-confidence and an illusion of full control over ourselves. From this ensues a sort of hubris, inasmuch as perfect self-control implants in us a conviction that we are able and naturally entitled to control others as well. For he who knows everyone's place in society, within the political elite, is surely the ideal leader. However, this is a safe way to lose actual control, making us incapable of shame, which, in turn, will suggest to everyone else that something has gone awfully awry. What is required is a sense of non-knowledge, an openness to shame. Thus, the virtue of moderation is not identical with full moral knowledge. On the contrary, we need it as a moral virtue precisely in order to maintain the possibility of moral self-knowledge by making us forgetful of our own moral character embodied in and also entangled within its various descriptions.

The little story of Charmides's answering Socrates's personal question contains, therefore, both the element of representation of his moral self by being forced to give of himself a moral description—an account of his moral character—and the element of the reflection that is essentially tied to the virtue of moderation. Representation is making a commitment, therefore, an obvious constraint on the moral self. Reflection on awareness and knowledge of one's moral self is partly disowning commitments, emancipating oneself from the world but at the same time realizing that too much knowledge can be detrimental. First, because too many descriptions (the content of knowledge) amounts to too many commitments, which results in disorientation, an excessive fear of shame, an inability to act and thus to govern. Second, because it may make us overconfident, prideful, and plunging us into hubris. Thus, we find moderation intrinsically tied to moral self-knowledge and the problem of how and why to constrain it.

## CREON AND ANTIGONE, THE DUKE AND ANGELO: SHAME, MODERATION, AND SELF-KNOWLEDGE

### Antigone

In order to track shame transforming into a reflective mode of self-knowledge out of which moderation as a virtue may emerge in politics, rather than simply in ordinary social and moral life, let us turn again to Sophocles's and Shakespeare's plays and see how their intellectual insights and instincts work.

Shame is referred to directly in the *Antigone* only twice. First, in the first dialogue between Antigone and Creon. Creon confronts her with his conviction that she is alone in Thebes with holding her action right. Antigone rejects his thesis saying that the citizens "keep their mouths shut for fear of you." Creon: "Are you not ashamed to think so differently from them?" Antigone: "There is nothing shameful in honoring my brother" (556–559). However, it is not the word that matters when shame is around the corner. Creon described her position earlier with citing her "insolence" of breaking the law, coupling it with yet another act of insolence, namely, of being prideful of her act, and "laughing" at it. In other words, Antigone's demeanor was, in Creon's eyes, utterly shameless. And there is a third level of being shameless inasmuch as Antigone is a woman, provocatively presenting herself publicly in opposition to the king, a man, wherefore Creon feels—or anticipates—the intolerable shame of not being able to vindicate his rule against a woman. There is no doubt that shame and the fear of shame are centrally important in the drama, and it is very easy to identify ourselves with both Antigone's view that honoring her brother is an action opposite to shame, and that she may feel guilt and shame of not honoring Polyneices's body (a feeling she may want to impose on or arouse in Ismene, too); as well as with Creon's view that, given the ancient context, tolerating the defiance of his rule and questioning his competence in ruling the city as a man would have been gravely shameful. Fear of losing honor, fame, social, and political standing adumbrates shame. Thus, the topic of shame permeates virtually every act and every scene. The moral self or selves are always on public display.

Shame, as I argued, is a threshold event (event horizon, to use a modern metaphor taken from physics) that brings us into the inner world of self-awareness and self-reflection (which is, to many people, surely a sort of a black hole). It is triggered by a loss of a favorable description of the moral character. Compare the two main antagonists of the play. Antigone has an extremely strong and strongly controlled moral character. Her self-description includes love (though her reference to it is to her brothers and not to his fiancée), honor, and loyalty to her family, with a touch of defying shame (of her father and the circumstances of her conception that were shameful themselves, seriously harming the honor and reputation of a royal family). Does this imply that she knows her place in Thebes? Would she be competent to rule it? Certainly, female rule was a historical impossibility but though her defiance of Creon's orders, even her assuming the role of rendering the final burial to her brother, might have been interpreted as an unruly attempt to transgress the traditional barriers. In any case, she sticks to her public image carved out by her moral character, and no one questions its validity and truthfulness (her later lamentations are not considered signs of weakness or fear). She never feels shame, but nor does she display a single sign of moderation, of knowing anything but her sole purpose. She does not govern herself: all control is given up to fate, to the curse that she wishes to see accomplished, and this itself is a symptom of the lack of moderation, and hence her inability to be able to govern anything or anyone. It is very much possible that defying a corrupt or evil government, single-minded resistance is necessary from a practical point of view. However, from a theoretical point of view, this is a circumstantial possibility, which all governments should take into account. In other words, Antigone's resistance is, from Creon's point of view, a factual barrier to his government, something that he is well-advised to take seriously. He can overcome it with various means. Putting Antigone to shame would require a credible challenge to her moral character, something that Creon does not attempt to do. In one way, it is a reasonable omission: for making the other alert to her fault (if the attempt is successful) amounts to making her reflect on her moral self, her knowledge and its boundaries, and thereby her capability of control. Ismene might turn out to be a more capable and formidable opponent, exactly due to what seems to be her weakness: she is able to moderate her resentment, anger, and self-identification with the cause she is otherwise loyal to.

Creon's self-description is something that we search for in vain in the play. But we know from Creon's own words that he was consciously testing his self-knowledge by politics. In his speech from the throne, he very explicitly renounced all his personal relations, invalidating all the descriptions any-one might have had about him, including himself. The carte blanche policy sounds in many cases indeed very promising. What turns out quickly is that short of any personal bindings, without anchoring his public personality in the moral descriptions of him, he has nothing to stick to but his principles. Would he inspect his own self, Creon would find nothing but the austere and hollow-sounding principles and the laws derived from them in which he wished to ground his rule. Whereas Oedipus, another self-searcher, has a history, indeed, he has almost nothing but a personal history, which is very explicitly tied to the fate of his city, is a character we pity, has compassion with, and with whom emotional identification is possible, Creon never really achieves this. The only person who has affection for him is his son, Haemon. Therefore, his reaction to his father's appearance at the dead body of Antigone is especially relevant here. The Messenger tells about it. Creon cried out to his son groaning and in horror. Then

> the boy glared at him with savage eyes, and then / spat in his face, without a word of answer. / He drew his double-hilted sword. As his father / ran to escape him, Haemon failed to strike him, / and the poor wretch in his anger at himself / leaned on his sword and drove it halfway in, / into his ribs.
> (1307–1313)

The silent and frantic gesture of spitting is, by the way, exactly what Creon advised to him to do, metaphorically of course, when teaching a lesson to him about how to rule a household:

> The embrace grows cold / when an evil woman shares your bed and home. / What greater wound can there be than a false friend? / No. Spit on her, throw her out like an enemy. (704–707)

Spitting is surely a cross-cultural expression of contempt that is thought to be well-deserved because of some severely shameful act or behavior. It amounts really to throwing, casting out the other. Thus, the fiercest outburst of passion and pain not only in the *Antigone* but the whole trilogy is that of contempt and putting the other to shame (the sheer power and energy released in Haemon surpasses that of Oedipus and his action of self-blinding).

And this is not the end yet. Creon returns to his palace as the most hated person on earth and hated by his son whom he truly loved. But we soon learn from the Messenger that upon hearing the news, his wife, too, retires *without a word*, to kill herself. Spitting and denial of communication: these are extreme reactions to show one's contempt and to put the other to shame, once words are no more capable of carrying the weight of it. Creon becomes a non-person, as it were, someone about whom no one wishes to know anything more, anymore.

But was he *someone* before? We shall never learn because Creon acts and talks *always* as a political leader and never as a private person. He refuses to take counsel from anyone as a matter of principle. He commits himself but not to his moral self (that he already abandoned) but to what may be called his presumed political self. *That* is, however, vacuous. His political self is nothing but the law, which cannot have a character. The perfection of law consists in its being a sort of a knowledge *an sich*. Justice is blind, but for that reason, justice does not know anything else but justice. Moderation is impossible under such conditions because it entails, as I argued, non-knowledge as well.

Could he have been saved? Haemon offered him the argument:

> A man who thinks that he alone is right / or what he says, or what he *is* himself, / unique, such men, when opened up, are seen / to be quite empty. For a man, though he be wise, / it is no shame to learn—learn many things / and not maintain his views too rigidly. (762–766)

These lines and this reasoning, confirmed by the Chorus after the speech, make the point very straightforward. Haemon warns his father of emptiness—that is, having no knowledge whatsoever. Without knowledge, always constrained (one's views are always context-tied, contingent), no governing is possible: this is the root of moderation. And although *it does feel* shameful not to know something one is expected to know, it is *no less shameful* to know (or pretend to know) everything. Knowing non-knowing is, paradoxical as it may sound, helps us remain within boundaries, the transgression of which threatens with losing control over ourselves and over others, and put ourselves to shame. In this case, Creon's shame was dramatically marked by the wordless contempt and rejection by his son and his wife. His government was immoderate and proved to be shameful.

## Measure for Measure

In *Measure for Measure*, we have a more complex scenario and, of course, the ending is not tragic. Nonetheless, it may strike the reader who happens to read the two pieces in a sequence that notwithstanding their moral qualities, Angelo resembles Antigone in terms of the strength of their public characters; and that much like Creon, the Duke evades all attempts of characterization.[34] Moreover, whereas Creon loses his son and his wife, and with them, every human bond he has, the Duke does not have such bonds but establishes the first one by marrying Isabella. These parallels may give the reader the initial and tentative suggestion that character, self, and the problem of knowledge and non-knowledge tested in the business of government are equally strong topics in both plays.

As far as Angelo is concerned, the Duke introduces him by referring to his character, pouring praise on him, face to face—something that is difficult to imagine not to cause some blush on anybody's face:

> Angelo, / There is a kind of character in thy life, / That to the observer doth thy history / Fully unfold. Thyself and thy belongings / Are not thine own so proper as to waste / Thyself upon thy virtues, they on thee. (I.1.)

Angelo does not report about feeling shame, however, though he does try to evade the Duke's laudation by what might be a gesture of courtly politeness. Again, the Duke later calls him "[a] man of stricture and firm abstinence."[35] We still do not know whether he is serious. What we do know is that not everyone is so enthusiastic about Angelo. Lucio reports that Angelo's public image is less than favorable:

> A man whose blood / Is very snow-broth; one who never feels / The wanton stings and motions of the sense, / But doth rebate and blunt his natural edge / With profits of the mind, study and fast. . . . They say this Angelo was not made by man and / woman after this downright way of creation. . . . Some report a seamaid spawned him; some, / that he / was begot between two stock-fishes. But it

is / certain that when he makes water his urine is / congealed ice; that I know to
be true: and he is a / motion generative; that's infallible (III.2.).

Lucio's remarks are malicious, and he is far from being a reliable source
on anything, but Angelo's public appearances are in conformity with these
descriptions. They do not yet rule out that the Duke is right, after all. Angelo
is very strictly committed to his own public image, and the Duke obviously
wishes to look convinced that Angelo's character makes him particularly fit
for governing. His virtuousness may appear to be icy, yet very close to the
necessary sobriety and cool moderation we expect of a good (though not
exactly likable) government. However, even his descriptions contain something portentous, a bit inhuman, some deep and disturbing inconsistency.
Later again, the Duke himself seems to be aware that Angelo might not be
looked upon with appreciation by this subjects: "Lord Angelo is precise; /
Stands at a guard with envy; scarce confesses / That his blood flows, or that
his appetite / Is more to bread than stone" (I.3.). We later learn that he knew
about Angelo's vices, especially his greed. This is what makes one wonder
how Angelo would have responded to Socrates's question of whether he
holds himself a moderate or temperate character.

The answer would probably have been "no." Angelo would have thought
that virtuousness requires the denial of possessing that virtue. But a flat
denial would be hypocritical, much as the affirmation of having moderation.
In any case, neither position opens the gates toward self-knowledge. And
Shakespeare makes it very clear that Angelo does not possess sufficient self-
knowledge. He is genuinely surprised by the arousal of his own lust. He is
completely overcome by it. He is not mature enough even to love Isabella
(by extension, any human person), he desires only her body, he can lose
control over himself suddenly and totally, and he does not even feel shame,
only wonder, surprise, and some pity for himself. His moral self does not
exist yet, therefore, all the descriptions were imposed upon it, including his
own. Therefore, what looks virtuousness is in fact an ideal, no different from
the principles of Creon. Angelo, once in government, also identifies himself
with the law ("it is the law not I condemn your brother," II.2.). His journey
has not begun yet, he must be publicly humiliated to feel shame. This is what
happens with a force and to a degree that Angelo genuinely wishes to die.
Instead, he is led away to marry Marianna but, unlike Lucio's marriage, his
wedding is not a shameful act. Was the Duke about to teach a lesson to him,
or more generally, to educate him? It is indeed possible that Shakespeare's
personal message was that moderation is politics and government must begin
with a moderation over oneself, and that moderation is intimately linked with
knowing one's non-knowledge that begins with feeling shame. Of course,
nothing precludes further surprises, but surprises—Machiavelli would say

Fortuna—can be overcome only if we are in control of ourselves sufficiently. The lesson is not, therefore, that Angelo ought to have been a *genuinely* (perhaps an all-the-way-through) virtuous person to qualify as a ruler because that would have committed to him to some descriptions unnecessarily, even dangerously. Had he not fallen, his judgment of Claudio would have been no less harsh and somehow no less inappropriate. The law knows no exceptions, it cannot do anything but condemn, hence it has no freedom of action, and if it acts, it acts blindly. Much as a full identification of principle and governing is either impossible or tyrannical, perfect virtuousness is both disabling and blinding.

As was said, the Duke's character or personality has ever puzzled or embarrassed not only readers but commentators as well. Lucio tells him (unaware of his identity) that the Duke had his secret life, which was anything but virtuous, and Friar Thomas also seems to have hinted at the possibility that going around in a monk's habit may be merely a cover for some flirting adventures. None of these descriptions and assumptions sound very solidly grounded. Lucio seems to be right about Angelo, yet his "information" about the Duke whom he says to be intimate with sounds more based about gossips, though some of them seem to be quite well-detailed. And princes have always been supposed to have the power for satisfying their personal desires, those of the flesh included. There is nothing personal, therefore, about this behavior. It is, then, especially interesting that the Duke (still disguised) enquires Escalus about his image and personality. Significantly, this comes right after the Duke's words on the riddle that governs world, which is perhaps the main political and philosophical message of the play.

> I / pray you, sir, of what disposition was the duke?—One that, above all other strifes, contended / especially to know himself. /—What pleasure was he given to?—Rather rejoicing to see another merry, than merry at / anything which professed to / make him rejoice: a / gentleman of all temperance. But leave we him to / his events. (III.2.)

At last, we are confronted with our core concepts of self-knowledge and temperance.[36] Even if Escalus may have some interest in attempting to give a good impression about his prince to the envoy of the Holy See (his partner introduces himself as such), he does not mention religiosity, piety, or chivalry, valiance, not even wisdom and justice as the most relevant qualities of the Duke. Much like, again, the later Prospero, the Duke is portrayed here as a passive onlooker who is entertained by his subjects, strangely, by their joys and happiness. That is not the pleasure Lucio had in mind, and not the pleasure any of his subjects could really understand: however, Shakespeare might have thought of the logic of theater that helps us learn how to be happy without interest and second thoughts simply by thinking about the happiness of other people.

But this proves to be an illusion, if pressed too far. Why would the Duke so inclined start the whole plot? Probably because the lack of something, which is similar to what Creon thought. Without politics, that is, without throwing ourselves literally into the life of others, there is little chance to learn much about ourselves. It is not really Angelo but the Duke himself who needs to be taught something. And busy as he becomes with his subjects' lives, he makes a number of mistakes. He is able to correct them, otherwise the play would immediately turn into a tragedy, but his corrections are either of a supernatural nature (he must use his seal, an act that he probably wanted to avoid); or providential: the benevolence of his subjects is something he could not have predicted. He begins to govern. Governing means both some knowledge of himself but also some non-knowledge, an openness to mistakes, even Fortuna, which teaches him the constraints of his own government. He can achieve a lot, but he is far from being an omnipotent and omniscient ruler.

The Duke is never shamed, that is true, though we may sense a bit of shame on his part due to his failure of ruling well, and his subjects' indifferent, perhaps even poor opinion of him does not help dispel this. Unlike Angelo whose public character was strong, the Duke's character is, at the beginning, almost non-existent, hollow, and therefore neither benevolent, nor malevolent. Escalus praises him, yet we are rightly embarrassed by his words: what sort of a government is it whose head rejoices in seeing others' merry? Aesthetic pleasure is doubtlessly valuable; selfless rejoicing in others' bliss is perhaps a sign of moral perfection, yet there is no further clue to the Duke's intentions, motivations, in short, to his character, in which these qualities would make sense. Actually, he has this to tell Escalus in the first scene: "I love the people, / But do not like to stage me to their eyes: / Through it do well, I do not relish well / Their loud applause and aves vehement; / Nor do I think the man of safe discretion / That does affect it" (I.2.). Is this a laudable sort of temperance? Or an idle, even idiotic sort of a mind? Both are compatible with these descriptions. He is uncommitted to any reliable description, yet this freedom from commitments makes his "rule" weak and ghostly. He is not, however, a devilish manipulator, an "old fantastical duke of dark corners,"[37] to cite Lucio's words that are somehow enigmatic enough. Rather, he is a sort of a non-person, an ineffectual institution, about whom, or which, neither knowledge, nor non-knowledge is verifiably predicable. But running the government, doing politics, navigating the ship needs a flesh-and-bone person of recognizable character, and a proof of being capable of control, in the first place, over himself. If anything, this is a great lesson to the Duke. True temperance requires self-knowledge, which requires accessible descriptions without a complete and irrevocable commitment to any of them, which is both a philosophical task to go down the way between knowledge and non-knowledge until the end, and a political virtue of governing, without falling into either the trap of tyranny or the trap of anarchy.

## SUMMARY

After considering how political theory in its toughest conceptualist forms, which present us with the most powerful and over-imposing images of government, I directed the focus on the image of the captain or navigator, on the assumption that we should expect most people to imagine the government first and foremost in personal terms. It soon turns out that the adjective "personal" is not entirely unequivocal. On the one hand, it suggests something truly individual, unrepeatable, and unique (something that "charisma" refers to); on the other hand, most probably people have fairly strong "objective" expectations of what qualities a person "doing governing" should possess. But again, these qualities or properties are considered to be "personal." In effect, personality and office are very tightly intertwined. A well-known historical example is the difference between "imperator-emperor" and "Caesar-Kaiser/Tsar": in the first case, the office becomes personalized; in the second case, a person's character becomes institutionalized. The question to which an answer was searched in the chapter was whether this centaur-like idea of the governor (captain) incorporates a similarly inherent constraint as political theory was shown to have.

I discussed the notion of character first. We learn about ourselves from the various descriptions of our characters. Most people are doubtlessly very much interested in having favorable descriptions of them. It is not a privilege or a special feature of the politician or the political leader. Thus, not having a favorable description, or losing it is something most of us try to avoid or prevent. In this respect, shame is a crucial emotion and experience. Through shame we are not only taught certain—often painful—lessons but enabled to look into ourselves—our moral selves. Shame teaches us that we need to control ourselves, but also that a loss of control occurs in spite of our efforts, sometimes due to simple bad luck. Thus, the vicissitudes of politics and governing begin within our own souls. This provides the bridge between self-governance and governing others.

Following Plato's story and dialogue of Charmides, as well as re-reading *Antigone* and *Measure for Measure*, I found that the experience of shame is closely related to moderation, which is the most reliable way of governing both ourselves and others over the unpredictable waters of reality. Moderation means to be able to know our limits. In its absence, we are more likely to come to believe that a full knowledge is possible, which is, of course illusory, threatening us with overconfidence on the one hand, and inability to act on the other hand. Thus, the constraint we have been looking for consists in the nature of governing that begins with self-reflection and self-control. The idea, first expounded by Plato, is that we must steer clear of both the illusion of perfect or full knowledge, and the illusion of total ignorance. All governing, including self-governance and control, takes place in a reality where total rule and total anarchy are equally shameful, resting on illusions. Since governing is not mystically or metaphysically different from self-governance, shame remains an equally strong and powerful reminder of intellectual, moral, and political transgressions.

## NOTES

1. Bernard Williams, "Politics and Moral Character." In S. Hampshire et al. (eds.) *Public and Private Morality* (Cambridge: Cambridge University Press, 1978), 54–70.

2. Edward Hall, "Integrity in Democratic Politics." *The British Journal of Politics and International Relations* 4 (2018): 385–98.

3. Ibid., 401.

4. Ibid.

5. Mark Philp, *Political Conduct* (Cambridge, MA; London: Harvard University Press, 2007).

6. Ibid., 39.

7. Ibid., 49.

8. Ibid., 51–52.

9. Non-realist conceptions work with different categories, such as tropes. The ontological problems are, however, irrelevant here.

10. It turns out that the utilitarian tradition is essentially tied to the notion of "goodness" or "the good." The deontic tradition cherishes a similarly central value, that of the infinite worth of the human person.

11. This presupposes that we have such a character. Let us assume that this ontological precondition is given, that is, everyone has a moral character, no matter whether it is morally bad (or overwhelmingly bad) or good (or overwhelmingly good).

12. For an overview of various metaphysical positions about the self, see *Self-Knowledge*, ed. Quassim Cassam (Oxford: Oxford University Press, 1994). Talking about "the self" smacks, much as the abstract concepts of political theory discussed in the previous chapter, of some unnaturally sounding philosophy. But Galen Strawson observes: "The problem of the self doesn't arise from an unnatural use of language which arises from nowhere. On the contrary: use of a phrase like 'the self' arises from a prior and independent sense that there is such a thing as the self." In: "The Self." In S. Gallagher and J. Shear (eds.) *Models of the Self* (Thorverton: Imprint Academic, 1999), 3–45. Strawson is concerned with the "mental self" as the essential sense of the self. He argues that contrary to the common assumption according to which

memories and plans, a sense of past and future, temporality, or minimally a "stream of consciousness" is necessary for there being a self, a simple consciousness of one's being there is enough. However, the problem of how to account for the existence of the self has remained tightly connected with time and temporality, as identities, obviously also very central to the notion of the self, also evolve and develop temporally. Discussing these problems is beyond the scope of this book, yet the insight that we are capable of introspection, of a demarcation and detachment of our inner life from the roles and "offices" we identify ourselves with but with the "right" of reservation, suspension, and abolition, is necessary for the reasoning. By the term "moral," I wish to add the evaluative dimension to the ontological or existential awareness of ourselves—or of our selves. "Normative self" might be an alternative but it appears to be unnecessarily technical. By "personal," I wished to stress the importance of what is at stake.

13. When it comes to deliberate and decide over our responsibility for actions taken, passions used, emotions given room to, and so on, the moral self works as our conscience. Our habit, customs, narrative and moral commitments, and memories are usually to be evaluated as constraints and limitations of our culpability (if an immoral action is at the foro interno).

14. *Somewhat* inconsistent: the New Testament does not "refute" or reject the Old Testament's concern with good reputation as a sign of God's blessing. It deviates from it in many respects by exalting the instrumental value of suffering, but the concepts of glory and victory are essentially no different (glory is translated as doxa—opinion—in the Septuaginta.) Of course, it is the glory of God and not that of men that is the highest value; nonetheless, His glory shines through His saints and His People—or His Church.

15. John Kekes argues that shame is an emotion that moral maturation or progress should constrain: "moral progress leads us away from shame toward other moral responses" because "shame undermines self-direction, reduces the chances of moral reform, and weakens our selves." "Shame and Moral Progress." In P.A. French, Th.E. Uehling Jr, H.K. Wettstein (eds.) *Ethical Theory: Character and Virtue.* Midwest Studies in Philosophy Vol. XIII (Notre Dame: University of Notre Dame Press, 1988), 282–96. His reasoning is, however, deeply embedded in a conception of moral progress at the center of which stands a well-entrenched conception of good life. Moral progress may entail that; however, shame remains important in launching this progress. And, as will be argued, in politics, shame remains essential.

16. *A Theory of Justice*, 388–89.

17. Ibid., 390.

18. Gabriele Taylor, "Shame, Integrity, and Self-Respect." In Robin S. Dillon (ed.) *Dignity, Character and Self-Respect* (New York: Routledge, 1995), 157–81, 161.

19. John Deigh, "Shame and Self-Esteem: A Critique." Ibid: 133–57, 152.

20. Cheshire Calhoun, "An Apology for Moral Shame." *The Journal of Political Philosophy* 2 (2004): 127–46, 145.

21. David Velleman, "The Genesis of Shame." *Philosophy and Public Affairs* 1 (2001): 27–52.

22. Phillip Galligan, "Shame, Publicity, and Self-Esteem." *Ratio* March (2016): 57–72. "Shame is a feeling of low self-esteem, experienced in response to the subject's perception that he is not thought of in the way that he intrinsically values himself for being thought of by some relevant other" (65).

23. Such as David A. Graham's article: "Trump Has No Shame" in which he argues that shame—apparently?—not working in the case of the Donald Trump, and other constraints are necessary to look for, and indeed, he finds them in the institutions. This may be an important observation, demonstrating the shame is by no means the only constraint in governing. But one also wonders why shameless behavior is supposed somehow to extirpate or lessen the importance of shame. On the contrary: shamelessness makes shame more important than ever. https://www.theatlantic.com /ideas/archive/2019/09/trump-fears-only-consequences/598657/ Accessed 2.11.2020. Jill Locke, the author of *Democracy and the Death of Shame: Political Equality and Social Disturbance* (Cambridge: Cambridge University Press, 2016) argues that the current (2020) President may feel shame for failing to achieve various things (in his pre-presidency life), which might drive him to overcompensate and overcome shame; but she also argues that bringing shame back in to politics may backfire, as it may amount to buying in the childishness argument about the president, which, she writes, is disarming: children are forgiven more. Therein lies the danger of deprecation with shame. See: https://krisis.eu/donald-trump-is-not-a-shameless-toddler-the-pro blems-with-psychological-analyses-of-the-45th-us-president/. Accessed 11.20.2020. However, the present argument is that shame indicates serious problems with control, thus, its disarming-infantile effect in the "adult world" is limited.

24. For a useful comparative analysis, see Aurel Kolnai, "The Standard Modes of Aversion: Fear, Disgust and Hatred." *Mind* 427 (1998): 581–95. The brief analysis of fear is based on this article.

25. Judith Shklar rejects the view that fear can justify the Leviathan; nonetheless, her liberalism is centered around it. The fear of fear (of cruelty, violent death) is the ultimate justification of the liberal order. See "The Liberalism of Fear." In Nancy L. Rosenblum (ed.) *Liberalism and the Moral Life* (Cambridge: Harvard University Press, 1989), 21–38.

26. Plato, "Charmides." In Benjamin Jowett (tr.) *The Dialogues of Plato*, Vol 1 (London: Oxford University Press, 1892), 1–38, 15.

27. Voula Tsouna, "What is the Subject of Plato's Charmides?" In Y. Z. Liebersohn, I. Ludlam, and A. Edelheit (eds.) *For a Skeptical Peripatetic. Festschrift in Honour of Johan Glucker* (S. Augustin: Academia Verlag, 2017), 34–63. "Socrates' search for self-knowledge kept him away from politics, whereas Critias' idea that temperance endows one with supreme cognitive authority eventually brought him to the leadership of the Thirty" (61).

28. The point is made succinctly by Gabriel Danzig: "After showing the difficulties involved in knowledge of knowledge, Socrates argues that such knowledge is politically useless anyway. Even if one possessed knowledge of knowledge it would not enable one to know oneself, or to know what someone else knows or does not know. It would enable one to know whether someone has knowledge or not, but not what kind of knowledge he has." "Plato's Charmides as a Political Act: Apologetics

and the Promotion of Ideology." *Greek, Roman, and Byzantine Studies* 53 (2013): 486–519, 514.

29. *Charmides*, 26.

30. Alan Pichanick, "Sôphrosunê, Socratic Therapy, and Platonic Drama in Plato's Charmides." *Epoché: A Journal for the History of Philosophy* 1 (2016): 47–66, 16.

31. For a dissenting view, however, see Thomas Tuozzo, *Plato's Charmides: Positive Elenchus in a "Socratic" Dialogue* (Cambridge: Cambridge University Press, 2011). Tuozzo also argues that the knowledge at issue is that of the good and the bad, which is objective enough (in a Platonic view), yet the emphasis on non-knowledge as part of knowing seems to be at variance with this reading. Saying that Critias talks about objective knowledge, while Socrates talks about knowing the method of knowing appears to be only a verbal compromise. Critias might have meant it well, like Creon, when he claimed to be able to run a republic on the grounds of moral goodness and badness, yet he proved to be, much like Creon, wrong on account of not knowing where even good governments are to be constrained.

32. "The political significance of moderation in the Charmides follows from the political cast of characters, the dramatic date, and the recurrent idea that good government is sophron, whatever sophrosyne turns out to be. But it follows especially from the fact that Critias' core idea about sophrosyne—doing one's own things—was an aristocratic-oligarchic slogan in an on-going political struggle in which Chaerephon, Charmides, and Critias were actors on different sides and of which, ultimately, Socrates was a victim. The dialogue, with its ultimate refutation of that idea, suggests that sophrosyne should not be used as political cover for an oligarchy of technical expertise and, more importantly, enacts a nonauthoritarian commitment to principles and individual humility about one's own knowledge, importance, and reputation" [Greek letters are transcribed]. Gerald A. Press, "The Enactment of Moderation in Plato's Charmides." *Acta Classica Universitatis Scientarum Debreceniensis*, 54 (2018): 5–34, 30.

33. Danzig's conclusion is therefore, in my view, misleading: "it seems clear that the would-be political expert should look in another direction for political expertise. Socrates swiftly offers a better option, arguing that what is necessary for political rule is the knowledge of good and bad. . . . Just as previously Socrates argued that the good and not the self provides an adequate standard for action, so too here he argues that the good and not the self provides a useful object of knowledge" (*Plato's Charmides as a Political Act*, 515). Being obsessed with one's self is of course a safe way to tyrannical thinking, and it cannot be a "standard for action." However, knowing how *not to* think that we know everything about ourselves is a precondition to moderation.

34. No wonder that the character of the Duke has been one of the main foci of the scholarly literature on *Measure for Measure*. Commentators are divided on the moral quality of the Duke's character. Ervene Gulley points out that notwithstanding some occasions of derailment, the Duke remains the mastermind of the story as the denouement demonstrates (" 'Dressed in a Little Brief Authority': Law as Theater in Measure for Measure." In B. L. Rockwood (ed.) *Law and Literature Perspectives* (New York: Peter Lang, 1996), 53–80. Nigel Bawcutt insists that the Duke is benevolent and rejects the Machiavellian parallels: " 'He Who the Sword of Heaven Will

Bear?' The Duke Versus Angelo in Measure for Measure." Shakespeare Survey: An Annual Survey of Shakespearian Study and Production 37 (1984): 89–97. Stephen Cohen thinks that the topos of the disguised king was Shakespeare's main dramaturgical instrument and in that sense, this figure is neither morally good nor bad. "From Mistress to Master: Political Transition and Formal Conflict in Measure for Measure." *Criticism* 4 (1999): 431–64. Others consider him a more fallible character, yet someone who wishes to learn how to better govern (Cynthia Lewis, "'Dark Deeds Darkly Answered': Duke Vincentio and Judgement in *Measure for Measure*." *Shakespeare Quarterly* 3 (1984): 271–89. Some critics regard him a much more sinister figure: Andrew Barnaby, Joan Wry, "Authorized Versions: *Measure for Measure* and the Politics of Biblical Translation." *Renaissance Quarterly* 4 (1998): 1225–54. Also Brian Holloway, "Vincentio's Fraud: Boundary and Chaos, Abstinence and Orgy in *Measure for Measure*." *West Virginia Shakespeare and Renaissance Association, Selected Papers* 21 (1998) www.marshall.edu/engsr/SR1998.html.)

35. 102.

36. Gibbons points out the connection between James I's person, his *Basilikon Doron*, and the play's moral lesson in which moderation or temperance is pivotal. The king's famous work itself "emphasised the importance of temperance. Acknowledging the element of public display required of a prince, James stressed nevertheless that a prince should show virtue in action and cultivate it as a private inward state, warning against hypocritical outward show and empty words. He also confessed that he had been insufficiently strict at the beginning of his rule, and expressed strong disapproval of 'unreverent speakers'; these are elements which Shakespeare gives special emphasis in his Duke at the beginning and end of Measure for Measure, and which were no doubt intended to be recognised as allusions to the new king." *Introduction*, 26.

37. 175.

*Chapter 4*

# Character and Office, Normalcy and Exceptions

In the previous chapter, I tried to show how and why knowledge and self-knowledge is related to self-rule, from which the necessity of moderation arises. In its absence, either tyranny or anarchy threatens. This is not an earth-shaking discovery, of course, but the confirmation of a traditional wisdom, hopefully from a new angle. As this book generally, the argument of the previous chapter is meant to be an exploration of parts of our common wisdom, something that not only political theorists and their reasonings but also the everyday intuitions and experiences of citizens can support. This is why the personal, more accessible dimension of every government had to precede this chapter, which brings us closer to the more customary topics of contemporary political theory.

This chapter will shift a focus on the more institutionalized and routinized aspects of governing, here, on the offices. The central idea is the possibility and naturalness of this shifting or switch: as usually, if such a possibility arises, then we need to make some conceptual and image-related distinctions, which help us understand something of reality and guide us in our practice. Three such distinctions will be proposed and explained in the first part of this chapter. The first is the by-now familiar one between the personal and the institutional aspects of governing. The second is the distinction between time-perspectives. It is quite customary to distinguish between normal and exceptional times both in our own private lives and politics/governing. The two distinctions do not overlap, though the personal aspect of governing is generally thought to be more important, at least more apparent, in exceptional than in times; whereas the institutional aspect is considered to be more relevant in normal than in exceptional times. The third distinction is made between governing and anti-governing. The latter refers to the private sphere of individuals. The insight is that all sorts of governing activities "take place" there as well, which mirror or mimic governing in the traditional sense, and which will be called here political governing. It is not necessary to regard anti-governing is strictly opposing political governing. The image of mirroring suggests parallelism and similarity but also non-identity and distinctness as well. These three distinctions, so it will be argued, constitute conceptual and practical constraints of governing. How these can help us in discerning these limits will be discussed in the second part of this chapter by help and in terms of the legislator, the executive and the judge as three public characters and offices that any government (broadly understood) needs and works with. As always, the Sophocles and Shakespeare will help us relate these issues to our everyday life.

## DISTINCTIONS

### Character versus Office, Normal versus Exceptional Times

My presumption was that most people think of government in rather personal terms, especially in times of crisis or *ecstasis*, crying out for someone to help, to create or restore order, correct the failing or corrupt institutions, resist an invasion, defeat a virus, and so on. At other times, that we may call normal times, the personal aspect wanes, and people want their leaders to let them go about their everyday business, and are content with the usual complaints about the incompetence of the state, its bureaucracy, the authorities, the decision-making bodies, courts, public servants, and officials, without any particular desire to have someone reform the whole system urgently and from the grounds. However, when a crisis sets in, for whatever reason (remember: rulers can themselves instigate crises, as *Measure for Measure* suggests), then the characters of political leaders and their ways of governing becomes more important and interesting in the eyes of many than the quality of the institutions, and there does not seem to be any compelling argument for wishing to suppress or ignore this interest. It *is* now simply important who is "the executive," or who holds the executive power, who is the president, the prime minister, the party chairman, not because of the office but because it confers rights and powers to act on the person occupying the post.

Thus, the considerations discussed in the previous chapter are especially relevant to make a case for the inherent constraints of political leaders that are derivable from the very notions of leading and governing. What emerges out of these simple observations are two distinctions: the one between the personal and the office/routine-based dimensions of governing, and the other between exceptional and normal times. The two distinctions do not overlap perfectly, though as has been argued, normal times tend to obfuscate the personal dimension of politics and governing, whereas exceptional or critical situations and times have the opposite effect. Let us briefly spell out these two distinctions.

The importance of *personality*, *character*, and leadership qualities in politics has never been forgotten in political theory though it has not been in its center recently. With the rise of what is commonly called populist-authoritarian regimes, the interest in it is growing. What a "character" is, how "it" (in the form of an office, of an institutionalized post or role) looks like, is a matter of descriptions that are given in terms of virtues, vices, professed principles, and values. However, the traits and information are validated and justified in terms of actions. Governing and leading people consists in acting for them, on behalf of them, with them, and so on. Popular persons, also known as celebrities, are often acclaimed with the words "X for President!"—which suggests that they are considered to have done certain admirable things (often but not always actions praised for their moral excellence), which, in turn, are seen as reflecting some admirable character traits.

The phrase "for President" means, thus, that they are thought to be fit for a position where those traits are deemed somehow desirable. However, once they are indeed in power, holding the (or some) official-governmental post, the expectations change. They are supposed to "govern," which is different from vying for the post, holding inspiring or moving speeches, meeting people in the streets, and so on. Most people would find it weird that a good and popular humorist for whom they voted—perhaps half-humorously but half-seriously—and who indeed won the post should continue making jokes wherever he goes. His personal charisma, in whatever it consists, should somehow be used in and for governing. It should not vanish, on the contrary: being devoured by the elite and its games (with the more common metaphor, the "deep state") is a danger; yet something must change, the charisma is expected to be used and applied for a reform or a revolution in governing. A famous actor may be idolized for his achievements, his talents, and even his moral deeds (e.g., generosity and support of certain good causes), yet he must successfully transform or adapt his charisma, his moral behavior, and even his cherished special goals to the business of governing and leading, which involves, among others, much listening to others as well as making "unpopular" decisions, a deliberate and cool anticipation of becoming rejected by certain social and political groups. An excellent military commander may be highly popular and win the elections by high margin, yet even an experience with leading an army that requires strategic thinking, tactical skills, logistic, and administrative capabilities does not necessarily prepare him well for political leadership: Ulysses Grant is probably a case in point here.

In normal times, no matter how sympathetic or attractive the personality of the new politician is, once she is in power, we expect her to think in terms of utilitarian or consequentialist ethics. Promoting the public good is her main duty, and this duty requires constant activity. We usually describe such leaders as "serving," "working," "laboring," "negotiating," "administering," "running," and so on: such skills figure often on the list of realist mirrors for princes (see the first section of the previous chapter). Their character is expected to be in conformity with such activities. Even in emergency situations, or exceptional times, such as wars, leadership requires more than personal bravery, perseverance, dedication, and the like; a great deal of administrative, coordinating, negotiating work awaits the leader. Dwight D. Eisenhower, unlike General Grant, is often considered to have been a successful military commander for his "political skills," which shows that no matter how critical a situation is, how decisive a war is, the nature of people does not change, wherefore politics and efficient governing may remain a precondition to military success. Still, in exceptional times we tend to desire a political leader to whom virtue or value-centered ethical thinking is more important. She may be dedicated to a cause or to a principle, rather than a duty (or "the" duty) and we are highly interested in her personal reasons, biography, character development, charisma, and so on. And we eagerly expect her to perform actions in conformity with her ethic and her character. If she gets immersed in the routines of politics and governing, and sinks in the "empire of mud," people are likely to become disappointed. Yet again, exceptional, or simply innovative actions are also likely to become routinized, repeated, analyzed, and taught at schools and academies. They may become models for others and enter manuals (i.e., especially striking in military history and business textbooks). Charismatic actions are often repeated and continued as rituals. Thus, the distinction between person and institution, or between personality and office, is constantly shifting in practice, yet this is how governing and political leading are identifiable, and kept in the focus, in terms of emotions, images, concepts, and arguments within a political community.

Certain political systems, especially the presidential and the chancellor-dominated parliamentary ones, are institutionally more open to the personalization of politics and government, putting the character and person into the center of governing even in normal times. Innovative, creative, unexpected actions that break rules, protocols, customs are not at all alien to "normal" politics and governments. It is even tempting to conclude that real or genuine politics is creative and innovative, whereas governing means administration, legality, and decision procession. But neither the institutionalized openness, nor the truly exceptional times make politics merely a personal issue. Leadership tends to be consumed by routinized actions, and running governments is a political issue all the way through. There is, thus, no one-to-one correspondence between the personal/institutional and the normal/exceptional dimensions of politics. The lesson is that our changing and often contradictory attitudes to and expectations of government have a confusing effect on it, which is responsible for the Fortuna-like aspect of politics that caused so much headache to Machiavelli.[1] But this constitutes an important barrier to the omnipotent and all-powerful government. Routinized, institutionalized governing has its limits because it cannot substitute for the personal dimension, and vice versa: personal politics is limited because of the inevitable routinization and institutionalization of all governments.

Let us briefly put the other distinction, the one between normal and exceptional times, into the focus. Whereas the argument for moderation being the key virtue of governing holds for both, we generally expect and tend to accept that actions permitted, even required in exceptional times are different from those allowed and held necessary in normal times. There is, thus, a distinction between the competences of the government *diachronically*, rather than, for instance, *functionally*. The distinction suits well Machiavelli's insight about the different behavior of fox-like and lion-like political leaders, the former being more suitable to normal circumstances, the latter more in demand in exceptional circumstances. Of course, whereas he struggled with the problem of how to integrate what appeared to him fundamentally different types of human nature into a single leader character, our more institutionalized political realities allow for a greater room for a diachronic perspective. "Ecstatic" times justify not only a more personalized government but also special functions, offices, rights, and prerogatives. Dictatorship is usually considered to be constitutionally illegal or unmanageable but the regular office of the president/prime minister may be modified, with extended competences and empowerments, adequate to critical times. Though even normal times do not make politics and governing wholly impersonal and institutionalized, as was argued, yet surely different types of actions, roles, methods, and styles of doing politics are expected. This is not to blind us to the possibility that certain crises emerge due to political efforts, intentions, and manipulations: think of the host of prophets, anarchists, revolutionaries, as well as hysterical, visionary, or simply refined politicians and other insiders to governments not only hoping for but also actively contributing to the atmosphere of crisis. It is also possible that a more or less natural, or non-political crisis is carried on in politics: a natural disaster or an economic setback may cause deeper repercussions in politics, by which long-standing changes can be introduced that serve the interests of the leader. The crisis may be over, yet the political atmosphere may continue to be artificially hectic and tense. However, these possibilities can be put aside for the moment, the main point being here the analytical one, namely, that in terms of actions and rules, institutions, and functions, we are able to distinguish between governments suited to various needs of times. Not everything is permitted in normal times, and exceptional times must end and give way to normal times: these are the two meta-rules that suggest an effective constraint to both governments.

## Anti-Governing[2]

There is a third distinction I wish to make for the forthcoming discussion. It needs a separate subsection because it has a logical structure different from that of the two distinctions discussed earlier. Whereas the previous two distinctions rest on an opposing relation (personal *versus* institutional, normal *versus* exceptional), the present one rests on a parallelism. It is no less germane to the intuition that governing is a limited activity as the two others. The distinction to be introduced and discussed here is made between governing and anti-governing.

Traditionally, we do not think that only the government should govern, or rule, administer, or take care of various issues. First of all, we like to think of our lives being under our own government. This has been a classical liberal conception, which has its roots in the various autonomous communities of the Middle Ages, justified by a variety of arguments, beginning with the distinction between temporal and spiritual authority. Modern moral and social philosophy, inspired by Kant's concept of the autonomous will, Rousseau's exaltation of the citizen, Mill's humanist ideal, and Nietzsche's aspirations to create the modern self, has made much of the concept of the autonomy of the individual. Although such conceptions have an elitist flavor, and many people are content with legal guarantees that protect their small circles of freedom, modern welfare societies do provide individuals with an ever-growing set of opportunities and choices to select from, and construe their own lives, as it were. Thus, being the originator and source of meaningful decisions becomes a way and a constitutive element of self-governing.

All this is a well-known story that needs no detailed recapitulation. The substantial point that was added to it here was the argument outlined in the previous chapter, namely, that moderation grows out of self-knowledge and is essentially related to self-rule and *self-government*.

Secondly, and perhaps more interestingly, though the more traditional, or patriarchal approach to family may be on the wane in many parts of the world, with the model of the pater (sometimes mater) familias in charge of the family, with extensive rights over the members; yet the idea that there can be groups of people with some *natural ties* that entitle them to govern themselves may be not at all outdated. As a matter of fact, even modern families may have their common good, parents have various "governing" responsibilities over their children, and much as a modern constitutional democracy, families may be "run" according to the principles of "power sharing"; deliberation over the common good; calculating the benefits and harms of individual members of certain programs, projects, and undertakings; and use perhaps even the instrument of voting. No less natural are ethnic communities, many of which claim or enjoy rights of self-government. Their institutions vary greatly across countries, but the idea of having self-governing as a precondition of collective survival and existence remains the same. Whereas families are not (or no longer) "meant" to perpetuate themselves over generations, hence their self-governing activities are more similar to a search of the actual and short-run common good, as well as running a sort of a business, for ethnic communities, the existential purpose is arguably the primary one.

*Non-natural* collectives—corporations, associations, churches, unions, universities, movements, parties, and various forms of local/municipal governments—may have their own types of self-governing activities, with often highly sophisticated institutional and organizational systems, diverse interests, traditional and modern techniques of leadership, goal-setting, determining of the common good, and so on. The basic point is the same: much governing takes place outside of "the" government, and much politics goes on outside of politics writ large. Unsurprisingly, the distinctions outlined earlier, namely, the one between the normal and the exceptional cases and situations, and the one between the personal or agency-related and the action/institution-related dimensions of governing, are easily applicable to many of these collectives. Examples could be cited ad infinitum. On the one hand, a firm may enter a financial crisis or be on the brink of bankruptcy, which constitutes an exceptional situation where special abilities and even charisma are necessary. On the other hand, however, even during normal times, human resource management is an operative unit in many business organizations, not only for administrative but "character-related" reasons. Its job is not only to administer issues but on the basis of the firm's "philosophy," to actively seek for potential employees and evaluate hired ones. Searching of special talents, understanding how various capabilities and competences can be integrated in the best ways is itself an activity that is difficult to carry out according to "rules," but without them, the specific job of human resource management becomes impossible. Who are the best such managers? How to select them? To these paradoxical questions, we may add that many jobseekers also try to learn how to be "individual" by using "methods" and consultants who give streamlined personal advice to them. The upshot is not the impossibility of the task but the distinction we try to maintain between the personal and the institutional, the agency and the functional dimensions of running an organization.

I subsume these activities under the label of anti-governing. The term is meant to capture two ideas. One is some obvious opposition to governments suggested by the qualifier "anti." Anti-governing is an evident constraint on political governments and political governing. It stresses that there are spheres and fields of life that are, in an essential sense, exempt from the authority of governments, and this sense is essential because it is truly a sort of governing, a rival to the central one. This is the second idea: what we are talking about is a *parallel activity* of ruling and deciding and tending to collective issues, and many more. Much as the famous and so far undetectable antimatter is a form of matter, anti-governing is a form of governing.

How are the two related? The idea of constraining by distinguishing is the principal one, and it is not necessary to suppose that whatever anti-governing involves must be diametrically in opposition to political governing. This is why the metaphor of parallelism is perhaps better. But it is also important to observe that in many cases, the ways and ideas of anti-governing is an imitation, a mimicking of political governing—and vice versa. For instance, "leadership" is a concept equally important to organizational and to political studies. Being concerned with how to perpetuate a community is similarly constitutive of political and non-political governing (governing and anti-governing). The time-honored distinction between laws and customs reflects another mimetic relation: positive laws as man-made institutions often mirror existing norms preserved and protected by customs.[3] Ruling by laws is an important constitutional principle of constrained governing, but then ruling by customs is, in turn, a form of government, too. Thus, anti-governing is an activity with which most people are presumably pretty familiar, and by participating in its various forms and levels, they experience the essential distinction between normal and exceptional times and situations, as well as the distinction between personal and institutional aspects. These experiences form an important conceptual background for them in interpreting the political government's activities, competences, and responsibilities. The distinctions being applied to the political government become constraints, presumptions, and exceptions that the government needs to respect. The distinction between anti-governing and governing is thereby also engendered, since the objects of reference are obviously different: although individual, or communal hardships may overlap with political, social, and wide-scale crises, they remain clearly distinct issues. What is an exceptional situation or time for a firm, for instance, may have nothing to do with general business climate, which may be relentlessly optimistic. A government crisis arising from leadership issues, perhaps rooted in the governing party's internal struggles, may leave most people rather unaffected. The problems may look and sound familiar, yet remote and in some ways normal, thus, whereas governments may be in trouble, anti-governments are just fine—and vice versa.

## Foucault and Schmitt

The concepts and reality of governing and anti-governing can be related to two influential conceptions in political theory. Before discussing the various activities characteristic of governing and anti-governing by applying the distinctions that have been introduced in this part, let me briefly make these two excursions. The first conception is what may be called the *Foucauldian* approach to the study of government, with his concept of governmentality on the banner.[4] It originates, of course, from Foucault's various writings and lectures, and is a highly idiosyncratic concept, which has become like a lens through which all social phenomena can be studied. Barry Hindess formulates the concept in a useful way:

> Foucault maintains that, in spite of the different specific objectives and fields to which the term is applied, there is a certain continuity between the government of oneself, the government of a household, and the government of a state or community . . . . . Principles of political action and those of personal conduct are intimately related.[5]

Everything hinges upon how the predicate of "related" is interpreted. On the one hand, one can happily accept the idea that self-government, indeed, the government of so many natural social groups and communities, as well as artificial collectives, and organizations, whatsoever, are "related" to the political or central government. There is nothing terribly surprising, let alone worrying about it. On the other hand, this relation or parallelism can be interpreted as a more menacing phenomenon. According to this interpretation, a gigantic and seamless network of power emerges in modern societies, which makes it largely senseless to insist on the differences between political and non-political governing; or governing and anti-governing. For Foucault, the nature of power remains basically the same and the only interesting thing.

True, he does not directly propose the idea of a single totalitarian power supervising, controlling, and even animating everything and everybody. There is no center of power, no single will, no person or institution "has" or possesses "the" ultimate power or authority. Foucault himself remained a social theorist and rejected political activism as largely illusory insofar as modern governments cannot be simply abolished at will because, at least according to the theory, there is no such thing as a government in the strict sense of the word. What we call political governing is as much a product of governmentality as are other forms of it. Thus, what reigns is power as such, and governmentality is meant to capture the ubiquity and phenomenological semblance of all sorts of governmental activities, from self-government to political government. Governing and anti-governing are merely forms or illusions of governmentality.

It is hard to refute such extremely broad assertions or theses. However, two general remarks are perhaps defensible. First, social theory may dispose of the relevance of political theory making a distinction between governing and anti-governing as being similar and, say, *ontologically non-opposing*, yet distinct and *politically opposing* phenomena, it remains intelligible and practicable. Naturally, a political theoretical interpretation of the Foucauldian explorations will doubt that governing and anti-governing are happily operating side by side and will suspect that it is the government, or the state, that is becoming the dominant agent, wherefore what looks a parallelism is in fact an imitation: discipline becomes self-discipline. But the logical chain of causation can work the other way as well. Political theorists from Aristotle to Machiavelli, Montesquieu or Tocqueville have emphasized the long-run impossibility to govern a state or a people in complete contradiction to, or rejection of, their customs, including their self-governing practices and activities. This suggests that the form and style, but also the substance, of political government cannot be absolutely out of tune with how anti-governing both in normal and exceptional circumstances goes on.

The second remark is that the Foucauldian approach works with the very same distinction it wishes to de-substantiate, and this inadvertently confirms at least the significance of the distinction. We need a theorist to tell us that our distinction between governing and anti-governing is illusory or irrelevant. Hence a special emphasis is put on the distinction as something whose existence must be refuted. However, the logic of detachment and demarcation remains crucial here. This has a real political effect. Let me illustrate this point by a fictional case.

Suppose there is a wide discontent with the actual government's policies regarding crime. To make the case even more salient, let us suppose that an overwhelming majority of citizens wants capital punishment to be restored (perhaps a particularly vicious serial killer has been arrested recently and is being tried). Many people think or are convinced that if they had the opportunity and right to do so, they *would* vote for the reinstatement of this form of punishment. And they keep telling that this is what they expect their representatives to do. For all sorts of reasons (international commitments, constitutional court rulings, and individual conscience barriers), no such proposal is made in the legislature. A Foucauldian way of explaining this discrepancy could be to argue that these reasons are merely superficial and illusory, because the reality is that although we are prone to all sorts of wild emotional outbursts, resentment, and there is perhaps a mob mentality in all of us, and lynching is common desire, yet deep in our hearts we know that such forms of behavior are disruptive and impermissible, hence they must be suppressed, and despite all our protestations, in fact we are practicing self-discipline. Further, paradoxically perhaps, the abolition of death penalty may have bereaved us of certain ugly but pleasing spectacles, yet our resentment over the abolition is nonetheless enjoyable. We are disciplining ourselves and we know that it hurts; yet we are compensated for it by the enjoyment of resentment and anger aimed at the political elite. The upshot is that the seamless network of governmentality catches everybody, and there is no rea-son to make a distinction between governing and anti-governing.

Now it is indeed possible that the case explained in this Foucauldian inter-pretative framework captures some sound psychological truths. However, the political theorist may also argue plausibly that the de-substantiation of the distinction between individual judgment and conditional action on the one hand, and collective conscience, social superego and actual non-action on the other hand *is itself* a way of confirming the distinction. We may think that it is right that our self-legislation (which would include the restoration of capital punishment) and the collective legislation (which refuses to do so) are distinct, and even though we may revolt against a non-compliant legisla-tion (our representatives not voting for such a law), we cherish this right of revolting, based on our emotional reactions, in need of taming and disciplin-ing perhaps, yet not belonging to the government, and much less created by it. They are ours, and it is us who rule them. Hence, the distinction remains valid and relevant, as it helps us keep "the" government outside of our own governmental activities.

The other conception that appears to be relevant here is the influential idea of *Carl Schmitt* about the content of "the political."[6] Just by way of reminding the reader: in Schmitt's view, governing is principally a leadership issue, and politics is defined in terms of the exceptional state, or the state of emergency. His /in/famous distinction between friend and foe, which is said to consti-tute "the political" also bears the mark of the personalist understanding of politics. This personalism results from two aspects. First, "friendship" and its opposite bear an obviously personal dimension. As a matter of fact, Schmitt does not dwell much on friendship, he devotes his attention to the figure of the "enemy" but he stresses that the enemy is a public one and by no means a private adversary.[7] Notwithstanding the conceptual contextualization he is attempting at, and the strange but undeniable "official" or "institutional" aspect of "the public enemy," it is impossible to get rid of the rather strong personal aspect of an *enemy*.[8] Secondly, *choosing* one's enemy, at least inso-far as in is one's power, or declaring the other an enemy (again, if he—or it?—has not yet done so) is clearly a decision that cannot be explained away by simple institutional procedures and welfare calculations. Picking the best policy solution is obviously different from picking one's enemy, how-ever "public," that is, "impersonal" the choice is said to be. Evidently, the Schmittian way of thinking about politics is very much partisan itself, with an overemphasis on the character of the leader and his sovereign actions—mainly decisions.[9]

Schmitt does not deny that political actions need routinization. Complex societies cannot be governed by simple personal instructions and commands. Further, Schmitt does not hold emperors such Caligula or Elagabalus the true models of the divine-political sovereignty. Notwithstanding his contempt for the parliamentarian business-like politics, he also conceded, at least implicitly, that governing has an impersonal, normalizing and orderly dimension. Of course, everything flows from the ultimate and sovereign will of the leader. However, this image is closer to fiction than to reality. Thus, although Schmitt is considered as a theorist today who relentlessly and rightly warns us of the irreducibly conflictual nature of politics (and for this reason, indispensable to understand democracy), or alternatively, a theorist defending the autonomy of politics (a forerunner to a version of modern political realism), his thinking remains controversial because of its inherent imbalance.[10] One of his early critics, Aurel Kolnai, pointed out this imbalance by emphasizing the other side:

> *The question of the detailed structure of the "order" in the state, the question of how it is ruled and ought to be ruled*, how far, for example, there should be master and inequality, with what material qualifications or kinds of value power should be especially bound up, how far it should be concentrated or divided: *this is the proper object of politics*. The working out of this does not mean armed struggle, but the *contrast and comparison of the ideas of order, that is,* primarily, *social discussion* [original italics].

If the balance and parallelism of governing and anti-governing is recognized and theoretically accounted for, then the problem of the autonomy of politics is also more properly understood. The crucial question for Schmitt is whether anti-governing possesses and displays the main characteristics of political governing. First, there does not seem to be a "right" (or political opportunity) to decide about the public enemy in the private life of citizens comparable to the politicians' rights or opportunities (criminals are public enemies but not because they are chosen to be), and consequently, ordinary citizens have no right to legitimately and seriously curtail anybody's freedom according to their political judgment. This is one of the cornerstones of the Rechtsstaat. However, in his later work, *The Theory of the Partisan*, Schmitt himself allows for the possibility of the political becoming private, and for that, in the most controversial area of killing other people.[11] The partisan is not a criminal, and not even a figure like Michael Kohlhaas, waging his private war for justice. The partisan fights for his country, his political cause (such as a revolution), and most interestingly, for his "world" (more precisely, for his "land"). However, Schmitt continues, the partisan needs a third party to justify his case—a movement, an army, a political party. Thus, reluctantly perhaps but he, too, is compelled to admit that the "political" can flow to the private sphere and bring with itself the characteristic autonomy of politics (the partisan begins to act as lawmaker, executive, judge, and military commander), though he tries to maintain the primacy of organized (governmental) politics—which is actually a return to the "normal" and in his view, liberal theory of the state and government. It goes without saying that the problem of the partisan war remains largely a theoretical one in constitutional democracies, yet civil disobedience, some forms of violence, at least active defiance of certain laws are more common and in principle even accepted. Such phenomena support the view that not only the normal but also the extraordinary or exceptional dimensions of politics do *not* remain within the boundaries of government. Consequently, whether and when these forms and dimensions are tolerable is an issue within the sphere where anti-governing takes place, making the constrain implied by the distinction between normal and exceptional times discernible and efficient in the private sphere of citizens.

Secondly, the personal dimension of governing is even more obviously discernible within the realm of anti-governing. Ever since Locke announced that "every Man has a *Property* in his own *Person*,"[12] sovereignty ceased to be a distinctly political concept in theory. But actually it was his opponents, such as Robert Filmer, among others, who worked with the theory of patriarchalism in which monarchical rule, a form of political governing, is shown to have historically emerged from family rule, that is, political anti-governing. Therefore, against the overblown idea of political leadership being fundamentally or essentially different from non-political leadership, including governing, both the "liberal" and the "conservative" traditions testify. Further, within the anti-governing sphere we also find the distinction between individual and personal decisions versus routinized and institutionalized procedures, both in the form of customs and cultural norms as well as the various forms of nongovernmental organizations and structures. Once again, the argument is not meant to show that governing and anti-governing are *in*distinct activities. They remain distinct, yet not for the distinction between personal/institutional being inapplicable in and for anti-governing. The really relevant insight is that since we know how to lead others, and how to constitute and operate institutions without the intervention and supervision of politics and political governments; and are able of realizing how these distinctions arise and are practically relevant, we are better equipped to realize them in the sphere of political governing, and use them accordingly, to constrain it.

Hence, once the distinctness of governing from anti-governing is not conceived in terms of antagonism and contradiction (the physical possibility and right of killing being constitutive of political existence), then the autonomy of politics can be conceptualized in a more realistic and normal way. Politics—political governing—is in fact a different business, yet not beyond the intelligible, on the contrary: its specificity or distinctness arises from its similarity to anti-governing.

## CHARACTERS AND OFFICES

In the second part of this chapter, I shall briefly consider and discuss three prominent characters, and the same time, offices of the government, broadly understood. The concepts of the legislator, the executive, and the judge capture the traditional doctrine of the separation of the three main branches of power. It is a defensible doctrine and I shall deal with it in the next chapter, for now, it merely serves as a customary frame of reference to the activities of any government. In each case, my purpose is to show how these offices are constrained due to the three distinctions outlined and explained earlier. As always, I shall use the topics raised in, and party by help of, the *Antigone* and *Measure for Measure* to give flesh to the bones of the abstract distinctions.

### The Legislator

*(Rousseau)* There is perhaps no better example of wrestling with the role of the legislator in political theory than Rousseau's discussion in the second book of *The Social Contract*. Many commentators have found the role of the "Legislator" puzzling, or inconsistent with the general argument for the democratic sovereignty that the treatise is famous for.[13] Rousseau repeatedly claims that laws are valid only if approved by all citizens: the "populace that is subjected to the laws ought to be their author."[14] However, from the end of chapter 6, he begins to raise doubts about the rationality and reasonableness of the whole as a legislator. Sudden inspirations, lack of foresight, and knowledge of the common good—all these possibilities seem to worry him increasingly. He fears that the democratic regime can hardly accommodate and redress such anomalies. At the end of the paragraph, his concludes with an almost Platonic argument:

> Private individuals see the good they reject. The public wills the good that it does not see. Everyone is equally in need of guides. The former must be obligated to conform their wills to their reason; the latter must learn to know what it wants.[15]

And indeed, Rousseau cites Plato (*The Statesman*) and Lycurgus and other ancient models of supreme lawmakers in the subsequent chapters.

On the first reading, these observations and views are inconsistent with the theory of the sovereign general will commanding and governing itself. It may be argued, then, that the inconsistency is mitigated if we distinguish between what we call here "normal" and "exceptional" (i.e., constitutional) or foundational legislation.[16] Or else, that the extraordinary role of the "Legislator" is closer to that of a facilitator, a counselor, as indeed, Rousseau himself refers to the Roman decemvirs who "never claimed the right to have any law passed on their authority alone."[17] Thus, Rousseau seems to want to separate legislation proper from the more general "rules of society" that need to be "discovered" as being the "best suited to nations."[18] However, he continues to call the role he discusses the "Legislator" whom he compares to a divine figure, having a "great soul" and a supreme knowledge and insight of human nature in general, and the nature of the people or nation to be governed in particular. His makes use of even more personalizing metaphors: "father of the nation," "architect," "wise man," and "master," which put further flesh on the bones of the "office."

These usual, somewhat conservative-aristocratic and yet commonsensical observations and thoughts may, albeit hardly, be reconcilable with the general legislative competence of the democratic polity. However, all these attempts are suddenly bracketed by a stunning outburst of Rousseau, which makes the inconsistency-charge inevitable and impossible to deny:

> He who dares to undertake the establishment of a people should feel that he is, so to speak, in a position to change human nature, to transform each individual (who by himself is a perfect and solitary whole), into a part of a larger whole from which this individual receives, in a sense, his life and his being . . . . In a word, he must deny man his own forces in order to give him forces that are alien to him and that he cannot make use of without the help of others.[19]

Extraordinary as this argument is, and pleasing and inspiring as it must have been to Robespierre and his fellow revolutionaries, the idea stands in contrast not only to Rousseau's exaltation of the legislative power and capability of all citizens on other pages of the *Social Contract* but also to his former remarks on the importance of being intimate with the people's history and nature. But to add puzzle to surprise, Rousseau claims that the founding legislator may be a fatherly figure or a wise old man, or a heroic and mythical actor, with superhuman abilities and science, his activities constitute an *office*, which is, according to the philosopher,

> neither magistracy nor sovereignty. This office, which constitutes the republic, does not enter into its constitution. It is a particular and superior function having nothing in common with the dominion over men.[20]

I do not think that it is worth trying to reconcile Rousseau's inconsistencies with one another or resolve them somehow within the confines of his theory. The failure to present us with a unified and consistent theory is an implicit argument in favor of the intrinsic constraint of governing, in this case, within the sphere of legislation. There are thresholds, distinctions, and differences that make us alert when there is a shift within legislation from personal to institutional, from normal to exceptional modes of operation. No wonder, thus, that Rousseau wavers between the agent-oriented, creative, perhaps exceptional, and the action-oriented and rule-guided description of legislation. What remains to do, then, is to observe and record these modes of operation with the constant shifts between them.

(*Person versus office*). When Creon issues his order, which is equivalent to making a law in Thebes, he seeks to explain and justify his act in two ways. First, he refers to the eternal or divine moral law of good and evil being in a fundamental opposition. Lawmakers must respect this difference and their laws must be consistent with it. Second, he refers to his own will, implying that even if we were ignorant of what goodness and evil consist in, there must be a single, ultimate, and public will, which puts an end to all controversies. However, even such a justification rests on a publicly accessible and assessable argument that we may call the utilitarian one. This asserts that everyone is better off having someone in the position of an arbitrator, or referee, regardless of his or her personal character, rather than face anarchy and chaos.

In absence of a consensus about the meaning of good and evil, or about how these abstract distinctions can be translated into positive law for complex cases, and if the purely utilitarian idea is not persuasive, then there is a third, no less time-honored alternative. In political theory, especially in its classical conservative and liberal tradition, and perhaps more conspicuously in the common law countries, lawmaking is sometimes interpreted and justified in terms of a sort of a discovery, a distillation and understanding of a rich and objective reality, which includes the human nature, the natural relationships, as well as the extant norms and customs of a given society.

In each case, we see how the personal dimension of legislation is questioned and restricted. In the *first* case, the lawmaker himself acknowledges and stresses that the laws are not "his" but derivations of a *higher law*. Therefore, legislation is essentially a refinement of higher laws, and by no means a sort of creation ex nihilo. In the *second* case, trust is obviously a prerequisite of a successful *utilitarian* solution and trust needs someone to be trusted, which again presupposes impartiality and incorruptibility, which are personal character traits but essentially making the individual and personal aspect of the "person" as irrelevant as possible. Finally, in the *third* case, the freedom of the lawmaker is evidently restricted by the *customs* and facts he must reflect and legally express, thus, his role is closer to that of a spokesman than of an absolute sovereign. In fact, this already points to the anti-government constraint of governing.

Still, lawmaking is a political activity and part of governing, and it has a personal dimension. This dimension is also discussed in great length in Andrew Sabl's book written in the realist tradition via the ideal form or figure of the "Senator."[21] I take the liberty to identify the "Senator" with the lawmaker or legislator (though Sabl emphasizes that he has specifically the U.S. Senator in mind). Here are his observations: a Senator pursues long-term aims (consistent with the idea of the legislation as an embodiment of constancy), and wishes to achieve fame by his legislative activities (the "extensive and arduous enterprises for the public good").[22] At least in democracies, constitutional stability, the commitment to good government, and democratic responsiveness are further marks of the Senator-character. Also, equality being the cornerstone principle of democracy, a certain degree of populism, the rejection of aristocratic pretensions, as well as the lure of the big money are required. Listening to others is another feature of accepting equality, and it also opens the gates to compromise-readiness and bargaining capacities, where bargaining over principles is also among the options.

Though Sabl restricts his discussion to the democratic constitution, his characterization of the legislator is easily applicable to non-democratic regimes as well. No doubt, Creon wished his name to remain splendid and he be remembered as a good ruler, and much like Solon and others, supreme lawmakers are truly remembered as great statesmen because of the "goodness" of their laws. This was obviously an obsession of Machiavelli, searching for the secret of the endurance, stability, and greatness of Rome. Some sort of responsiveness to the public good that includes everyone is clearly a requirement in any politically sound regime, and being able to listen to others, especially the good advisors, has always figured among the top counsels listed in the mirrors for princes. However, these character traits are quite unspecific. We can imagine a host of other jobs and offices where these qualities are in demand or serve well the agent doing the job or holding the office. The point is exactly this: notwithstanding the occasionally important personal aspects of legislation, it does not favor the character-dimension of politics, and it belongs to the normal, rather routinized aspect of governing (to the chagrin, even worry, of some political thinkers and commentators who hold romantic ideas about laws emerging out of undistorted communication and deliberation). There is no Swiss equivalent to the U.S. Senator, and perhaps not even a Swiss equivalent to the British MP (and there is no Westminster or Capitol Hill in Switzerland). In the inventory of democratic images, it is the Swiss citizen whose self-governing capabilities are thought to include in the very first place the legislative competences and the ensuing activities. The "Swiss citizen" has no name, no desire for fame, no recognizable character (only one "citizen of Geneva" has a proper political name), yet he or she is the model of self-governance by participating in the legislation actively and constructively. And he or she legislates for normal times, rather than exceptional cases.

It is, therefore, questionable that the sort of the charismatic lawmaking that Weber seems to have had in mind when he defined his concept of charisma in fact works following the logic of surprise, contradiction for its own sake, miracle-making, and other unexpected and unpredictable interventions. Weber cites the Sermon of the Mount: "It has been written . . . but I say onto you." By this reference, he means to capture the essence of charisma, but he does not make the distinctions we do (and common people do) concerning governments and governing. Executive decisions, especially those of making exceptions, might be closer to this type of action but norm-setting and general legislation cannot follow this pattern. Jesus's "legislation" on the mount is better characterized as a purifying action, with the intention of leading his audience back to the intentions of the original lawmaker, or of bringing out the true meaning of the written law. For what "is written" is already a distortion and corruption of what is written "in the heart."[23]

(*Normal versus exceptional times*). The whole thrust of Rousseau's theory is to give the right to legislate to the citizenry. The credibility of his theory rests on the insight that, after all, there is nothing exceptional, extraordinary, or unusual about making laws. In fact, legislation is to a large part merely a solution to coordination problems and the problem of time discrepancies. Andrew Sabl argues that "we should (and in fact do) arrange and support political institutions, as well as more informal social practices, that help us achieve our long-term desires in the face of short-term temptations."[24] Sabl's discussion does not target at a comprehensive analysis of legislative activities, but it can easily be interpreted as an argument for the incessant continuity of legislation as a function of the government, since average citizens simply have no other ways to secure their long-term purposes. Sabl connects this long-term horizon of legislation to the virtue of constancy. Constancy is

> a "middle" virtue, involving not extremes of nobility or self-denial but the kind of steady attachments to goals, persons, and salutary habits of which most people are capable. . . . In basing politics on constancy we seek to make possible the satisfaction of long-term interests and the more complete fulfillment of existing values.[25] [It has three aspects, namely] consistency of character, consistent attention to certain political relationships, and long-termism in the pursuit of political goals [which] reinforce one another through the mechanism of popular politics.[26]

In anticipation of the third distinction let it be noted that this argument also captures well the governing and anti-governing parallelism argument, which is latent in Rousseau's more theoretical and certainly more extravagantly made argument about popular sovereignty. At the same time, Sabl's observations underline the discontinuity aspect, underlying the distinction between normal and exceptional times as well: although most people are capable of developing and fixing rules, even little children can invent new games by defining its rules, laws are nonetheless special rules insofar as they are meant to constrain our autonomy and freedom for our own long-term interest. Criminal law provisions, inheritance, and property laws are textbooks examples. Sabl makes the point even more succinctly when he writes that

> the advantage of a deliberative senate is not that it decides better than the people would in the long term, but that in enables the people to get to the "long term" before they make decisions they would reject *by their own standards* (italics in the original).[27]

From this perspective, it is of a secondary importance whether such laws are made by legislative bodies or by an "enlightened" (read: up-to-date) ruler such as Napoleon. Senate or monarch, the point about the *rationality of legislation* is the same. The government as a legislative agent is bound by a number of expectations and standards, but at the same time empowered by those very expectations and standards.

The overwhelmingly impersonal dimension of the legislator is in consonance with the predominance of normal times for legislation. By definition, laws are meant to maintain order and make it operative. Legislating for exceptions is itself exceptional. If it happens for some personal reason, it is often considered to be nepotism or favoritism, and a sure sign of tyranny, that is, of an abuse of government.[28] If it is justified by public good, such as a law of amnesty, it is closer to making an exemption from law, granted by the legislative power, rather than genuine lawmaking. There are symbolic and definitive laws as well, but these are executive acts of the legislative body rather than proper laws. Since many cases of emergency are foreseeable, it is also possible to create laws for such cases. However, such laws are also normalized rules, subject to considerations, reasons of prudence, and moral judgment, similar to non-emergency cases.[29]

The only case where legislation appears to be truly exceptional is the foundational act. History books know a number of great lawmakers, from Solon to Suleiman the Great, from Moses to the American Framers. And the books about the history of political thought give ample space to Plato and his *Laws* and *The Statesman*, to Cicero and his Scipio (and Scipio's Romulus), to Machiavelli and his reflections on Rome, to name but a few classic examples. These figures are, however, typically founding fathers, constitution makers rather than ordinary legislators, as Rousseau himself pointed out. Moreover, the emphasis is precisely on their achievements of laying down institutions and procedures that have proved to be enduring and binding the actions of the heirs. Little is told about the characters of these founders (exceptions are those where they were, like Suleiman, also outstanding political or military leaders). Their personality recedes into the background, besides the vaguely circumscribed virtue of wisdom attributed to them, there is little we know, and the tradition of political theory deems necessary to tell us, about them.

Cicero is an ample example here. In his *De re publica*, Book II, Scipio analyzes Romulus's founding deeds, particularly his choice of site to build Rome, his establishment of the "institutions" of the *Senate* and the *auspicium*.[30] Romulus's personality is wholly ignored. His decisions are explained as having resulted from good calculations and sound insights. In principle, such calculations and insights are not miraculous revelations but open and available to anyone for discussion and understanding. However, when Scipio tells his audience about his famous dream, in which he is given a warning and an inspiration to save the republic as a dictator, he points to his own person indirectly. He must suspend the legal order, and in that sense, he becomes the supreme lawmaker (or lawbreaker), yet this action is already provided for by the Roman constitution, and in that sense, it may be an extraordinary executive action but with the aim of restoring the normal legal order. Thus, the point returns and remains: making or creating laws is predominantly an impersonal and rule-guided activity, even though there are borderline cases that need to be accounted for. Such distinctions and assertions about what is and what is not predominant already suggest to us important limitations of and for governments.

(*Governing versus anti-governing*). There is nothing surprising about even the great legislator being an impersonal person, as it were. Establishing the foundational laws of a polity, or constitution-making are not ex nihilo creative acts. On the one hand, these laws are meant to be the model laws of the community, as well as the frames of normalcy, and in that sense, they are not part of normalcy. On the other hand, precisely because they are meant to regulate normalcy, they cannot be extraordinary. In the *Deuteronomy*, we read: "For this commandment I give you today is not too difficult for you or beyond your reach. It is not in heaven, that you should need to ask, 'Who will ascend into heaven to get it for us and proclaim it, that we may obey it?' (30: 11–12)." As exceptions already presuppose normalcy, even foundational or cardinal laws are tied to the normal mode of governing and, contrary to the assumption discussed above, perhaps even more so than "normal" laws. As a matter of fact, foundational acts and constitutional legislation (not counting here minor revisions) often, and historically, have a restoring nature, much as in the case of the Duke's re-establishment of order in Vienna. Even the French revolutionaries had partly historical models in mind (such as Rome), and partly a philosophical-moral view of the human nature, which served as the "natural normalcy" assumption behind the political constitution. Political science, especially its game theory tradition, has been very fruitful and useful for analyzing the various possibilities of defining rules, especially decision-making procedures, and its consequences, both in theory and in practice.[31] This tradition is known for its explicitness of its axioms or presumptions that include some degree of rationalism, utilitarianism, consequentialism, and egoism (pursuit of self-interest). Personal ambitions are parts of everybody's calculations; however, there is no single founder with an exceptional knowledge or charisma. Even in cases that seem to be supporting the special role of the Founder and his personal character traits are less persuasive on a closer look. Gandhi's India is a case in point: Gandhi's political ideals are far from what has become constitutional and political reality, and he is revered for his moral righteousness as well as political achievements (e.g. independence) than for the constitutional principles and frames that legislation means. It would be hard to imagine him endorsing the atomic bomb and the massive arming policy India has been pursuing since the late 1940s.

It is still very much possible that creating foundational laws requires special qualities that are not easily replicable or learnable, and though such laws are "normal" rather than "exceptional," making them is closer to the personal, rather than the office-related dimension of legislation. Such legislators are irreplaceable and creative agents for, perhaps, a single extraordinary moment: no one else possesses the authority, persuasive strength, insight that he has. However, even in this moment, the legislator is bound by the "nature" of the people, the nation, the matter at hand, and she is not free to frame the fundamental laws at his pleasure. The special quality she needs is not at all creativeness or originality but understanding and attentiveness. To govern well presupposes the knowledge of people govern themselves.

Creon's turning into a tyrant is to a great part explained by Sophocles in terms of hubris. How could he have avoided this fatal flaw? What Creon should and could have done was to realize that legislation as a governmental activity, even in its "founding" moments, has an *anti-governmental* dimension or parallelism. Ignoring here the complex context of the drama, Antigone and Haemon may be considered as representing this dimension. Creon appeals first to common sense that embodies natural law and then to the utilitarian argument of how to escape chaos and anarchy. Neither Antigone nor Haemon challenges him or his arguments. Antigone, however, questions his first argument by referring to the divine laws, and Haemon warns his father of the slippery slope of making his rule a personal business rather than an impersonal service. Further, Antigone places the divine law into the context of Thebean (and Hellenic) religious practices and traditions. She does not refer to a personal intuition, a vision as it were, on which her claim rests; she argues that natural bonds between family members cannot be ignored as they are "created" by nature (her reference to love), and in that sense, positive law or government-sanctioned law must respect that act of creation. The "divine law" is not unintelligible, it is there to be discovered, and Creon should simply look into his own heart. Haemon supports this by his reference to the popular rejection of Creon's methods and governing philosophy. Unintentionally perhaps, even Creon admits the validity of this argument when he attempts to justify his case to Haemon in terms of tradition (which makes a woman's rule illegitimate).

It is crucial to see that neither Antigone nor Haemon wants to replace Creon in his lawmaker capacity or topple him. On the contrary, what they do is to confront him with the pluralism of justifications and *his* being restricted by the necessity to meet, to use Bernard Williams's term again, the basic legitimation demand.[32] Making this demand, anti-governing is operative, and thereby it forces legislation as a governing activity to be, at least to pretend to be, impersonal. Creon's failure to manage the conflicting and "legitimate" demands for "legitimizing" his laws consists in over-personalizing legislation and making himself a destroyer rather than a founder.

Normal legislation in governments has, unsurprisingly, a great deal in common with anti-governing. Laws belong to the pool of norms, rules, and patterns of behavior, in other words, they are, by definition, routinized actions, either invented or discovered. Even if we could imagine laws being created really ex nihilo, by simple fiat, they are meant to make life predictable, both for the governors and for the governed. Laws are inherently order-creating and normalcy-oriented. Laws themselves have an impersonal style and manner, a passive-active flavor, which means that they have, or pretend to have, no author except the lawmaker, an unidentified, functioning rather than acting agent.

Finally, let us have a short look on Shakespeare's drama in this subsection, too. When the Duke assigns Angelo the responsibility of government in the presence of Escalus, he refers to the (established) institutions of the country and to the supposed personal virtues and qualities of his regent. In this context, however, it is *his* further actions that are the important part of the story. He aims at preparing himself for the great re-founding act that takes place at the denouement. Although he remains an inscrutable person throughout the events, and partly so because notwithstanding his ubiquity and continuous activity, his main ambition is to observe and learn about human nature, through moving his subjects. He enquires, interrogates, immerses into various conversations and discourses always with second thoughts. And he makes ample use of his newly gained knowledge in the final scene: without inventing new laws and proclaiming a new world to usher in, he is able to assert a general feeling of re-founding normalcy.

## The Executive Leader

I do not have such a fascinatingly inconsistent introduction to the figure of the executive leader as Rousseau's thoughts about the legislator in the second book of *On the Social Contract*. Machiavelli's tormenting reflections on how to reconcile the contradicting but equally necessary virtues and qualities in the Prince (cited in the first subsection) may serve a point of departure, with the tentative conclusion that the distinction, so keenly observed and in demand, already anticipates the point about objective constraint being inherent to the position of the executive leader. Since no one can be fully and perfectly both a lion and a fox, the two natures being very different from one another, Machiavelli argues, every leader will be inevitably ousted by his or her rival once the occasion arises, usually in the form of the sudden change of times. This is not a minor point at all, yet it does not really cut to the heart of the matter, namely the distinctions we are working with.

*First*, let us consider the *character/office distinction*. In the previous chapter, shame and moderation were discussed in detail. Arguably, it is mainly in the public character of the executive leader where the person or agent-related character traits are the most prominent in making him or her fit or unfit for this office. Earlier in this chapter, it was further argued that ordinary people may often vote for people for this office in virtue of their achievements in other areas of life, which presuppose different character traits, yet they expect, obviously, ex post festum, that the new leader displays virtues adequate to his or her office. Of course, different times and different regimes require different virtues in this role, but if the importance of shame and the deriving virtue of moderation was convincingly presented, then we have at least one—there can be more—decisive quality that is expected of all executive leaders.

To see how character and office can be distinguished in an appropriate manner here, let me briefly discuss Eric A. Posner's and Adrian Vermeule's rather provocative thesis about the *The Executive Unbound*.[33] The title is perhaps alarming but the intention was not to beware us of the dangers of the growing power of the presidency understood as an office. On the contrary, they argue that, first, one should not deny the reality of the incredible power in the hands of the modern executive ("the gigantic complex of national political institutions");[34] second, that this power is very much necessary in exceptional circumstances (e.g., an economic crisis); and third, that the traditional-legal constraints, such as the separation of powers, are neither useful, practical, and reliable, nor necessary because there are other, more efficient and reliable political constraints of the executive power. Moreover, they argue that

> political constraints, unlike most legal constraints, operate even in times of crisis. Indeed, counterintuitively, some political constraints actually increase during perceived emergencies. Crises tend to produce broad delegations to the executive and cause the public and the officials to rally round the flag. Yet crises create pressure for bipartisanship and an appearance of public solidarity across

ideological lines, which in turn pressure presidents to offer concessions necessary to bring legislators from other political parties on board.[35]

Further, they contend, the wealthy and educated population or citizenry, as
well as the need to convince it, which presupposes credibility, constitute further constraints on the executive power.

It is certainly true that if the chief executive is indeed the supreme political leader, briefly, the captain or navigator of the ship, then his being able to
steer the ship clear of all dangers involves, among others, virtues of rhetoric
(to convince others of his abilities, to unleash emotional energies, to inspire
his crew, etc.), of determination and resolution (being able to resist opposing
wills, to fire the weak and unwilling, to punish rebels) and lot more. These
traits are virtues precisely because they need practicing, and practicing means
facing difficulties—in a trivial sense, constraints. Some of these constraints
are indeed related to the distinctions we are discussing here. Nonetheless, it
seems to be overloading the concept of the constrain specific to governing
if we suppose and argue that every human activity, including doing politics,
exerting power and governing, is "constrained" by objective and subjec-
tive difficulties and circumstances. In the long run, death is a very effective
constraint of every rule and every ruler, and, as Hobbes reminds us, since
every human being is equally vulnerable during sleep, wherefore we spend
a considerable part of our life in an unconscious state, similar to death, we
have another strong natural and objective constraint "threatening" or at least
"blocking" the activities and "freedom" of all executive leaders. However,
such constraints, hard as they can be (e.g., in ancient Rome, the probability of
being killed in office was very high among emperors), fail to work as devices
that can be reckoned with, that are calculable, that can help us discern and
make sense of *government*. They are constrains of human life, and hence
rather unhelpful in matters of governing.

The root of the problem is that Posner and Vermeule do not really explain
the meaning of constraint. "Credibility" is surely a constraint that is closely
related to the *person* and not the office (though as was also argued, we attribute moral qualities to certain offices; however, credibility is not sui generis
associated with any *political* office). Many political constraints that they refer
to in the quotation mentioned above, and to several others, are in fact merely
political possibilities, context-dependent, circumstantial calculations rather
than constraints on the government. The concessions that they allude to may
be in some sense power constraints but at the same time sources of power. For
instance, they *may* be costly to the president (to "buy" the opposition's votes),
however, they may, in another sense, obviously increase his power. The net
outcome is politically indeterminate. These are surely constraints within the
game of power and as such, very important to any politician. But what we

need are constraints on government as far as the character *and* office of the executive leader is concerned.

In this respect, Richard Pildes's review—in fact, a long polemical discussion—of Posner and Vermeule's thesis is very helpful.[36] Pildes recalls that the justification of the strong presidency has a long history, though the ideological pressure behind it changed. In Roosevelt's time,

> it was the Progressive movement, first at the state and then at the national level, that turned to executive power as the institutional vehicle through which to bypass corruption-plagued, paralyzed legislative bodies and status quo-affirming courts [but later] just as liberals began to have second thoughts, conservatives propelled the expanding presidency further.[37]

In fact, the history of American presidency shows an even longer record of such expansions. This is a minor, though important point, because it already reflects on the underlying issue of what it means to act as the chief executive leader. Pildes thinks that Posner and Vermeule's criticism affects the assumption that *legal* constraints, in our terms, the *office-related* constraints that make the executive leader part of the government are effective at all. The criticism consists in the rejection of this assumption. Pildes argues, however, that we simply *do not and cannot know* how the legal, office-related constraints in fact work.

> What we will observe is presidential compliance with law. The actual reasons for that compliance, however, are likely to remain mysterious, absent access to internal deliberations, let alone internal access to the minds of presidents.[38]

The problem is, Pildes continues, that the authors' "framework relies upon a sharp separation of law and politics (or public opinion or public reactions)."[39] But in emphasizing the political constraint, they lose sight of the fact that legality and legal constraints are also partly political since "perceptions about lawful authority—about whether the President is following the law or not—are inextricably intertwined with political and public responses to presidential action."[40]

The point is very pertinent to the distinction between character and office: no matter how personal the executive leader's role is, with its internal (often glaringly and painfully ineffective but discernible) constraints, there is a legal, office-related constraint, which consists in the need to adjust the leader's role to the general framework of the government, usually in some legally constitutionally entrenched form of an office. Transgressing the legal limits is of course possible. Creon's self-identification with his office shows the need for such limits, and vindicates the superiority of an Athenian democracy, perhaps any constitutional polis, with a sophisticated system or structure of the executive power, over the primitive government of Thebes. In Angelo's case, we see how he transgresses the shame-moderation constraint. And he quickly forgets about the advice of the Duke to "enforce or qualify the laws" (I.1.) according to what looks "good" to his soul—which does not imply a wishful but rather a reasonable governing. His governing activity is basically judging (more about judges below), besides ordering the destruction of the houses of immorality, and he proves to be a harsh ruler. No one questions his authority, his office, and he does not trespass its limits (which are extremely widely drawn, for sure). Yet much as Creon did, Angelo identifies himself with the law, as was cited several times, which is, again, a good indication of not being sufficiently aware of a transgression, here, between office and person. What everybody waits for and certainly desires thus is that Angelo *breaks* the law by granting mercy to Claudio. This does not happen, the constraint inherent to the character/office distinction is also ineffective, yet all the more evident.

*Second*, considering the normalcy/exceptionality distinction, and the constraint that it involves, a similar lesson emerges. It is possible to have a constitutionally defined office of the executive leader for exceptional times, with powers and prerogatives different from the office defined for normal times. However, there are all sorts of crises and exceptional times. Both the characters and the offices may change and may have various types and forms. The Roman example of how a new office emerges is particularly striking: from the assemblage of various constitutional posts (consul, imperator, dictator, pontifex) the least significant one (princeps) turned out to be the most powerful and useful one, yet not without the personal authority conferred by the name of Caesar to his heirs in the princeps' chair. Cromwell's Protectorate did not survive and vanished with him, yet the way he used his powers became part of how the Kingdom was later to be governed by the prime minister's office. Ever since Lincoln, American presidency has been different; but it is also arguable that the meaning of the executive power has never been as clearly defined as one expects it to be; indeed, an interpretation of the president having no executive power is also possible.[41] Alexander Hamilton's formulation is remarkable and frequently cited:

> Energy in the Executive is a leading character in the definition of a good government. It is essential to the protection of the community against foreign attacks; it is not less essential to the steady administration of the laws.[42]

Hamilton refers to both the personal and the institutionalized aspects of the executive power and its holder, virtually using the distinction between normal and exceptional times. Energy is a personal attribute (though meant to vitalize and penetrate the office) as well as a force and personal strength protecting the community against foreign attacks, which implies that this personal virtue ("energy") is needed especially in extraordinary circumstances. In such times, the executive leader executes chiefly his or her *office*. But "the steady administration of the laws" refers to the normal business of the executive leader: "steady" and "law" suggest normalcy and institutionalization. In normal times, the executive leader executes chiefly the *law*.

We must never forget the much as the character/office distinction, normalcy and exceptionality are also intertwined. "Times" should not be taken in either historical or physical terms. It is always political as Shakespeare reminds us. Sh. Prakash concludes his overview with observing that

> after ratification, Washington assumed his role as chief executive of the laws and others recognized the obvious. No one regarded him as a constitutional usurper when it came to law execution. Despite his seemingly empty title, the president is a powerful constitutional creature who wears many hats. Because he wields the veto power, he is the chief legislator. Because he is commander-in-chief, he is the nation's generalissimo. Because he enjoys executive power, he is the nation's chief diplomat. But first and foremost, he is the chief executive empowered by the executive power to execute Congress's laws and to control the law execution of executive officers.[43]

Indeed, it is a meaningful question how Madison's abstract (abstract? what images did he have in his mind?) conception of the executive power and the chief executive merged with Washington's personal qualities, authority, charisma, wisdom, and whatever else "others recognized [as] obvious." The result is neither an office, nor a theoretical concept but a "constitutional creature," that is, a powerful image. It has many hats—again, a good choice of metaphor—but wearing each on top of the other *at the same time* would not make the executive leader a discernible figure but a monster or a clown. That is, once again, the trouble with the Duke's new government that he instates after Angelo's fall: our instincts remain confused as to whether we have been witnessing exceptional times, that is, disorder; and if yes, in what sense; and finally, whether disorder was itself caused by the government (of course: which one?) or by the collapse of social mores and the legal order. The Duke returns. Vienna is also back in normalcy but we are unsure whether this is the result of the Duke's political illusionism or something real.

The play is subversive in this sense. It presses on us the need to make distinctions, in this case, a distinction between political times. It is possible that parallel times are running; and politics is sometimes more complicated than cosmology. But that's how it works. The White House and the Air Force One are not only the two strongest symbols of presidential power but symbols of political times running—or stopping concomitant of one another. The House stands, resists history, and suggests normalcy, whereas the plane is meant to fly and be moving whenever the president is on board, suggesting the fluidity and immediacy of exceptional times. The two are different, and no executive leader can be at both places—perhaps in both times—concurrently. Attempting to do so or to be such indicates a transgression of a constraint that everyone knows it exists.

*Thirdly* and finally, we need to take stock with the constraint inherent to the distinction between governing and anti-governing with respect to the executive leader. Consider here a remarkable account of the mirage of Napoleon written by Ralph Waldo Emerson:

> Every one of the million readers of anecdotes or memoirs or lives of Napoleon . . . . Napoleon is thoroughly modern, and, at the highest point of his fortunes, has the very spirit of the newspapers. He is no saint . . . and he is no hero, in the high sense. The man in the street finds in him the qualities and powers of other men in the street. He finds him, like himself, by birth a citizen, who, by very intelligible merits, arrived at such a commanding position that he could indulge all those tastes which the common man possesses but is obliged to conceal and deny: good society, good books, fast travelling . . . what is agreeable to the heart of every man in the nineteenth century, this powerful man possessed. . . . Bonaparte was the idol of common men because he had in transcendent degree the qualities and powers of common men. There is a certain satisfaction in coming down to the lowest ground of politics, for we get rid of cant and hypocrisy. Bonaparte wrought, in common with that great class he represented, for power and wealth—but Bonaparte, specially, without any scruple as to the means. All the sentiments which embarrass men's pursuit of these objects, he set aside.[44]

Emerson's insight is that the attraction Napoleon had and the spell he exerted over his and the next generation lied not primarily in his special genius and talent but in his extraordinary closeness to the spirit of his age, living in everyone else. Was this the secret of his astonishing rise and fall, his power over Europe, his authority over France, his influence over the imagination of so many, from the last grenadier of his army to Goethe and Beethoven? In any case, he was one of the greatest executive leaders of history, more of an anti-ideologue than Metternich or Donoso Cortes, and at the same time, a model for so many imitators. Napoleon was the common man's chief representative, yet the Emperor; a ruler who was both an "office" (recall the capital "N" designating also the "N-model" of a new generation of emperors throughout the world) and a person (Bonaparte)—again, we find here the first distinction working. It is very appropriate, therefore, that Napoleons and American presidents have something very common and very princely about them at the same time, as Harvey Mansfield observed.[45] In this classic piece,

Mansfield puts the point very succinctly already in the preface: "The beauty of executive power is, then, to be both subordinate and not subordinate, both weak and strong."[46] In his view, the true inventor of the executive power *as a tool* is Machiavelli. Every political regime needs strong executive power and although we may not like it, or like it to hear, modern statesmen are often democratic princes. Mansfield stresses the importance of the personal side of leadership (in his view, the president is an executor of his office rather than of the law) and argues that one of the principal purposes of Locke and his heirs has been to teach—to tame—its users.[47] However, not even this tradition can blur the brute fact that the executive leader has, or is expected to have, the power to use violence, again, mostly but not exclusively in exceptional times. Mansfield repeats the paradox:

> The popular humor *per se* is not the desire to rule but the desire not to be ruled; nonetheless, the people must be ruled. This difficulty defines the political problem: how to rule the people without their developing the intolerable sensation that they are being ruled.[48]

If this is true, then governing is really an almost impossible task. Let us remember: Creon judged Antigone, sentenced her to death, yet oddly shrank from his own ruling in the last moment, trying to pretend that he had nothing to do with death. There was something inordinate about his sentence, although its justification and legality was flawless. People expected him to be able to use violence, as he was their chief executive, yet they also expected him not to do something irreversible, to tread upon the demarcating line between life and death. Oedipus's anger and murder, however justified it looked to the very end (Oedipus still defends it at Colonus), wrought misery upon Thebes, and Creon remembered this. Who can predict how violence and death impacts law and order, peace and life? The ambivalence, perhaps incompatibility of our expectations of what the executive leader is supposed to, or allowed to do, reflects the parallelism of governing and anti-governing. As Mansfield contends, our wish to be governed is in contrast to our wish not to be governed, and this contrast takes the most evident form about the leader's decision over life and death (to a lesser extent, over causing suffering deliberately, ordering quarantines, taking away freedom, declaring an emergency, making a choice about preferences that involves life-affecting issues such as health, etc.)

Napoleon did not seem to have qualms and scruples about deciding over life and death. This brought him fervent admiration, yet hatred as well, from the Spanish guerillas to Beethoven. He was a common man, yet an alien being: unifying governing and anti-governing in an uncanny way that could not last long. This is an inconvenient lesson to all political governments:

anti-governing, the wish to govern ourselves, to have the last word on our life, including our relationship to others and society, is a formidable and constantly active instinct, passion or urge, which slowly but inevitably demolishes every government grounded in a single person and his or her charisma best suited to extraordinary times and circumstances.

## The Judge

The judiciary is generally considered to be one of the branches of power. However, it is usually taken to be a sine qua non condition of constitutional government and the rule of law that this branch is strictly separated from the political branches of the government. For this reason, it may sound somewhat unusual to consider the judiciary as an organic part of the civil government.

Political theory has never denied this, but it has also accepted the clause of the depoliticized and independent judiciary as a normatively necessary requirement of a well-governed polity. Moreover, with the rise of constitutional courts and the idea of constitutional review, with the increasing influence of judicial decisions on the legislation, and with the more and more entrenched civil rights and the liability of the state, especially its executive organs, an observer from the past would probably conclude that the modern judiciary has de facto become independent of the government.

Some contemporary theorists acknowledge this tendency but criticize it for its illusory nature.[49] According to them, the independence of the judiciary is merely institutional and instrumental to promoting certain political and moral ideas, or on a more modest reading, to adjusting the laws to the changing social and political consensus. Conservatives, nationalists, and populist thinkers, on the contrary, lament the influence of liberal moral and political philosophical views over judicial decisions. They urge that these ideas spreading within the judiciary should be somehow contained. Arguing from a different angle, political constitutionalists, republicans, and radical democrats reject the tendency that small judicial bodies decide over political issues, and for want of a better alternative, by way of voting, which makes it even more absurd to deny this right to the legislature or the populace in general. They argue for the reduction of constitutional barriers in order to make legislation "free" again. The judiciary, so the argument may go, has been "abusing" its constitutional rights and mandates. Eventually, all these objections aim at purifying the judiciary of the political contaminations, and restore the good order where judges are truly without any political responsibility.

However, if the judiciary is a principal branch of the government, and no serious political theory has denied this, then a perfect depoliticization of the judiciary is neither possible, nor desirable. Some *political* principles—such as the separation of powers, the rule of law, the sovereignty of the commonwealth and others—should be very much on the minds of judges, especially, of course, judging on constitutional matters. It simply belongs to the nature of government and the activity of governing that the role of the judiciary remains an ever-contested issue, and that the independence of the judiciary is a public, *hence a political*, good as it is a moral desideratum over which legitimate and important discussions should be had.

Thus, it is very natural to consider the office and character of the judge especially for the present purposes of exploring how governments are inherently constrained. As with the legislator and the executive, the usual distinctions between character and action (and office), between normal and exceptional states, and between the mirroring aspect of "judging" are applicable for the judge as well. Let me begin with the two dramas now.

In the *Antigone*, we also see Creon both as the legislator, the executor of the law, and the supreme judge, though in this capacity, he does not have a difficult job because Antigone freely confesses her "crime." Hence, Creon as a judge needs only to evaluate it and condemn the "crime" and the "criminal." The investigative role of the judge is less relevant than, for instance, in the case of Oedipus, whose political greatness consists just in his being able to transform himself from the chief executive to the supreme judge. That story is practically nothing but a criminal investigation, leading open the question of culpability, however. Creon does not commit a crime, yet his verdict and condemnation of Antigone brings upon him another sentence, raising the possibility of divine judgment. Judges will themselves be judged, and the legal clauses cited are rather nebulous, so the lesson may go, and the *Antigone* remains of the most memorable reference to the limits of any government for its transgression of norms unwritten yet sacred. For it is not making the law, nor the execution of it (i.e., Creon's orders to watch over Polyneices's corpse), but the judgment that proves to be to the ultimate test of governing. Neither the legislator, nor the governor, the chief executive in doing her job of administration, steering, tending to various affairs, nor even her decisions over life and death that was discussed in the previous section have that high mark of divinity, of the sacred the judge has, even in the smallest affair the judge rules. In Christian theology, it is The Judgement that is the greatest event awaiting us individually and mankind, the Doomsday, which every judicial decision anticipates. More universally, such decisions have a quality of finiteness everywhere. The judge's ruling, in the last instance, has an unappealable nature, notwithstanding the judge's lack of executive power and right to use force. This lends to this office a distinct dimension of sacredness that no other governmental office can boast of.

Now *Measure for Measure* covers the two phases (investigation and sentencing) of the judge's job, although it uses three characters to this purpose.[50] Angelo considers himself a mouthpiece of the law, identifying himself almost literally with it, and he has no patience to listen to arguments, to dissect a case, to uncover the complications of adultery, prostitution, and other criminal, but widespread activities. He is not doing his job, he leaves Escalus with Elbow and his company with the derisive words: "I leave you to the hearing of the cause; / Hoping you'll find good cause to whip them all" (II.1.). Escalus does it, however, without making a judgment or a verdict, in an almost diametrical opposition to Angelo's conception of what it means to be a judge. Then the Duke's grand judgment in the final scene is, however, a feat of judging, but also governing, which involves investigation, the uncovering of truth and sentencing without lenience and mercy yet pardoning those who are worthy of it: this is how the law is rendered efficient (again). The Duke is able to make every criminal confess publicly, punishes most of them severely though without meting out death penalty, and basically rearranges Vienna, which, as was argued, may be interpreted both as restoring order (which may or may not have been necessary) or creating a new order (at least making matters look that way). Investigation and rendering judgment, and in virtue of this, establishing order, is, at least according to the Sophoclean and the Shakespearean understanding of the role of the supreme judge, the principal part of the judge's job and points of orientation for exploring this character.

Such is the office, the job or vocation of the judge. Like the legislator, the character recedes to the background.[51] Iustitia, blind by default, is impersonality personified, and the slightest flaw of partisanship or partiality is thought to have far-reaching corruptive effects on the judiciary as a whole. Modern legal systems are often very sophisticated and, especially in the continental tradition, aim to allow as little room as possible for the influence of personality over judicial decisions. Judges are mouthpieces of the law, or better, its administrators.[52]

At the same time Isabella's sympathetic and unrelenting pleas for pardon in *Measure for Measure* show that we do not always find it repellent to try to influence the judge, to bring her over the constraints of her office, and to make her understand our private reasons and share them, which is the essence of partiality. Our justification of this behavior is rooted in our belief that the final truth to be discovered during the investigation is personal, something that only another person can understand and fully appreciate, and which remains ever clouded for Iustitia. Hence, the deeper meaning of her blindness is that she cannot see the deeper truth. It is thus in the figure of the judge where the personal and the impersonal aspects clash, thereby revealing this almost unbearable distinction, which is a constraint the transgression of which the governed often fervently desire but at other times vehemently reject.

It is perhaps in response to this ambivalence that modern legal systems have tried to institutionalize the personal aspects well. The expansion of individual rights helps judges to pretend to remain impartial yet appreciate as much of the impartial dimension of their cases as possible. Individual rights are expected to serve vicariously our personality within the legal process, especially but by no means exclusively in the criminal processes. However, this does not seem to be a really viable solution insofar as the more rights are being represented in the courtroom, the more legal rules, norms, or at least conventions and precedents are necessary to steer clear among them, and the judge is inevitably pressed to rely on them. Hence, the official and institutional aspect gains the upper hand again.[53] There seems to be no escape, and yet this is through which the whole misery and glory of governing in the courtroom as an inherently constrained activity is revealed. Wherever and whenever personality begins to dominate, people cry out for legality, formalism, impartiality, justice, and equality. Wherever and whenever impersonality begins to dominate, people want understanding, appreciation, fairness, compassion, mercy, and inequality. Personality cannot be fully institutionalized, as the development of individual rights shows, and it is no less obvious the impersonality cannot be personified or humanized all the way through, no matter how detailed and compassionate our laws and procedures are.

The office of the judge is essentially restoring, aiming at normalcy by eliminating exceptions, extraordinary, and emergency times. In cases of civil conflicts, the governmental aim of the judiciary is to put an end to it by applying the law, and in a sense, to annihilate the law itself. In other words, making cardinal or fundamental laws such as the civil or the penal code amounts to anticipating conflicts that are, of course, inevitable but resolvable. Such laws are instruments to resolve conflicts and help people return to a conflict-free state, and in that sense, restore a natural order where laws are in principle unnecessary. This is similar to Locke's idea of the social contract, which looks both unnecessary (the state of nature is governed by Reason via the law of nature) and necessary (the law of nature is insufficiently executed). Thus, the idea emerges according to which the judge must have a natural (i.e., normal) sense of justice, something that precedes and often overrides the law. In cases of criminal conflicts, the restoring nature of the office of the judge is even more evident. Criminal offenses are, to various degrees, against nature and natural order, and usually regarded as extraordinary and exceptional. In another sense, what is exceptional, surprising, or just unconventional, has already a *ceteris paribus* aspect of criminality. The judge is there to determine and pronounce this aspect, and annihilate the exceptionality. This protective, restoring, and annihilating power of the judge gives to her office the aura of sacredness and poses at the same time the problem that Creon had to face: what does the natural order prescribe? Antigone's resistance based on her argument for the anti-natural, revolting, extraordinary content of Creon's law is perhaps the most universal and persuasive feature of the play, appreciable to modern readers as well, since she successfully appeals to the natural sense of justice and order we all share. In effect, Antigone represents the anti-judge, making an anti-sentence, declaring Creon the criminal, the revolutionary, and hence the tyrant. Therefore, it is a safe conclusion that the office of the judge is very clearly an embodiment of normalcy vis-à-vis exceptionality, to the point that where laws are born in the legislation, they must die in the judiciary, whereas laws have an aspect of exceptionality, during their application they are meant to dissolve in the normality of everyday life.

Evidently, then, the anti-governing mirror to the judiciary as part of governing is constituted by the evaluative activities of individuals. Rawls writes about a sense of justice being necessary for his theory to work, implicitly admitting that the political government based on the principles of justice presupposes certain evaluative capacities on the part of the citizens. But of course, it is not only a sense of justice that operates in our evaluative decisions. As a matter of fact, Rawls's idea of a sense of justice is perhaps closer to a sense of fairness, whereas the sense of justice that most people feel, especially in criminal cases, has a powerful retributive aspect as well. There is a difference between Claudio's violation of the law and Angelo's abuse of the law, and whereas we positively wish to see Angelo punished, we not only want Claudio be forgiven or pardoned but also think it would be unjust to his fiancée and his unborn child to lose a husband and father without any serious natural reason; but behind our sense of injustice to them we feel compassion, pity, or simple benevolence. We expect the judge to have, share, or appreciate these feelings, and let herself be guided by them, to act as a mouthpiece not only of the law but as everybody else. Indeed, the institution of the jury, from the ancient times onward, has been an institutionalized way of anti-governing in matters of the judiciary. But even the legislative body or person who creates laws is expected to let herself be governed by her conscience formed, on assumption, within the anti-governmental spheres of life. The decision to, say, punish intentional manslaughter more severely than incest; or the act of decriminalizing divorce, are judgmental in essence, arising from the natural conscience of legislators as private persons. Thus, when they make decisions of this kind, legislators act as judges, distorting perhaps an essentialist-substantialist approach to the separation of powers (more about this doctrine in the next and final chapter), yet thereby they highlight the constraint every government must face: in virtue of personal conscience, however effective it may be, the evaluative anti-governing activities intrude into the government, and make the judiciary an eminent example of how governing is impossible without imitating, following, and giving room to the natural sense of justice (and other evaluative sentiments).

## SUMMARY

This chapter explored constraints of governing arising from it as an activity. After having discussed the personal stakes of governing as done by politicians as persons in the previous chapter, here I proceeded to a perspective that is often neglected in political theory. Since before the more institutionalized and routinized aspects of governing may be addressed, there are some familiar and quite ordinary distinctions by help of which governing is approached and conceived of by individuals. One need not be well-versed in political theory and the arcani imperii of governments to be able to distinguish between requirements of office and character, between exigencies and imperatives of normal and critical times, and between the sphere thought to be properly under the authority of governments and the sphere that belongs and that must remain under our self-government. The no less trivial and traditional offices of the legislator, the executive leader and the judge were then used to highlight how these distinctions become visible and sensible in these offices and roles. All this confirms, so the argument goes, the idea that, however, vaguely and context-dependently, most people do not think of governments as unitary agents, with unshared responsibilities, spelling over different phases of history and historical times. The idea of constrained government precedes constitutions and preempts all theories of politics that wish to outline the institutional and procedural specificities of such governments.

## NOTES

1. "[One can see] a certain prince today fortunate and tomorrow ruined, without seeing that he has changed in character or otherwise. I believe this arises in the first place from the causes that we have already discussed at length; that is to say, because the prince who bases himself entirely on fortune is ruined when fortune changes. I also believe that he is happy whose mode of procedure accords with the needs of the times, and similarly he is unfortunate whose mode of procedure is opposed to the times. For one sees that men in those things which lead them to the aim that each one has in view, namely, glory and riches, proceed in various ways: one with circumspection, another with impetuosity, one by violence, another by cunning, one with patience, another with the reverse . . .. One sees also two cautious men, one of whom succeeds in his designs, and the other not, and in the same way two men succeed equally by different methods . . . which arises from the nature of times, which does or does not conform to their method of procedure." Niccolo Machiavelli, *The Prince and the Discourses* (New York: The Modern Library, 92). For interpretations of Fortuna here, see Timo Airaksinen, "Fortune is a Woman. Machiavelli on Luck and Virtue. Essays in Honor of Hannu Nurmi." *Homo Oeconomicus* 3–4 (2009): 551–68.

2. I introduced and defined this concept in my previous book: *The Principle of the Separation of Powers. A Defense* (Lanham; New York; London: Rowman and Littlefield, 2016).

3. See Charles de Secondat, Baron the Montesquieu, *The Spirit of Laws*, tr. Thomas Nugent (1752) (Batoche Books, Kitchener, 2001), esp. Book 28, Chapter 12.

4. *The Foucault Effect: Studies in Governmentality* (Chicago: Chicago University Press, 1991). Also Danica Dupont, Frank Pearce, "Foucault Contra Foucault. Rereading the 'Governmentality' Papers." *Theoretical Criminology* 2 (2001): 123–58.

5. Barry Hindess, "Discipline and Cherish: Foucault on Power, Domination and Government." In *Discourses on Power: From Hobbes to Foucault* (Oxford: Blackwell, 1996), 96–136, 105.

6. *The Concept of the Political* (Chicago: The Chicago University Press, 2007).

7. "The enemy in the political sense need not be hated personally, and in the private sphere only does it make sense to love one's enemy, i.e., one's adversary." Ibid., 29.

8. As I argued in chapter 2, the personal dimension of the image of the political leader entails a strong, though unwanted constrain of governing: this is the loyalty problem. Schmitt himself was on delicate terms with the Nazi elite, to say the least; and it is well-known that Hitler was a target of countless assassination attempts, probably of more than any other politician in the twentieth century.

9. A lot more should be said about how choosing one's enemy in politics happens. Public choice theory is concerned with policy choices; one wonders how it could be applied to enemy choices. For admitting the personal side of picking one's enemy, Schmitt had a virtual point about the "institutionalization" of such decisions. It seems to be a reasonable hypothesis that in normal times, policy choices predominate, whereas in exceptional times, enemy choices are more in the forefront. In any case, the distinctions between character or person versus office, and normal versus exceptional time, look sensible, accessible to everyone, and have substantial explanatory potential. The point here is that they enable shifts and switches, which, in turn, can work as constraints.

10. Aurel Kolnai, "What Is Politics About?" [originally written in German and published as "Der Inhalt der Politik" in *Zeitschrift für die Gesamte Staatswissenschaft* in 1933]. In F. Dunlop and Z. Balazs (eds.) *Exploring the World of Human Practice* (Budapest-New York: CEU Press, 2004), 17–46, 28.

11. Carl Schmitt, *Theory of the Partisan* (New York: Telos Press Publishing, 2007).

12. John Locke, *Two Treatises of Government*, ed. Peter Laslett (Cambridge: Cambridge University Press, 1992), 287 (original italics).

13. Christopher Kelly, " 'To Persuade without Convincing': The Language of Rousseau's Legislator." *American Journal of Political Science* 2 (1987): 321–35. Kelly argues that Rousseau's main intention was to inspire citizens and create the spirit of legislation. A similar view is expounded by Harvey F. Fireside, "The Concept of the Legislator in Rousseau's Social Contract." *The Review of Politics* 2 (1970): 191–96.

14. *On the Social Contract*, 162.

15. Ibid.

16. Steven Johnston, *Encountering Tragedy. Rousseau and the Project of Democratic Order* (Ithaca, London: Cornell University Press, 1999).

17. *On the Social Contract*, 164.

18. Ibid., 162.

19. Ibid., 163.

20. Ibid., 163.

21. Andrew Sabl, *Ruling Passions* (Princeton: Princeton University Press, 2002).

22. Alexander Hamilton, "The Federalist Paper No 72." In G. Wills (ed.) *The Federalist Papers* (Bantam Books, 1982), 367. Sabl quotes this sentence and passage from where his book's title is taken.

23. Lawrence A. Scaff, *Weber and the Weberians* (New York: Palgrave Macmillan, 2004), 101. See also Andrew McCulloch, "Jesus Christ and Max Weber: Two Problems of Charisma." *Max Weber Studies* 1 (2005): 7–34.

24. Sabl, *Ruling Passions*, 63.

25. Ibid., 56.

26. Ibid., 49.

27. Ibid., 75. Original italics.

28. Not all acts of a legislative body amount to law-making, despite the legal status of an "act." In other words, constituting an institution, honoring a person, granting privileges to the royal house as an expression and protection of sovereignty, and so on *by law* are, in political theoretical terms, executive rather than legislative actions (sovereignty-related actions are perhaps different).

29. Rules in emergency situations are stricter, usually granting greater freedom of action to the authorities and restricting personal liberties. Characteristically, however, constitutions that have provisions for such cases retain as much as possible of the authority of the legislative body.

30. Cicero, *The Republic and the Laws*, Oxford World's Classics (Oxford: Oxford University Press, 2009).

31. The pioneering work is G. Tullock's and James Buchanan's *The Calculus of Consent* (Ann Arbor: The University of Michigan Press, 1990).

32. *Realism and Moralism in Political Theory*.

33. Eric A. Posner, Adrian Vermeule: The Executive Unbound. After the Madisonian Republic. Oxford, Oxford University Press, 2010.

34. Ibid., 5.

35. Ibid., 13.

36. Richard H. Pildes, "Law and the President." *Harvard Law Review* 125 (2012): 1–42.

37. Ibid., 1, 4.

38. Ibid., 13.

39. Ibid., 27.

40. Ibid., 28.

41. For a very useful and thorough overview of the problem, see Saikrishna Prakash, "The Essential Meaning of Executive Power." *Illinois Law Review* 3 (2003): 701–820.

42. Federalist Papers 70.

43. Prakash, *The Essential Meaning of Executive Power*, 820.

44. Ralph Waldo Emerson, "Napoleon: Man of the World." In *The Complete Works of Ralph Waldo Emerson: Representative Men*, Vol. 4 (Ann Arbor, MI: University of Michigan Library, 2006), 223–58, quotation: 225–28.

45. Harvey C. Mansfield, *Taming the Prince. The Ambivalence of Modern Executive Power* (New York: Free Press, 1989).

46. Ibid., xvi.

47. Of course, Mansfield has a longer and broader story to tell. He begins with Aristotle and concludes with the lesson that political science should learn more from sociology (the nature of power and the nature of the subjects to be governed)—the lesson that Rousseau also realized.

48. Ibid., 140.

49. See John Ferejohn, "Judicializing Politics, Politicizing Law." *Law and Contemporary Problems* 65 (2002): 41–68.

50. For the sake of making the argument shorter, I shall ignore the various possibilities of how judges may take part in the investigative procedures in different legal systems. At least in the last phase, in the courtroom, there is still much to investigate and discover, despite the evidence that has been unearthed by the authorities and the affected actors (litigants, plaintiffs, defendants, accused persons, their lawyers, prosecutors) themselves.

51. David Dyzenhaus asks this question: " 'What is a judge?' This question, somewhat curiously, receives only an oblique answer in much legal theory." See "The Very Idea of a Judge," *University of Toronto Law Journal* 1 (2010): 61–80, 64. He continues that a strong tradition in legal theory does imply that judges be only mouthpieces of the law, and that even the common law tradition holds that judges are there to discover and reveal the law: again, a fundamentally impersonal and an institutional role.

52. In such a system, judges "are simply the officials charged with interpreting the law and their task is to determine a content that can represented as the one intended by the powerful." Ibid., 63.

53. However, the justification of these rules and norms is different: "judges have a role in legal order as guardians of . . . 'fundamental,' even 'transcendent,' 'constitutional values.' " "Judges are no more than an instrument through which the (moral) content of the law manifests itself in the world" (Dyzenhaus 64, 66). Dyzenhaus recommends a Hobbes-inspired version of the office of the judge, which rests on the analogy between the judge and the arbitrator. It soon turns out, however, that the arbitrator is bound by the natural law (it is important the stress that this conception is better suited to the civil law than to the criminal law procedures; however, the personal "truth" and searching for the two parties' own "truth" is as important in a civil case as is the "final truth" about a crime and the perpetrator's person). Natural law is, so Dyzenhaus/Hobbes, practically nothing but "sound reasons, reasons that include the principles of legality" (70). We are still miles apart from the genuinely personal aspect of being a judge.

*Chapter 5*

# Political Principles of Constrained Government

In this last chapter, I wish to discuss the political principles of constraining governments or the constraints of governing. In the previous chapters, I have used the *Antigone* and *Measure for Measure* as texts of inspiration for political theoretical reflection and argued that they highlight, sometimes directly explain, the reasons for thinking that governing broadly understood is an inherently constrained activity. These reasons have been formulated in moral and political philosophical terms, with a constant eye on the importance of images in and for political thinking, especially because they help us in our discerning mode of reflection. Discernment is about finding (rather than making and imposing) distinctions, differences, forms, and shapes in reality. Still, if our reflections, our distinctions, images, as well as our reasons remain merely explorations, arguments bound to contexts and stories, political exigencies, and historical experiences; they may appear to be weak, both practically and theoretically. To cut a long story short, it is a legitimate expectation that a book on constraining the government should conclude with some more explicit and robust conception of how such a government looks like and should look like.

## IMAGES OF A CONSTRAINED GOVERNMENT

The first thing to recall, once again, the importance of the image. As I argued in chapter 2, some political theories of government are apparently overconfident about their convincing force, and behind this self-confidence we can discover a particularly suggestive and powerful concept and image. However, as I tried to argue, all shapes and forms, including those associated with the government "out there" or with the state, have boundaries and limits, and in this primitive, almost useless sense, constraints. Notwithstanding our suspicion of the uselessness of this idea, namely, that contours are already constraints, our reactions to the forms and figures are not at all unreal and irrelevant. A leader in the square is certainly more inspiring than a Watchmaker in his little shop around the corner.

However, these images are not exactly those of a government. Or perhaps they make it easier for the modern citizen to think something about it, to have the assurance that someone is in control of it. The Leviathan is, as we saw, both an image of the sovereign as a towering political figure and of the state that is essential unpolitical, and in that sense, it is not only a multitude unified in one person but also an assemblage of the various institutions and agencies, as Hobbes calls them, the magistrates, unified in one image. Such images and the political theories behind them exert considerable influence on our political thinking and behavior. To some extent, as I argued, they work as constraints. However, these effects are inchoate, often contradictory and disorienting. For the most memorable and poignant description of these disorienting effects, the uncanny feelings we have toward the authorities, the external agent controlling our life to unfathomable depths we may turn to Franz Kafka. His last, unfinished novel, *The Castle*, begins with K., the main character, arriving in a village. It is winter and late evening.

> The village lay deep in snow. There was nothing to be seen of Castle Mount, for mist and darkness surrounded it, and not the faintest glimmer of light showed where the great castle lay. K. stood on the wooden bridge leading from the road to the village for a long time, looking up at what seemed to be a void.[1]

Next morning, K. is able to have a look at the Castle. The invisible becomes visible. What is the form like? Kafka does not spare us a detailed description, but with one of his usual twists:

> Altogether the castle, as seen in the distance, lived up to K.'s expectations. It was neither an old knightly castle from the days of chivalry, nor a showy new structure, but an extensive complex of buildings, a few of them with two storeys, but many of them lower and crowded close together. If you hadn't known it was a castle you might have taken it for a small town. K. saw only a single tower, and could not make out whether it was a dwelling or belonged to a church. Flocks of crows were circling around it. His eyes fixed on the castle, K. went on, paying no attention to anything else. But as he came closer he thought the castle disappointing; after all, it was only a poor kind of collection of cottages assembled into a little town, and distinguished only by the fact that, while it might all be built of stone, the paint had flaked off long ago, and the stone

itself seemed to be crumbling away. K. thought fleetingly of his own hometown, which was hardly inferior to this castle.[2]

The novel tells the story of K.'s repeated and ever-frustrated efforts to get there. One reading of the novel is that K. is already *in it*, having already become part of the Castle, with his job of a land-surveyor. On this interpretation, K.'s relentless attempts to ascend from the village to the Castle are in fact attempts to get out of it. Therefore, the image that Kafka uses is a trap: there is no escape from the reality of being governed, since the Castle is not out there, it has no castle-form, it has nothing ideal, beautiful, impressive, or attractive, not even special about it. However, K.'s almost maniacal preoccupation with the Castle[3] literally captures his mind and fantasy, never letting him free.

Kafka's several other writings are variations of this image (he was particularly impressed by the Chinese Empire and the images associated with it, from the Great Wall—the greatest physical constraint of a government—to the illusion of central control over the Empire). There are no limitations, there is no escape from a modern government; and this truth is expressed in terms of a non-image, a ramshackle and almost shapeless habitat of people with the self-evidence of unintelligibility.

In view of the omnicompetence of the modern state or government, which arguably exceeds Kafka's worst nightmares or his fantasy, and seems to confirm Foucault's visions of governmentality and biopower, the case for a credible conception and a visually convincing image of a constrained government looks almost impossible. Montesquieu's *The Spirit of Laws*, which I shall briefly discuss later here, has received generally positive reviews and supportive treatments, yet its impact has been significantly lower, at least within political theory, than that of Hobbes or Locke or Rousseau. It is highly probable that Montesquieu's way of discussion, notwithstanding the eloquence and clarity of his prose, is one of the causes of its remaining in the second row: though he compared himself to a painter in Introduction, he simply did not produce the necessary metaphors, images, concepts for his conception, and persuasion of the need of a constrained government. For those in favor of such a government, Edmund Burke is a better exploit. It is now a commonplace argument to point out that Burke's aesthetic views heavily influenced his political thinking and vice versa.[4] As is known, his guiding "principle" for describing the English, and in his opinion, well-governed commonwealth was beauty. This quality incites gentle love, which is so necessary for good governance: "There ought to be a system of manners in every nation which a well-informed mind would be disposed to relish. To make us love our country, our country ought to be lovely."[5]

It is important to bear in mind that Burke was suspicious of images directly meant for the eyes. Paintings, as opposed to words, leave less room for the imagination and can often have unintended and incorrigible effects (what was intended to be sublime results in being ridiculous).[6] Hence, a description of the constrained—and beautiful—government does not aim at creating a single and simple image. Rather, Burke works with several metaphors and rhetorical instruments. "Government is a contrivance of human wisdom to provide for human wants,"[7] he writes, among which a want, or wish, to be restrained, especially due to the excesses of our own passions, is a prominent one (the parallelism between governing and anti-governing is easy to discover here). Hence, "in this sense the restraints on men, as well as their liberties, are to be reckoned among their rights."[8] Those responsible for governing have a specific job to do, and Burke joins forces of some traditional authors who work with the image of professional-elitist politics, arguing that in matters of government, "I shall always advise to call in the aid of the farmer and the physician rather than the professor of metaphysics."[9] Yet governing is more than administration, it needs more than management skills and experiences. Returning to aesthetical concepts in discussing unintended consequences of political decisions, Burke argues that "very plausible schemes, with very pleasing commencements, have often shameful and lamentable conclusions. In states there are often some obscure and almost latent causes, things which appear at first view of little moment, on which a very great part of its prosperity or adversity may most essentially depend."[10]

The image behind this description is the old organic vision of the state as a body, and Burke's precept is to recommend the politician as a physician supervising and curing, rather than governing and controlling, the body. Besides the images of diligent and dedicated leaders working for the public good, and the doctors intently observing every symptom, change, and nuances of the body, Burke invokes the sacral imagery as well, taken again from the English tradition in which state, church, and state-church merge: "That sense not only, like a wise architect, hath built up the august fabric of states, but, like a provident proprietor, to preserve the structure from profanation and ruin, as a sacred temple purged from all the impurities of fraud and violence and injustice and tyranny, hath solemnly and forever consecrated the commonwealth and all that officiate in it."[11]

It is highly improbable that these images would have the same imaginative force today as once they had or might have had. Politicians are not really thought of as wise men, architects, let alone doctors or priests. Consequently, governments are hardly ever considered to be bodies of the wise, the elect, a masonry corps working on the cathedral for centuries, a staff of a hospital, or a temporal clergy. Nonetheless, we are witnessing the emergence of special roles associated with a well-ordered government, especially certain agencies with special tasks (ombudsmen, so-called whistleblowers; judges sitting in Supreme or Constitutional Courts, and so on). Further, politicians must enter the ring with some "vision." In crises, the government is still looked upon as the sole agent possessing the cure, although the ancient metaphor of the ship and her captain has also lost its force (modern ships are perhaps too automatized). Instead, we are exposed to much ritualism, formalism, preaching, moralization, exhortation, and other gestures in contemporary politics, which evoke a strangely secular version of sacral authority.

Such and similar images may not be compressible into a single picture. Some of them are, however, suggestive of a more relaxed and unimposing, yet dignified and respectable version of thinking about governing. To appreciate this imagery for both its aesthetic qualities and political virtues, Burke's no less impressive negative visions and wordings are particularly helpful. He is especially derisive of the National Assembly of France in which

> there appears a poverty of conception, a coarseness, and a vulgarity in all the proceedings of the Assembly and of all their instructors. Their liberty is not liberal. Their science is presumptuous ignorance. Their humanity is savage and brutal.[12]

As to the new constitution of France, Burke finds a remarkably harsh metaphor, and continues with a counter-point to his former list of noble governors:

> All these considerations leave no doubt on my mind that, if this monster of a constitution can continue,[13] France will be wholly governed by the agitators in corporations, by societies in the towns formed of directors of assignats, and trustees for the sale of church lands, attorneys, agents, money-jobbers, speculators, and adventurers, composing an ignoble oligarchy founded on the destruction of the crown, the church, the nobility, and the people.[14]

A particularly interesting parallel lies in his anticipation of a wholly mechanized government (remember the Watchmaker metaphor), which is unable to rule the popular passions properly, that, in turn, makes those passions all the more intimidating and ominous:

> Let us now turn our eyes to what they have done toward the formation of an executive power. For this they have chosen a degraded king. This their first executive officer is to be a machine without any sort of deliberative discretion in any one act of his function. At best he is but a channel to convey to the National Assembly such matter as it may import that body to know.[15]

Both the executive power and the law without a face are ruinous inasmuch as no personal relations are possible to bind people to their governments. That was something that both Creon and Angelo were striving for, to their detriment. For there is no such thing as a faceless government. It may be horrible, monstrous, soulless, and inhuman; for Burke, perhaps sublime; and therefore forbidding, impersonal, and hollow; yet it is always rooted in society, in our own behavior and readiness to obey.

The point is, let us repeat, not to substitute a gentle, pardoning, merciful, benevolent, kind face for the ruthless and deformed face of the revolutionary government because no such single face is available. Governing is not a bucolic and idyllic pastoral business, as another Shakespearean character, Gonzalo in *The Tempest*, fancies his utopian rule:

> I' the commonwealth I would by contraries / Execute all things; for no kind of traffic / Would I admit; no name of magistrate; / Letters should not be known; riches, / poverty, And use of service, none; contract, succession, / Bourn, bound of land, tilth, / vineyard, none; / No use of metal, corn, or wine, or oil; / No occupation; all men / idle, all; / And women too, but innocent and pure; / No sovereignty . . . . All things in common nature should produce / Without sweat or endeavour: treason, felony, / Sword, pike, knife, gun, or need of any engine, / Would I not have; but nature should bring forth, / Of its own kind, all foison, all abundance, / To feed my innocent people.[16]

"I would execute"—Gonzalo dreams, but without "sovereignty" because nature operates on its own; "bringing forth" everything necessary for life, yet again, not without him being the king there. This is, in fact, anti-government replacing government, which is a utopian illusion. Or, if we read Jonathan Swift's *Fourth Travel*, it is more portentous than one might think. The horses' legislative assembly rules by Reason alone, therefore without any political antagonism, except for the problem of the yahoos (and later Gulliver), which the horses cannot resolve, only vacillate between their wholesome extirpation and temporary toleration. Gentle as they are to themselves, they are tyrants to others.

Notwithstanding the illusions of pastures and the government by nature, of nature, and perhaps for nature, there is a feature or quality that the realist Burke and the dreaming Gonzalo have in common with regard to governing. This is *harmony*. Harmony presupposes some order, or orderliness, which, in turn, needs parts, pieces, components, and elements of a greater whole. No doubt, harmony as a meta-property is often quite difficult to realize and discern. In chapter 1, Mandeville's colorful description of the hive as a society was discussed. Is there order or disorder in it? The copresence of good and evil, both with high intensity, makes the question difficult to answer. Even if Mandeville (and his present-day followers) are right about the beneficial effects of such a state of affairs, the result—abundance and wealth—is not identical with harmony. But are they not related at least? There is, perhaps, a harmony in the peaceful co-existence of opposites. This is hardly a celestial symphony of praising melodies, only an earthly orderliness, yet under the supervision and assurance of providence.

The last question to be discussed is whether this vision of a *harmonious social* order can be applied to the government. We need to avoid the possible political conclusion of a communitarian or corporatist vision of society as a mystical whole governing itself (in fact, as was pointed out, such views end up with the rule of some narrow elite). Rather, the idea is a well-ordered government, with discernible functions that can be associated with certain professions and jobs, vocations and types of experience. As far as Mandeville is concerned, he addressed this feature of the hive and observed that

> This was the State's Craft, that maintain'd / The Whole, of which each Part complain'd: / This, as in Musick Harmony, / Made Jarrings in the Main agree; / Parties directly opposite / Assist each oth'r, as 'twere for Spight; / And Temp'rance with Sobriety / Serve Drunkenness and Gluttonny.[17]

Opposition and opposing passions, parties and partiality do not exclude state-craft and order, *harmony* and agreement within the government. It is not very easy to agree with him, however. In *Measure for Measure*, as we have seen, the problem of order is in the forefront but it is a problem of Vienna, rather than of its government. The new ducal government emerging out of the chaos is in the formation, but it does not look a very moderate and harmonious one. Some of the Duke's subjects are humiliated, others are elevated, but all stand in awe. Will the new government work in a way that would please Burke and Mandeville? This is the question hovering in the last moment and lingering on after the curtain falls. The Duke shall have to make his choice between the Castle's disarray and a court's fine order, between an unconstrained and ugly, and a constrained and beautiful, or at least harmonious, form of governing. It is telling that even Hobbes, the prophet of unconstrained sovereignty, could not entirely resist the lure of harmony in the government. After exalting the unlimited rights of the Sovereign, he lists the various offices and activities associated with practical governing:

> He is Judge of what is necessary for Peace; and Judge of Doctrines: He is Sole Legislator; and Supreme Judge of Controversies; and of the Times, and Occasions of Warre, and Peace: to him it belongeth to choose Magistrates, Counsellours, Commanders, and all other Officers, and Ministers; and to determine of Rewards, and Punishments, Honour, and Order.[18]

It is impossible to imagine a working, running government without some kind of an internal order that arises from the depths of times and traditions, no less so than the social order is said to have been formed in the furnace of history. No more is necessary. The image of harmony and order is perhaps less powerful and arresting than the images suggested by the triumphant absolutist theories of political science. The reason is clear: neither harmony nor order are proper images; rather, they are experiences and impressions that can have many sources, and thus, many political theories. Nonetheless, our sense of forms and shapes, of order and containment, of difference and distinction, of harmony and beauty is and remains the cornerstone of our resistance against the sublime and arresting, passionate and formless, and powerful and sweeping images of unconstrained governments.

## MODERATION

In chapter 3, moderation was discussed and shown to be emerging out of an experience of shame, which compels us to reflect on our innermost world, the moral self—or, more precisely, which compels the moral self to reflect on itself. This sounds technical and philosophical, as probably only a few people think about their "selves" in the third person singular. However, it must occur to most people that there is a difference between what they know and what they do not know, and perhaps quite a few of them (actually, of us) also reflect on the problem whether they should learn more, what their knowledge qualifies them to do, of whether non-knowledge or ignorance is a moral or intellectual barrier to their endeavors, and so on. In the end, we are confronted with the ultimate question of whether we are in control of ourselves, or whether full control over ourselves is possible at all. The experience of shame is a constant reminder that this is never the case, yet the temptation that it should be otherwise is no less perennial. I argued that Plato's insight that moderation is rooted in this very deeply rooted problem is sound, and more pertinent to the virtue of moderation than the simple wisdom that moderation entails being able to control our passions, period. In other words, moderation begins with the intellect and spirit, rather than with emotions, passions, drives and urges.

In his voluminous book on moderate governments, Paul O. Carrese, makes the same point, though without the analytics I offered earlier. He writes that "moderation is a philosophical as well as political and moral principle that we should take seriously in liberal, constitutional politics. We used to, we don't anymore, and we're paying the price."[19] His logic of inference takes philosophical extremism to be first mistake, from which a faulty political theory and science ensues, leading to bad practice. Immoderation in politics is a widespread experience, in the first place, in public (destructive) discourse. Although we still invoke moderation in politics and discourse [this] often occurs indirectly when criticizing the other side, in politics or thought, as extreme, single-minded, imbalanced—thus as unfair, unjust, uncivil, and unreasonable.[20]

Carrese also admits, though implicitly, that moderation as a political principle is a residuum, a lesson drawn from bad experience with extremism in thought and in practice:

> In the past century . . . moderation has been conceived at best a tactic rather than a central principle of a liberal-democratic theory and practice. This marks a revival of the radical Enlightenment spirit of Spinoza, Hobbes, Locke, Rousseau, and Kant among others.[21]

In view of this lacuna, he cites a vast tradition of moderate political thought, beginning with Socrates, Aristotle, adding to it the Scholastic thinking, the French thinkers from Montaigne to Tocqueville, and the American Founding Fathers, ending with the contemporary realist revival that I discussed in the earlier chapters. Indeed, what seems to be the strategy of political theorists defending or attempting to revive, or somehow formulate, principles of moderate governing is the in-depth analysis of this tradition. Besides Paul Carrese and Harry Clor,[22] Aurelian Craiutu has done a great service to this cause.[23] He also implicitly admits that moderation is guide, a compass, a virtue, rather than a principle, since

> it cannot be studied in the abstract, but only as instantiated in specific historical and political contexts and discourses. What is moderate in one context and period may significantly differ from what is moderate at another point in time, which is another way of saying that moderation is not a virtue for all seasons and for everyone.[24]

He cites his own personal experience with totalitarian extremism and argues that in "violent age of extremes," invoking and defending moderation is "a legitimate reaction."[25] He also rejects immoderation in philosophical thinking, contending that a preoccupation with and preference for the absolute, the authentic, or the adventurous is the bedrock for immoderate political practice. Moderation is a mental disposition as well. It is strictly different from cowardice or cautiousness; moderation requires courage. According to Montaigne, walking on the extremes is easier than walking in the middle where it is easier to get lost. Further, to make things even more complicated, moderation can itself be immoderate, at least when being "applied" in the wrong circumstances that would require, for instance, a disposition to act upon passions.

All this sits fairly well with the idea of moderation being essentially related to avoiding the extremes, though as I argued, the real hazard lies less in the extreme passions and more in the philosophical paradox of knowing and of unknowing, a faith in or suasion of full self-control, which tends to make us either overconfident and tyrannical, or frozen and incapable of acting. However, from these insights about the moderate character, or the virtue of moderation as a property of ordinary people and politicians, norms and style of political action are derivable, but not political principles in strict sense. Craiutu himself tries to describe, or perhaps distill, a specific style or code of political action that he calls trimming and that he illustrates with a num-ber of political thinkers (and, in the case of Vaclav Havel, political leader). Yet again, the art of trimming, a sort of mixture of caution, flexibility, and readiness to compromise but never losing the purpose can indeed be part of statesmanship but it is hardly identical with it.[26] How can moderation be tran-scribed as a political theory?[27]

Montesquieu is probably the most widely cited authority on moderation as a political principle of governing. However, his magnum opus does not expound an axiomatic theory, not even a Socratic analytics of concepts and arguments.[28] Nonetheless, the caveat of extremes is there on almost every page of the book, the advice to look for the middle is constantly on his mind.[29] About democracy, he writes that

> one great fault there was in most of the ancient republics, that the people had a right to active resolutions, such as require some execution, a thing of which they are absolutely incapable. They ought to have no share in the government but for the choosing of representatives, which is within their reach.[30]

About the two main branches of power, he observes that

> of the three powers above mentioned, the judiciary is in some measure next to nothing: there remain, therefore, only two; and as these have need of a regulat-ing power to moderate them, the part of the legislative body composed of the nobility is extremely proper for this purpose.[31]

About tyranny, his insight is that

> there are two sorts of tyranny: one real, which arises from oppression; the other is seated in opinion, and is sure to be felt whenever those who govern establish things shocking to the existing ideas of a nation.[32]

His famous thought about politics and governing being context-dependent is that mankind are influenced by various causes: by the climate, by the religion, by the laws, by the maxims of government, by precedents, morals, and customs; whence is formed a general spirit of nations. In proportion as, in every country, any one of these causes acts with more force, the others in the same degree are weakened. Nature and the climate rule almost alone over the savages; customs govern the Chinese; the laws tyrannise in Japan; morals had formerly all their influence at Sparta; maxims of government, and the ancient simplicity of manners, once prevailed at Rome.[33]

Later, Montesquieu discusses the pluralism of laws:

Men are governed by several kinds of laws; by the law of nature; by the divine law, which is that of religion; by ecclesiastical, otherwise called canon law, which is that of religious polity; by the law of nations, which may be considered as the civil law of the whole globe, in which sense every nation is a citizen; by the general political law, which relates to that human wisdom whence all societies derive their origin; by the particular political law, the object of which is each society; by the law of conquest founded on this, that one nation has been willing and able, or has had a right to offer violence to another; by the civil law of every society, by which a citizen may defend his possessions and his life against the attacks of any other citizen; in fine, by domestic law, which proceeds from a society's being divided into several families, all which have need of a particular government. There are therefore different orders of laws, and the sublimity of human reason consists in perfectly knowing to which of these orders the things that are to be determined ought to have a principal relation, and not to throw into confusion those principles which should govern mankind.[34]

Countless further examples may be cited from *The Spirit of Laws*. Four basic points seem to emerge from these extensive quotations. The first is about *constrained competences* (democratic electorate versus their representatives). The second is about some sense of *balance* (in the quotation, with reference to the legislative body). The third is about being *alert to the extremes* and the abysses of unfreedom and despotism (see the two forms of tyranny: they are both oppressive, the one, we may say, by way of physical force, reducing physical freedom; the other, by way of ideology, reducing the freedom of thinking). The fourth is *pluralism* (in the first part, Montesquieu refers to a sort of a global cultural and political pluralism, but it may be easily applied to smaller units of human societies; in the second part, we read about the manifoldness of norms governing human behavior).

Do these points make-up a "political theory of moderation"? Recent commentators of Montesquieu and his idea of moderation lean toward a position in which moderation is a cornerstone. For instance, noting the gross historical and factual inadequacies of Montesquieu's descriptions of past and contemporary Chinese and Japanese governments, Nathaniel Gilmore and Vickie B. Sullivan argue that the French thinker's purpose was to draw a comparison between Asian and European fanaticisms, with the intention "to guide his European readers by their very disdain for a cruel Other so that they might cure themselves of their own worst, most dangerous beliefs about punishment and correction."[35] Thus, historical parallels and comparisons are a device to make a theoretical point. Alex Haskins is less forgiving, he thinks that Montesquieu's inconsistency, in fact, his outright errors (probably deliberately misleading about the Asian regimes), is itself an immoderate act and method.[36] The moral aspect is the old dilemma of whether honesty can be taught or implanted into one's character by dishonest means, whether truth is sometimes served by untruth. Those who think that moderation sometimes endorses and needs passions, sometimes tolerates vices, or evil, and that what matters is the lesson of the tale and not its factual truth, would probably find no fault with Montesquieu's method. (Assuming that falsifying history or facts is an act of immoderation, which is, as far as I can see, not an evident truth.) The point is, nonetheless, the same: Montesquieu's intention was not historical accuracy but giving a teaching on what principles governments should follow.

However, the idea of moderation as a political principle does not develop into a theory of it. Montesquieu's insight and points do not form a closed set of principles or axioms. Craiutu himself discusses other ones as well, such as natural order and harmony (discussed in the previous section),[37] civil peace, the rule of law, public liberty, and a frame of mind committed to civilization (civilized manners and norms), as well as lucidity and transparency, and finally pluralism.[38] It is important to realize that none of these principles can be absolutes. For instance, he argues against a Hayekian type of thinking, which he thinks is based on the wishful belief in the impersonal rule of law. Further, as Isaiah Berlin used to point out, the pluralism of values is incompatible with the view of a harmonious order, as values themselves are often incompatible with one another. Thus, either we reconsider pluralism as an objective reality without harmony and say that governments should *respect pluralism* and at the same time try to *harmonize* conflicting values as much as possible (which indeed happens at every time a national budget is proposed and voted on), or we revise our concept of harmony, as was suggested earlier, to include antagonisms and conflicts in it. In either case, however, we can opt for admitting the inconsistencies between the Montesquieuian points and conclude the once moderation as a middle way of governing is accepted, we are committed to the rejection of single-mindedness and reductionism of any kind, including the rejection of governing according the strictly consistent theories of any kind.

This may not convince everyone. Moderation may be sui generis unfit for the role of being the cornerstone principle of a political theoretical conception of constrained government, yet it is efficient in guiding theoretical reflection and, perhaps, to make us more appreciative of a less axiomatic and more aesthetic kind of political theory. As Burke was highly consciously using metaphors and images in his rhetoric, Craiutu and Haskins both point out the less evident, yet appreciable aesthetic qualities of Montesquieu's writings. Haskins makes argument succinctly:

In his preface, Montesquieu fears his audience will dismiss his twenty-year work, pleading with them to consider the design of the whole work and how it reflects his broader role as an author. Montesquieu's artistic motif seems deliberate both here and at the preface's conclusion when he considers earlier French, English, and German writers and asserts that, like Correggio before him, "[he] too, [is] a painter."[39]

## SEPARATION OF POWERS

The common mood in political theory is not an enthusiastic appreciation of a Burkean-aesthetic vision of beautiful government, especially not as an effective constraint, and one may doubt that in place of beauty, harmony, and order would fare much better. Moderation and moderate governments have a more robust philosophical tradition but its main propositions and lessons are results of an experimental and inductive, rather than an axiomatic and deductive method. Perhaps unfortunately, the former method is generally considered to have less compelling and convincing force than the axiomatic one. It is quite easy to see why: in political science, we are accustomed to think in terms of constitutions, institutions, procedures, offices; as well as constructivism, policy models, projects and the like. This type of thinking prefers the axiomatic-deductive logic to the experimental-inductive method. Nonetheless, in this last part, I attempt at exploring how a long-cherished institutionalist-constitutional principle, the principle of the separation of powers, can be adjusted to the purposes of explaining and defending the idea of constrained governments.

The principle or doctrine of the separation of powers has two advantages. First, it is amenable to legal and constitutional thinking. It is a practically useful principle. It figures quite often in justifying decisions and rulings in constitutional review. Second, it has been traditionally thought to be buttressing the idea of constrained government. As is known, Aristotle's political theory, which is close to the ideals of moderate, at least non-tyrannical governing, describes the functional rudiments of the principle (legislative, executive, judiciary functions). The Roman constitution is famous for its logic of balance, an early, experimental model of checks and balances (especially in terms of institutional separations between legislative bodies and magistrates, as well as the different types of executive rights). Locke's and Montesquieu's theories contributed significantly to the theoretical formulation of the principle as a doctrine, which, then, was explicitly put into practice in the American Constitution (though the text does not allude to it; however, many state constitutions do so). Ever since, several written constitutions all over the world either explicitly or implicitly (e.g., by organizing the state according to the principle, without mentioning it expressis verbis) have followed the American suit.

Whether it is a doctrine that can indeed help constitutional review has, however, become a matter of legal debate and controversy.[40] Critics complain that the doctrine is still too theoretical, in both of its interpretations: the formalist interpretation insists on the purest possible separation of the three powers, trying to preserve their putative substantive purpose (making, executing, and adjudicating legal norms);[41] whereas the functionalist interpretation runs into the difficulty of finding the precise functions of the power branches within the constitutional whole. The simple fact that the doctrine can be interpreted in different, and often contradictory ways precisely when unambiguity is most demanded, namely, in constitutional review rulings, has led legal theorists to doubt is usefulness.[42] It is up to political theory, it seems, to find for the doctrine a more solid grounding and a more convincing justification.

How about, then, its second advantage, its natural closeness to the idea of constrained government? In fact, the doctrine has received serious criticism in political theory as well. One such attack (*The Executive Unbound*) was discussed in the previous chapter. Another detailed criticism was offered by Richard Bellamy.[43] His political constitutionalism and republicanism shares Posner's and Vermeule's trust in the long-run wisdom of the people that serves as a more solid bulwark against abuses of power and tyranny than the overly complicated, aristocratic, and elitist principle of the separation of powers. He does not dismiss the idea of sharing, dividing, and partitioning power but thinks that a horizontal-social division and balancing is better approach with more effective results. Such a horizontal distribution of power "involves either rival aspirants for power, as in competing parties, or rival centers of power, as in competing governments in certain aspects of federal arrangements."[44] In Bellamy's view, the traditional separation of powers leads to a blame-game, to on obfuscation of responsibility, which is further aggravated by the problem of a pervasive lack of clear demarcations between the branches of power. Thus, the judiciary makes law without clear mandate (especially worrisome in constitutional decisions such as legalizing morally controversial norms), whereas the executive may have unduly influence over judicial decisions—the examples of functional overlaps could be continued ad infinitum. Instead of such intricacies that cater for only legal and constitutional theorists, Bellamy calls for a clear demarcation of government as such and society, and for a stronger entrenchment of individual liberties.

The doctrine of the separation of powers has its defenders as well, however.[45] They usually aim at revisiting the basic concepts of the three branches. For instance, Christoph Möllers, after having recognized the problem of legal and political theory being largely disconnected, attempts to reformulate the separation of powers doctrine so that it can once again serve as a reliable guide for legal thinking. On the most general level, he views the three branches as representing a *continuum*, with the individuals and their fundamental interest in controlling their own lives on the one end and the collective interests of society on the other. Whereas individuals need the courts to defend their interests, the collective needs legislation to represents "its" interests. The executive stands in the middle, tending to the needs of the individuals, yet with an eye on the public good as well. Of course, courts also rely on the general norms, and the legislative body considers a variety of particular interests; however, in courts, it is the individuals who are the initiating agents; in the legislation, they are rather the passive agents (as against the "collective"). Möllers's theory may be a bit too speculative and abstract but it is a good example of how the principle of the separation of powers is invoked to give form to an idea, in this case, the distinction made between individual and collective sovereignty, in his term, self-determination. Actually, Möllers's basic political theoretical insight is not far from Bellamy's position, namely, that governmental power and social power should be kept separate. What they differ on is whether the formal doctrine of the separation of powers helps the individuals or the government.[46]

There is another argument, which apparently supports the doctrine of the separation of powers, though not via a revision of its political theoretical foundations. The insight is that the modern democratic constitutions contain a host of so-called independent or autonomous (often semi-autonomous) institutions with various functions. The historical antecedents are fairly well-known: the proliferation of such institutions and agencies reflect the expansion of the modern welfare state and its wide variety of administrative and welfare functions. Frank Vibert has called them "unelected bodies."[47] He records a number of functions such agencies fulfill, from whistleblowing to accounting, from information processing to security issues. He further argues that the sphere of these agencies form a new branch of power, with the general function of distinguishing between *facts and values*, where "values" are inherently political and contested, which makes "facts" somehow in need of defense and promotion. By operating in this way, the fourth branch of power serves the public interest or good in a way the other branches cannot. As

Möllers, Vibert also wishes to provide a political theoretical background to his argument, and like him, he also finds it in a distinction.

Actually, thus, both the critics and the defenders of the doctrine of the separation of powers work with the same logic and share the same concern with uncontrolled governing. Bellamy rejects the principle in its traditional forms in order to highlight and thereby defend the separation between social and governmental power. Möllers derives the justification of the principle from a "deeper" or more essential separation made between individual and collective self-determination. In Vibert's conception of the fourth branch, there is a natural distinction between facts and values, which provides the basic argument for the justification of "unelected bodies." Hence, at the end of the day, the principle looks stronger than ever, and even though neither the functionalist nor the formalist interpretation and defense of the traditional doctrine seem vindicated, and the new theories or interpretations preserve the initial inspiration of understanding—as Jeremy Waldron says, articulating[48]—governing in terms of distinctions.

I tried to explain why those theories and conceptions in the tradition of political theory that can be considered the less friendly (though not necessarily hostile) to the idea of the constraining the government, and, consequently, to the principle of the separation of powers end up with an implicit, perhaps reluctant, admission that theorizing over governments is itself a constraining activity, and, more importantly, that each theory constructs some constraints. In this last part of this chapter, it will be instructive to see that the principle of the separation of powers is particularly useful to illuminate these constraints with a special light, and therefore, the principle renders an unexpected service to the idea of constrained governing. In effect, it helps it become close to a political theoretical conception.

Hobbes's conception of the state (the Leviathan) was introduced and interpreted as an attempt to define a no-go-zone for politics, where political individuals cease to be political and become purely private persons, and from where the old-fashioned political aims of the government are also removed, since the state cannot have any other justification but order and peace. However, entering this zone or sphere has an unintended constitutive, even magical, effect: both the government as a political agent and the individuals as political agents must keep vigilant of each other as non-political agents. The state bureaucracy cannot accept political orders, and citizens cannot expect the bureaucracy to serve their political interests. A crucial distinction emerges, which suggests an important balance between the two sides.

Now the three traditional branches of the government cut across this distinction, which appears in each of them, but in different forms and ways, thereby helping each to find its special responsibility and character, and at the same time, contributing to the visibility and discernibility of the basic constraint at hand. Legislation *constitutes and regulates* the state, defines its structure and creates its legitimacy. To a large extent, however, the state *nurtures it* (providing it with information, policy proposals, reports, etc., articulating the needs of the individuals). The executive power *runs the state* as a non-political business but at the same time it also *"governs"* it as a "ship," generating agreement and disagreement alike among the citizenry. The judiciary is expected to be the most autonomous branch, almost falling outside of the state as operative agency, yet at the same time, it represents the ideal of a politically *neutral and arbitrator*-state in its purest form. The idea and ideal of the state as conceived by Hobbes thus sheds a peculiar light on the traditional branches of power that had been considered parts of the government. It has distorting and confusing effects, yet through the prism of the state, the variable and varying roles of the three (perhaps four) branches of power become more controversial, and thereby easier to be controlled by external agents.

Let us turn to the concept and image of the leader (I repeat that my intention was not to discuss Fichte's ideas of the state and its structure: in his writings he has various suggestions, much as Hobbes was also concerned with giving a more detailed analysis of how to build a system of what he called the magistrates). Obviously, a fully personalized idea of the state is incompatible with any separation of powers, not even perhaps a technical division of it (though in practice it is, of course, inevitable). The infamous Schmittian justification of Hitler's ruthless decision to annihilate the SA and have its leadership summarily executed explicitly states that the supreme leader, the Führer, must be the supreme judge. Schmitt quotes Hitler's address to the Reichstag in which he makes it a point that his decision was that of the chief judge judging, nota bene, the whole German people (and not only the "criminals").[49] I have argued that such an absolute and very emphatic merging of all branches of power into a single leader does, contrary to the first impression one may have, the internal constraint of making the problem of loyalty central to government. On this conception, it is within the judiciary where the loyalty issue becomes the most evident, of course, in a negative way. The twentieth century totalitarian regimes were notorious for their political/show trials, with the peculiar, even dizzy arrangement of the process that had to follow the judicial norms and forms, but it was clear that the verdict was a political issue. (Of course, history knows former examples, from the trial of the Templars to the trial of Charles I or Louis XIV.) Judges were expected to be the mouthpiece of the ruling class or the people, and not of the law; of course, their actual judgments and activities were closely supervised and controlled through the loyalty ties (to the party, and ultimately, to the supreme leader). Again, the principle of the separation of powers is only implicitly or negatively vindicated, in virtue of the "political shock" suffered by the people or the outside observers. In the case of the Stalinist purges, many "outsiders" were in fact Communists of other countries to whom these trials were the stumbling block—the constraint—that were highly effective in making them sever or weaken their loyalty ties to the Soviet Union).

The image of society as a whole (an organic body) has a different problem of separating powers. In itself, this conception is not compatible with a homogenous, undifferentiated society. On the contrary, it supports the various "natural" distinctions that natural, religious, local, or vocational communities produce and sustain. The problem is how the government should reflect on these distinctions, and how it is able to handle their potential and actual conflicts. The solution is inherent to the logic of the conception: actually, the various functions of the government are all understood in terms of professions and professional bodies. Judges, for instance, are not representing or operating a branch of power but are partly born, partly educated and trained personally to fulfill their tasks. Laws are made by the wisest and most competent spiritual and political elite. The state bureaucracy, Othmar Spann stresses, is reduced significantly, since a great amount of its work is done by the various lower-order collectives and communities. The traditional-legal doctrine of the separated power branches looks obsolete. However, as was pointed out, this organic conception smacks of idealization and romanticism and lacks convincing force. It does not have any serious mechanism for arbitration, conflict resolution, and interest processing, other than the reliance on the wisdom of the few and on the presumed communal instincts of the members of the society. Again, the more fears of such conflicts grow, the more responsibility judges will bear, and inevitably, their special profession will emerge as a crucial governmental activity. This goes against the very presumptions of this conception. Hence, the traditional separation of governmental functions can be expected to emerge no less naturally (like in the classic Greek cities) than the various corporations and communities do.

Finally, the Rawlsian theory has its own problems with the separation of powers. Some of its aspects were already discussed in chapter 2. I already referred to Rawls's own theory of a functional separation of government branches. The underlying idea is this:

> The basic principles of justice apply to the basic structure and regulate how its major institutions are combined into one scheme. . . . The social system is to be designed so that the resulting distribution is just however things turn out. To achieve this end it is necessary to set the social and economic process within the surroundings of suitable political and legal institutions. . . . In establishing these background institutions the government may be thought of as divided into four branches. Each branch consists of various agencies, or activities thereof, charged with preserving certain social and economic conditions. These divisions

do not overlap with the usual organization of government but are to be understood as different functions.[50]

Whereas the "usual organization of government" refers to the traditional doctrine on which Rawls says next to nothing, he outlines another fourfold structure with branches of allocation, stabilization, transfer, and distribution. These branches regulate and govern the spheres of social life most crucial to the promotion and defense of social justice. The political principles of governing are subordinated to the principles of justice because "the principles of justice regulate the whole structure; they also regulate the balance of precepts."[51] Apparently, these functions can be made perfectly compatible with the executive power's competences. The judiciary is supposed to be preoccupied with promoting social justice (probably entitled to constitutionally review laws that happen to be inconsistent with it), whereas the legislative body is supposed to control and distribute only surplus budget sources (Rawls later adds the "exchange branch," which resembles of this body). The negative justification of the doctrine of the separation of powers emerges from the possible resistance to this distributive tyranny of the government. Political debates and counter-interests will find their way to be heard and seen, if not in the legislative assembly under the control of the government so conceived, but in alternative forums. Similarly, the non-justice related functions of the government of the executive power will probably be seized by strong political leaders, notwithstanding the laments and complaints of those who are afraid of personalization and populism. Finally, if the judiciary becomes the ultimate decision-maker in matters of social justice, the single most important governmental concern, it will lose its special authority. The principle of the separation of powers is not justified in a substantial or axiomatic sense, again, but it helps understand how the inherent constraints of the Watchmaker Government are working.

## SUMMARY

This last chapter was meant to proceed toward a more comprehensive and normatively grounded account of constrained government. Since an axiomatic approach to political theorizing is neither necessary, nor purposive, and since the conceptual understanding of political theory was shown to be particularly close to an ordinary way of thinking about politics, in the first of this chapter, I made an attempt to use metaphors to suggest a distinction between an immoderate/unconstrained and a moderate/constrained vision of government. Edmund Burke's tradition is especially helpful because it strongly and consciously connects political theory to aesthetic experience. At its center, we discover some politico-aesthetic qualities such as harmony and order, which, however, are distinct from the more Romantic and grandiose idea of social harmony, central to the conception of society as a whole. Secondly, I tried to take stock with Montesquieu's views and argued that his "conception" of moderate government rests on precisely these qualities by which his arguably pluralistic approach to political theory, with a number of political principles working not as axioms but as guides and compasses, can be best and most convincingly summarized. Finally, I showed how the principle of the separation of powers today often vehemently attacked, but still widely considered to be a cornerstone of constrained governments, can indeed survive in the role of highlighting the constraints of governments especially within those theories, discussed in the second chapter, that are implicitly wary of, or explicitly reject, the constraints of governments as they, finally, get their institutional form in the constitutional doctrine of the separation of the branches of governmental power.

# NOTES

1. Franz Kafka, *The Castle*, tr. by A. Bell, Oxford World Classics (Oxford: Oxford University Press, 2009), 5.

2. Ibid., 11.

3. K. has endless conversations with various characters of the village, all with the sole purpose of learning about the secrets, the procedures and logic of the Castle. Kafka intended these to be comical features, yet as we rarely laugh about Gulliver's adventures, K.'s long monologues and stories are less than cheering. Sarcasm is not always humorous.

4. Neal Wood, "The Aesthetic Dimension of Burke's Political Thought." *Journal of British Studies* 1 (1964): 41–64.

5. Burke, *Reflections*, 78.

6. Paul Duro, "Observations on the Burkean Sublime." *Word and Image* 1 (2013): 40–58.

7. Burke, *Reflections*, 60.

8. Ibid.

9. Ibid., 61.

10. Ibid.

11. Ibid., 92.

12. Ibid., 80.

13. What is monstrous is not only the constitution, according to Burke, but the whole revolution and the masses doing it. See Mark Neocleous, "The Monstrous Multitude: Edmund Burke's Political Teratology." *Contemporary Political Theory* 3 (2004): 70–88.

14. Burke, *Reflections*, 196.

15. Ibid., 199–201.

16. *The Tempest* (New Haven, London: Yale University Press, 2006), 52.

17. *The Fable of the Bees*, 69.

18. *The Leviathan*, 252–53.

19. Paul O. Carrese, *Democracy in Moderation. Montesquieu, Tocqueville, and Sustainable Liberalism* (Cambridge: Cambridge University Press, 2016), ix.

20. Ibid., xi.

21. Ibid., 1.

22. Harry Clor, *On Moderation: Defending an Ancient Virtue in a Modern World* (Waco, TX: Baylor University Press, 2008). Moderation: balancing extremes, personal taming of passions, tempering one's mind—theory.

23. Aurelian Craiutu, *Faces of Moderation. The Art of Balance in an Age of Extremes* (Philadelphia: University of Pennsylvania Press, 2017).

24. Ibid., 3.

25. Ibid., 9.

26. In his earlier book, Craiutu offers an admirably thorough and insightful analysis of the French school of moderate governing and writes about the moderate spirit, concluding that "the moderation of the authors studied in this book was, moreover, neither a 'halting between extremes' nor a form of wavering lacking firmness or purpose. It is best described as a mixture between, on the one hand, *responsibility, prudence*, and *civility*, and, on the other hand, *enthusiasm* and *passionate commitment* to a distinctive set of principles and institutional arrangements." Aurelian Craiutu, *A Virtue for Courageous Minds. Moderation in French Political Thought, 1748–1830* (Princeton, Oxford: Princeton University Press, 2012), 219, italics added.

27. David Brooks titled his oft-cited and influential article "A Moderate Manifesto." The title is a bit paradoxical, as writing manifestos suits to a radical political style, though as Craiutu argued, moderate politics does not rule out radicalism in principle. Brooks writes in it that "those of us in the moderate tradition—the Hamiltonian tradition that believes in limited but energetic government—thus find ourselves facing a void. We moderates are going to have to assert ourselves. We're going to have to take a centrist tendency that has been politically feckless and intellectually vapid and turn it into an influential force." https://www.nytimes.com/2009/03/03/opinion/03brooks.html

28. Charles de Secondat, Baron the Montesquieu, *The Spirit of Laws*, tr. Thomas Nugent (1752) (Batoche Books, Kitchener, 2001).

29. Ibid., 176–77.

30. Ibid., 177.

31. Ibid.

32. Ibid., 322.

33. Ibid.

34. Ibid., 499.

35. Nathaniel Gilmore and Vickie B. Sullivan, "Montesquieu's Teaching on the Dangers of Extreme Corrections: Japan, the Catholic Inquisition, and Moderation in *The Spirit of the Laws*." *American Political Science Review* 3 (2017): 460–70, 462.

36. Alex Haskins, "Montesquieu's Paradoxical Spirit of Moderation: On the Making of Asian Despotism in *De l'esprit des lois*." *Political Theory* 6 (2018): 915–37.

37. Craiutu, *A Virtue for Courageous Minds.* Cicero and his vision about the Roman "political and legal architecture" is especially important.

38. Craiutu, *Faces of Moderation.* Berlin is cited, of course, because of his view that values cannot be reconciled with one.

39. Haskins, *Montesquieu's Paradoxical Spirit of Moderation,* 918.

40. John F. Manning is basically skeptical: "Separation of Powers as Ordinary Interpretation." *Harvard Law Review* 124 (2011): 1939–44.

41. Martin H. Redish, Elisabeth Cisar, "'If Angels Were to Govern': The Need for Pragmatic Formalism in Separation of Powers Theory." *Duke Law Journal* 3 (1991): 449–506. Elizabeth M. Magill, "Beyond Powers and Branches in Separation of Powers Law." *University of Pennsylvania Law Review* 150 (2001): 603–60.

42. For a defense of functionalism, and more generally, the context-dependent applicability of both interpretations, see Suzanne Prieur Clair, "Separation of Powers: A New Look at the Functionalist Approach." *Western Reserve Law Review* 1 (1989): 331–46.

43. Richard Bellamy, *Political Constitutionalism. A Republican Defense of the Constitutionality of Democracy* (Cambridge: Cambridge University Press, 2007).

44. 199, 200.

45. Eoin Carolan, *The New Separation of Powers. A Theory for the Modern State* (Oxford: Oxford University Press, 2009); Christoph Möllers, *The Three Branches. A Comparative Model of Separation of Powers* (Oxford: Oxford University Press, 2013); Jeremy Waldron, "Separation of Powers in Thought and in Practice?" *Boston College Law Review* 2 (2013): 433–68.

46. Another authority on republicanism, Philip Pettit, holds that the separation of powers is an efficient and usable principle in constraining governments. See *On the People's Terms* (Cambridge: Cambridge University Press, 2012).

47. Frank Vibert, *The Rise of the Unelected. Democracy and the New Separation of Powers* (Cambridge: Cambridge University Press, 2007).

48. Jeremy Waldron, "Separation of Powers in Thought and in Practice?" *Boston College Law Review,* 2 (2013): 433–68.

49. Carl Schmitt, Der Führer schützt das Recht. *Deutsche Juristen-Zeitung,* 1. August, 1934, frontpage.

50. *A Theory of Justice,* 242–43.

51. Ibid., 244.

# Conclusion

Moderation is a respected and unchallenged virtue. Plato (Socrates) asks this question to Glaucon: "Is it the rulers or the subjects of the community who, in your opinion, possess self-discipline?" "Both, he replied."[1] And Socrates goes on to argue that indeed self-discipline, or sophrosyne, with some liberality, synonyms for moderation/temperance, are a version of harmony, agreement, and an overarching quality of a well-ordered society. This is a virtue that can be acquired and practiced efficiently by many, unlike heroic virtues such as courage, or intellectual virtues such as wisdom. In political theory, the tradition of moderate government has enjoyed a similarly respected status, though unlike institutional-procedural political theories, such as social contract theory, public choice, constitutional theory (from the ancient ideal of mixed constitution to the modern ideal of liberal constitution), moderate government has remained an ideal to be venerated rather than expounded, analyzed, and systematically defended.

In this book, I made an attempt to redress this deficiency. To make the ideal more amenable to such a treatment, I decided to focus on the constraints of government, and governing as a process and activity, because the moderation is evidently a virtue of persons and institutions that is essentially the realization and respecting of constraints, limitations, and boundaries. The task is, therefore, to find the natural and inherent constraints of governing in our long and wide tradition. Political theory has the responsibility of addressing them and providing the general public with a systematic account of them, which, in turn, becomes a case for protecting them. This is an ever-acute responsibility because immoderation in morality, politics, and philosophy is always tempting. Person-based autocracies and institutionalized curtailments of individual autonomy and freedom present us with constant dangers.

In accordance with the Socratic insight about moderation—and logically, about its counterparts—being the most accessible virtue essential to good governance, I proposed to read and reflect on the *Antigone* and *Measure for Measure* as two outstanding dramas, guiding us throughout the explorations. They introduce us to the tragedy of tyranny and to the problem of how to distinguish between order and disorder, respectively. Tyranny is eminently a willful neglection, or outright rejection, of moderate government. Creon's decisions and actions reveal some of the most often cited boundaries of governing: the need of legitimacy; the inevitable confrontation with theology; the ultimate barrier to all political action, that is, death; and the hubris of politics, which threatens the ruler with becoming death and blind, with identifying himself or herself with the city, which pushes him or her to the void. Shakespeare takes us into a more complex world, where both Hobbes and Mandeville were called to help, to distinguish between various meanings of order. It is not always trivially clear whether there is a serious disorder in society, which calls for strong government and the removal of its constraints, or disorder is somehow "normal" and such a government would result in an even greater disorder. Shakespeare's play does not offer straightforward answers to the question of how to search for constraints of government when the basic concepts of order and disorder are obfuscated, and general social and political trust is shaken. But he does offer some clues: in case of a true moral chaos, which can be both a result of pervasive immorality and of a morally corrupt government, the strengthening of trust by natural ties (natural constraints), and need for the invigoration of the rule of law as well as consistency provide us with some constraints on the government. In case of moral panic, the pretension of moral chaos, however, the Mandevillean scenario sets in, where moral perfection is cried out for, and the government is looked upon as the last hope. However, there is no morally perfect government and governing (not even the new ducal government in Vienna is perfect), which becomes all-evident to everyone soon. Historically, reaching this conclusion has often been a result of a long and painful process of disillusionment, yet it is these historical lessons that reveal to the generation of the present that governments pretending to be morally perfect are too much disposed to claim omniscience and omnipotence for themselves. Instead of consistence, such temptations are best countered by inconsistencies, once a government is enlightened enough, creating for itself the constrains; and by a sort of skepsis and historically founded mistrust, once the citizens are enlightened enough to draw these conclusions. Shakespeare, in all certainty, leaves his audience with highly embarrassing and ambivalent impressions, which reveal the need to be wary of even the best government.

Sophocles and Shakespeare give us immensely important insights about how and why the lack of constraints on governments leads to tyranny and

chaos. To learn more about the inherent constraints of governing and government in our tradition, I next discussed political theories that, realizing the
necessity of efficient social coordination, and the prevention of social chaos
ensuing from the inherently conflictual nature of the interactions of individuals, argue for a (politically) omnicompetent and omnipotent government.
Such theories openly challenge the tradition of moderate governments. Since
I wished to remain faithful to the idea that political theory must be accessible
to non-experts, I proposed to work with an approach that I called here conceptualism, which, I tried to argue, has the advantage over normativism and
descriptivism as the two prevailing and confronting approaches in political
theory. Concepts, especially those that have solidified as images in our political tradition, condense both descriptive and normative aspects. They refer to
institutions, offices, structures, and to our attaching normative expectations.
I selected and discussed four such concepts, that of the state, of the leader,
of society (as a whole), and of the Watchmaker (the latter if, in all honesty,
a personal invention), to show and argue that even these concepts, embedded
in various theories of unconstrained governments, contain or develop inherent constraints. A common feature of these concepts is that by the very act
of their creation or exposure, their originators, the authors of the underlying
theories, have generated and imposed upon the governments, purported to
be unlimited, effective constraints. The state is not identical with the government. The leader is absorbed by politics. The society needs an elite. The
Watchmaker Government must constantly keep itself clear of politics. These
delimitations or demarcations, contrary to the intentions, reintroduce the idea
of governing as a constrained activity, and governments as structures with
limits.

As a virtue, moderation is eminently a personal, character-related issue.
Theories of the moderate government naturally relate moderation to the institutional make-up of the government, implying that it is an institutional virtue.
I proposed a more systematic treatment of how personal and institutional
virtue is connected. The explanation of the acquisition and practice of virtues
is rooted in Aristotle's ethical thinking. I made use of virtue ethics as a very
general framework to introduce the idea of moral character, its descriptions,
and the moral self as entailed by our capacity to reflect upon these descriptions. I argued that the experience of shame is particularly relevant to moderation. It is an essentially interpersonal occurrence and it always indicates a loss
of control, not necessarily of a moral kind, for which we may or may not be
culpable. Shame is a generic emotion that teaches us that we have no absolute
control over the descriptions of our moral characters, but this, in turn, enables
us to reflect on the constraints of our moral selves. Using Plato's Charmides-
dialogue, I further argued that in a proper reflection on these constraints, we
can realize that neither a complete knowledge of our moral self (in fact, a

pretension of such a knowledge) nor an immersion in our non-knowledge is desirable. The first leads to overconfidence and tyrannical action, the second leads to inaction and chaos. Once we learn to have do not and cannot have absolute or complete control over ourselves, we—as politicians, operators of governments—can better understand why neither full control nor the absence of control is possible in the long run. Thus, moderation as a personal virtue may yield an appreciation of constrained governing, both for the leader and the citizen.

It is very natural to think of governing as an activity pursued by professional leaders possessing offices. In fact, offices belong to the institutional structure and processes of governments and in that sense, they are easier targets of analysis in mainstream political science. However, they retain much of the personal aspect of governing. Legislation is done by legislators, and the executive is run by the chief executive, relying on countless officials who also execute not just the laws but also their own offices. A discussion of the offices of governing with the aim of searching for inherent constraints of governing was, thus, the next topic. For sake of convenience, I simply concentrated on the traditional roles—the legislator, the executive leader, and the judge—and applied two no less ordinary distinctions, first, between the personal and the institutional aspects of the office; and second, between the needs of normal and exceptional times. The third distinction drawn between governing and anti-governing is somewhat less straightforward. It is meant to capture the parallelism between what the central government does and what ordinary people do in the various areas of their lives, with the understanding and desire that the two levels remain distinct. Normal and exceptional decision-making as well as the differences between personal and official responsibilities are distinctions we routinely apply in non-political life, too. This is how we are able to recognize what the distinct branches of the central and political government (including the judiciary) is doing, and when it is and when it is not appropriate, for instance, to make a switch between normal and exceptional decision-making; or between the personal virtues and the office-related responsibilities. As a matter of fact, the three traditional branches have their own distinct emphases with regard to these distinctions (the legislative and the judiciary are predominantly less personalized offices, and they are safeguards of normality; whereas the executive office is prone to become more personalized and thought to be a guarantee of survival in exceptional times). These distinctions, mostly parallelisms rather than antagonisms, emerge as effective constraints for governments, helping them in some ways naturally yield to a sharing of powers and responsibilities (internal constraints), and making them aware of the reality of anti-governing.

In the final chapter, I reflected on the Burkean aesthetical-conservative and the Montesquieuean classical liberal conception of governing. Burke's characterizations of what governing means heavily rely on common aesthetic experiences, especially those that educate us to appreciate the forms rather than the forces, the more gentle emotions rather than the wild passions. Montesquieu's countless remarks and observations are similarly under-theoretized, yet they are extremely useful in making us—citizens and politicians alike—aware of the historical and cultural exigencies and contingencies of governing. His conclusions about the superiority of moderate governments may not convince every reader, yet no political conception can seriously reject the force of arguments taken from history. Finally, I took stock with the principle or doctrine of the separation of powers, relating it to the four concepts outlined and discussed in the second chapter, and argued that their being incapable of accommodating the doctrine is yet another argument for their potentially dangerous consequences, and vice versa: that the separation of powers is a principle that gives us a reliable check on the nature of governing.

Thus, even if authoritarian regimes are on the rise in the world—a claim that can be neither theoretically nor empirically evaluated here, and must remain a matter of perception and a spreading consensus in political science—is, actually, a good test of the central argument of this book that governing, at least within the broadly conceived Western tradition, has inherent constraints, and that defending and strengthening them is a normative duty that many citizens recognize with a sound political instinct.

## NOTE

1. Plato, *Republic*, tr. by Robin Waterfield (Oxford: Oxford University Press, 1993), 139.

# Bibliography

Ahrensdorf, Peter. "Blind Faith and Enlightenment Statesmanship in Oedipus at Colonus." *The Review of Politics* 70 (2008): 165–89.

Airaksinen, Timo. "Fortune is a Woman. Machiavelli on Luck and Virtue. Essays in Honor of Hannu Nurmi." *Homo Oeconomicus* 3–4 (2009): 551–68.

Alvis, John E. and West, Thomas J. (eds). *Shakespeare As Political Thinker.* Wilmington, Delaware: ISI Books, 2000.

Apfel, Laurel J. *The Advent of Pluralism. Diversity and Conflict in the Age of Sophocles.* Oxford: Oxford University Press, 2011.

Apolloni, Jessica. "Local Communities and Central Power in Shakespeare's Transnational Law." *Studies in Philology* 1 (2017): 124–47.

Armitage, David, Condren, Conal and Fitzmaurice, Andrew (eds). *Shakespeare and Early Modern Political Thought.* Cambridge: Cambridge University Press, 2009.

Ballengee, Jennifer E. "Mourning the Public Body in Sophocles' Antigone." *Colloquy* 11 (2006): 31–59.

Barker, Kye Anderson. "Of Wonder: Thomas Hobbes' Political Appropriation of Thaumauzein." *Political Theory* 3 (2017): 362–84.

Barnaby, Andrew and Wry, Joan. "Authorized Versions: *Measure for Measure* and the Politics of Biblical Translation." *Renaissance Quarterly* 4 (1998): 1225–54.

Baumgold, Deborah. "Hobbesian Absolutism and the Paradox of Modern Contractarianism." *European Journal of Political Theory* 8 (2009): 207–28.

Bawcutt, Nigel. "'He Who the Sword of Heaven Will Bear?' The Duke Versus Angelo in *Measure for Measure.*" *Shakespeare Survey: An Annual Survey of Shakespearian Study and Production* 37 (1984): 89–97.

Bellamy, Richard. *Political Constitutionalism. A Republican Defense of the Constitutionality of Democracy.* Cambridge: Cambridge University Press, 2007.

Bennett, Robert B. *Romance and Reformation: The Erasmian Spirit of Shakespeare's Measure for Measure.* Newark: University of Delaware Press, 2000.

Berlin, Isaiah. "Two Concepts of Liberty." In *Four Essays On Liberty.* Oxford: Oxford University Press, 1969: 118–72.

Bloom, Allan and Jaffa, Harry V. *Shakespeare's Politics*. Chicago, London: Chicago University Press, 1974.

Bossuet, J.-B. *Politics drawn from the Very Words of Holy Scripture*. Tr. by Riley, P. Cambridge: Cambridge University Press, 1999.

Brooks, David. "A Moderate Manifesto." *The New York Times*, 3rd March, 2009. https://www.nytimes.com/2009/03/03/opinion/03brooks.html

Brown, Carolyn E. Brown. "Duke Vincentio of Measure for Measure and King James I. of England: 'The Poorest Princes in Christendom'." *Clio* 1 (1996): 51–78.

Burke, Edmund. *Reflections on the Revolution in France*. Ed. L. G. Mitchell. Oxford: Oxford University Press, 1993.

Butler, Judith. *Antigone's Claim: Kinship between Life & Death*. New York: Columbia University Press, 2000.

Calhoun, Cheshire. "An Apology for Moral Shame." The Journal of Political Philosophy 2 (2004): 127–46.

Carolan, Eoin. *The New Separation of Powers. A Theory for the Modern State*. Oxford: Oxford University Press, 2009.

Carrese, Paul O. *Democracy in Moderation. Montesquieu, Tocqueville, and Sustainable Liberalism*. Cambridge: Cambridge University Press, 2016.

Carty, Anthony. "Alfred Verdross and Othmar Spann: German Romantic Nationalism, National Socialism and International Law." *European Journal of International Law* 1 (1995): 78–97.

Cassam, Quassim (ed). *Self-Knowledge*. Oxford: Oxford University Press, 1994.

Chanter, Tina. "Antigone's Political Legacies: Abjection in Defiance of Mourning." In *Interrogating Antigone in Postmodern Philosophy and Criticism*. Edited by Wilmer, S. E. and Žukauskaitė, A. Oxford: Oxford University Press, 2010: 19–47.

Charen, Hannes. "Hegel Reading 'Antigone'." *Monatshefte* 4 (2011): 504–16.

Cicero, Marcus Tullius. *The Republic and the Laws*. Oxford World's Classics. Oxford: Oxford University Press, 2009.

Claire Prieur, Suzanne. "Separation of Powers: A New Look at the Functionalist Approach." *Western Reserve Law Review* 1 (1989): 331–46.

Clor, Harry. *On Moderation: Defending an Ancient Virtue in a Modern World*. Waco, TX: Baylor University Press, 2008.

Cohen, Stephen. "From Mistress to Master: Political Transition and Formal Conflict in Measure for Measure." *Criticism* 4 (1999): 431–64.

Cohen, Mitchel. *The Politics of Opera: A History from Monteverdi to Mozart*. Princeton: Princeton University Press, 2017.

Craiutu, Aurelian. *Faces of Moderation. The Art of Balance in an Age of Extremes*. Philadelphia: University of Pennsylvania Press, 2017.

Craiutu, Aurelian. *A Virtue for Courageous Minds. Moderation in French Political Thought, 1748–1830*. Princeton, Oxford: Princeton University Press, 2012.

Danzig, Gabriel. "Plato's Charmides as a Political Act: Apologetics and the Promotion of Ideology." *Greek, Roman, and Byzantine Studies* 53 (2013): 486–519.

Deigh, John. "Shame and Self-Esteem: A Critique." In *Dignity, Character and Self-Respect*. Edited by Dillon, Robin S. New York: Routledge, 1995: 133–57.

Diehl, Huston. "'Infinite Space': Representation and Reformation in Measure for Measure." *Shakespeare Quarterly* 4 (1998): 393–410.

Dollimore, Jonathan. "Transgressions and Surveillance in Measure for Measure." In *Political Shakespeare: New Essays in Cultural Materialism*. Edited by Dollimore, J. and Sinfield, A. Manchester: Manchester University Press, 1985: 72–87.

Douglass, Robin. "Hobbes and Political Realism." *European Journal of Political Theory* 1 (2016): 1–20.

Dupont, Danica and Pearce, Frank. "Foucault Contra Foucault. Rereading the 'Governmentality' Papers." *Theoretical Criminology* 2 (2001): 123–58.

Duro, Paul. "Observations on the Burkean Sublime." *Word and Image* 1 (2013): 40–58.

Dyzenhaus, David. "The Very Idea of a Judge." *University of Toronto Law Journal* 1 (2010): 61–80.

Emerson, Ralph Waldo. "Napoleon: Man of the World." In *The Complete Works of Ralph Waldo Emerson: Representative men*. Vol. 4. Ann Arbor, MI: University of Michigan Library, 2006: 223–58.

Erman, Eva and Möller, Niklas. "Political Legitimacy in the Real Normative World: The Priority of Morality and the Autonomy of the Political." *British Journal of Political Science* 1 (2015): 215–33.

Feola, Michael. "The Body Politic: Bodily Spectacle and Democratic Agency." *Political Theory* 1 (2017): 1–21.

Ferejohn, John (2002) "Judicializing Politics, Politicizing Law." *Law and Contemporary Problems* 65: 41–68.

Fichte, J. G. *Foundations of Natural Right*. Cambridge: Cambridge University Press, 2000.

Fichte, J. G. *Characteristics of the Present Age*. Gloucester: DoDo Press, 2009.

Fichte, J. G. *Werke IV. Zur Rechts und Sittenlehre II*. Edited by Fichte, H. G. Berlin: W. de Gruyter, 1971.

Fireside, Harvey F. "The Concept of the Legislator in Rousseau's Social Contract." *The Review of Politics* 2 (1970): 191–96.

Freeden, Michael. "Failures of Political Thinking." *Political Studies* 1 (2009): 141–64.

Galligan, Phillip. "Shame, Publicity, and Self-Esteem." *Ratio* March (2016): 57–72.

Galston, William A. "The Populist Challenge to Liberal Democracy." *Journal of Democracy* 2 (2018): 5–19.

Galston, William A. "Realism in Political Theory." *European Journal of Political Theory* 4 (2010): 385–411.

Gauthier, David. *The Logic of Leviathan: The Moral and Political Theory of Thomas Hobbes*. Oxford: Clarendon Press, 1969.

Geuss, Raymond. *Philosophy and Real Politics*. Princeton: Princeton University Press, 2008.

Gibbons, Brian. "Introduction." In *Measure for Measure. The New Cambridge Shakespeare*. Edited by Gibbons, Brian. Cambridge: Cambridge University Press, 1991: 1–68.

Gilmore, Nathaniel and Sullivan, Vickie B. "Montesquieu's Teaching on the Dangers of Extreme Corrections: Japan, the Catholic Inquisition, and Moderation in *The Spirit of the Laws*." *American Political Science Review* 3 (2017): 460–70.

Goossen, Jonathan. "'Tis Set Down So in Heaven, But Not in Earth': Reconsidering Political Theology in Shakespeare's *Measure for Measure*." *Christianity and Literature* 2 (2012): 217–39.

Graham, David A. "Trump Has No Shame." *The Atlantic*, September (2019). https ://www.theatlantic.com/ideas/archive/2019/09/trump-fears-only-consequences/ 598657/

Gulley, Ervene. "'Dressed in a Little Brief Authority': Law as Theater in Measure for Measure." In *Law and Literature Perspectives*. Edited by Rockwood, B. L. New York: Peter Lang, 1996: 53–80.

Hall, Edward. "Integrity in Democratic Politics." *The British Journal of Politics and International Relations* 4 (2018): 385–98.

Hamilton, Alexander. "The Federalist Paper No 72." *The Federalist Papers*. Edited by Wills, G. Bantam Books, 1982.

Haskins, Alex. "Montesquieu's Paradoxical Spirit of Moderation: On the Making of Asian Despotism in *De l'esprit des lois*." *Political Theory* 6 (2018): 915–37.

Hawkins, Harriet. *Measure for Measure Harvester New Critical Introductions to Shakespeare*. Brighton, UK: The Harvester Press, 1987.

Hindess, Barry. "Discipline and Cherish: Foucault on Power, Domination and Government." In *Discourses on Power: From Hobbes to Foucault*. Oxford: Blackwell, 1996: 96–136.

Hindess, Barry. *The Foucault Effect: Studies in Governmentality*. Chicago: Chicago University Press, 1991.

Hobbes, Thomas. *Leviathan*. Introduced by MacPherson, C. B. New York: Penguin Books, 1977.

Holloway, Brian. "Vincentio's Fraud: Boundary and Chaos, Abstinence and Orgy in *Measure for Measure*." *West Virginia Shakespeare and Renaissance Association, Selected Papers* 21, (1998). www.marshall.edu/engsr/SR1998.html.)

Honig, Bonnie. *Antigone, Interrupted*. Cambridge: Cambridge University Press, 2013.

Honig, Bonnie. "Antigone's Two Laws: Greek Tragedy and the Politics of Humanism." *New Literary History* 1 (2010): 1–33.

Honig, Bonnie. "Antigone's Laments, Creon's Grief: Mourning, Membership, and the Politics of Exception." *Political Theory* 1 (2009): 5–43.

Honig, Bonnie. *Political Theory and the Displacement of Politics*. Ithaca, NY: Cornell University Press, 1993.

Honig, Bonnie. "Rawls on Politics and Punishment." *Political Research Quarterly* 46 (1993): 99–125.

Horton, John. "What Might it Mean for Political Theory to Be More 'Realistic'?" *Philosophia* 1 (2017): 487–501.

Horvath, Agnes and Szakolczai, Arpad. *The Political Sociology and Anthropology of Evil: Tricksterology*. London: Routledge, 2020.

Igor, Hector O. A. "Morality and State in the Fichtean Political Philosophy." *Araucaria* 1 (2019): 79–90.

James, David. "The Political Theology of Fichte's Staatslehre: Immanence and Transcendence." *British Journal for the History of Philosophy* 6 (2016): 1157–75.

Johnston, Steven. *Encountering Tragedy. Rousseau and the Project of Democratic Order.* Ithaca, London: Cornell University Press, 1999.

Jubb, Robert. "Playing Kant at the Court of King Arthur." *Political Studies* 4 (2015): 919–34.

Kafka, Franz. *The Castle.* Tr. by A. Bell, Oxford World Classics. Oxford: Oxford University Press, 2009.

Kaufmann, F. W. "Fichte and National Socialism." *The American Political Science Review* 3 (1942): 460–70.

Kekes, John. *Against Liberalism.* Ithaca, London: Cornell University Press, 1997.

Kekes, John. "Shame and Moral Progress." In *Ethical Theory: Character and Virtue.* Midwest Studies in Philosophy Vol. XIII. Edited by French, P. A., Uehling Jr, Th. E., and Wettstein, H. K. Notre Dame: University of Notre Dame Press, 1988: 282–96.

Kelly, Christopher. "'To Persuade without Convincing': The Language of Rousseau's Legislator." *American Journal of Political Science* 2 (1987): 321–35.

Kirkpatrick, Jennet. "The Prudent Dissident: Unheroic Resistance in Sophocles' Antigone." *The Review of Politics* 3 (2011): 401–24.

Knight, Wilson. *The Wheel of Fire. Interpretations of Shakespearean Tragedy.* London, New York, 1930.

Kolnai, Aurel. "The Standard Modes of Aversion: Fear, Disgust and Hatred." *Mind* 427 (1998): 581–95.

Kolnai, Aurel. "What is Politics About?" In *Exploring the World of Human Practice.* Edited by Dunlop, F. and Balazs, Z. Budapest-New York: CEU Press, 2004: 17–46.

Lewis, Cynthia. "'Dark Deeds Darkly Answered': Duke Vincentio and Judgement in *Measure for Measure.*" *Shakespeare Quarterly* 3 (1984): 271–89.

Lindsay, Adam. "'Pretenders of a Vile and Unmanly Disposition': Thomas Hobbes on the Fiction of Constituent Power." *Political Theory* 1 (2018): 1–25.

Locke, Jill. *Democracy and the Death of Shame: Political Equality and Social Disturbance.* Cambridge: Cambridge University Press, 2016.

Locke, Jill. "Donald Trump is Not a Shameless Toddler." *Krisis* 1 (2019). https://krisis.eu/donald-trump-is-not-a-shameless-toddler-the-problems-with-psychological-analyses-of-the-45th-us-president/

Locke, John. *Two Treatises of Government.* Edited by Laslett, Peter. Cambridge: Cambridge University Press, 1992.

Machiavelli, Niccolo. *The Prince and the Discourses.* New York: The Modern Library, 1950.

Mackenzie, Iain and Porter, Robert. "Dramatization as Method in Political Theory." *Contemporary Political Theory* 4 (2011): 482–501.

Magill, Elizabeth M. "Beyond Powers and Branches in Separation of Powers Law." *University of Pennsylvania Law Review* 150 (2001): 603–60.

Mandeville, Bernard. *The Fable of the Bees or Private Vices, Publick Benefits,* Vol. 1. With a Commentary Critical, Historical, and Explanatory by Kaye, F. B. Indianapolis: Liberty Fund, 1988.

Manning, John F. "Separation of Powers as Ordinary Interpretation." *Harvard Law Review* 124 (2011): 1939–44.

Mansfield, Harvey C. *Taming the Prince. The Ambivalence of Modern Executive Power.* New York: Free Press, 1989.

Marsh, Krystal. "Reconstructing the Morality Play and Redeeming the Polity in William Shakespeare's Measure for Measure." *Journal of the Wooden O* 13(1) (2013): 81–95.

Mason, Andrew. "Rawlsian Theory and the Circumstances of Politics." *Political Theory* 5 (2010): 658–83.

Maynard, Jonathan L. and Worsnip, Alex. "The Realist Narrative about 'Ethics-First' Political Philosophy." (2015). https://www.academia.edu/20790102/Politics_Ethics_and_Power_Making_sense_of_the_realist_challenge_to_political_moralism_through_Raymond_Geuss_Philosophy_and_Real_Politics?auto=download

McCulloch, Andrew. "Jesus Christ and Max Weber: Two Problems of Charisma." *Max Weber Studies* 1 (2005): 7–34.

Meilaender, Peter C. "Marriage and the Law: Politics and Theology in Measure for Measure." *Perspectives on Political Science* 4 (2012): 195–200.

Moggach, Douglas. "Freedom and Perfection: German Debates on the State in the Eighteenth Century." *Canadian Journal of Political Science* 4 (2009): 1003–23.

Möllers, Christoph. *The Three Branches. A Comparative Model of Separation of Powers.* Oxford: Oxford University Press, 2013.

Montesquieu, Charles de Secondat. *The Spirit of Laws.* Thomas Nugent tr (1752). Batoche Books, Kitchener, 2001.

Moore, Andrew. *Shakespeare between Machiavelli and Hobbes. Dead Body Politics.* Lanham: Lexington Books, 2016.

Neocleous, Mark. "The Monstrous Multitude: Edmund Burke's Political Teratology." *Contemporary Political Theory* 3 (2004): 70–88.

Nussbaum, Martha C. *The Fragility of Goodness.* Cambridge: Cambridge University Press, 1986.

Patterson, Cynthia B. Patterson, "The Place and Practice of Burial in Sophocles' Athens." *Helios* Supplement (2006): 9–48.

Pettit, Philip. *On the People's Terms.* Cambridge: Cambridge University Press, 2012.

Philp, Mark. *Political Conduct.* Cambridge, MA; London: Harvard University Press, 2007.

Pichanick, Alan. "Sôphrosunê, Socratic Therapy, and Platonic Drama in Plato's Charmides." *Epoché: A Journal for the History of Philosophy* 1 (2016): 47–66.

Pildes, Richard H. "Law and the President." *Harvard Law Review* 125 (2012): 1–42.

Plato. "Charmides." In *The Dialogues of Plato.* Vol 1. Tr. Benjamin Jowett. London: Oxford University Press: 1892: 1–38.

Plato. *Republic.* Tr. by Robin Waterfield. Oxford: Oxford University Press, 1993.

Planinc, Zdravko. "Shakespeare's Critique of Machiavellian Force, Fraud, and Spectacle in *Measure for Measure.*" *Humanitas* 1–2 (2010): 144–68.

Posner, Eric A. and Vermeule, Adrian. *The Executive Unbound: After the Madisonian Republic.* Oxford: Oxford University Press, 2010.

Prakash, Saikrishna. "The Essential Meaning of Executive Power." *Illinois Law Review* 3 (2003): 701–820.

Press, Gerald A. "The Enactment of Moderation in Plato's Charmides." *Acta Classica Universitatis Scientarum Debreceniensis* 54 (2018): 5–34.

Rawls, John. *Justice as Fairness: A Restatement*. Edited by Kelly, E. Cambridge, MA: Harvard University Press, 2001.

Rawls, John. *A Theory of Justice*. Cambridge, MA: Harvard University Press, 1971.

Redish, Martin H. and Cisar, Elisabeth. "'If Angels Were to Govern': The Need for Pragmatic Formalism in Separation of Powers Theory." *Duke Law Journal* 3 (1991): 449–506.

Reed, Valeri. "Bringing Antigone Home." *Comparative Literature Studies* 3 (2008): 316–40.

Rousseau, Jean-Jacques. "On the Social Contract." In *The Basic Political Writings*. Trans. Cress, Donald A. Indianapolis/Cambridge: Hackett Publ. Comp, 1987: 141–227.

Rowe, M. R. "The Dissolution of Goodness: 'Measure for Measure' and Classical Ethics." *International Journal of the Classical Tradition* 1 (1998): 20–46.

Rehm, Rush. "Sophocles' Antigone and Family Values." *Helios* Supplement (2006): 187–218.

Robjant, David. "What Use is Literature to Political Philosophy? Or the Funny Thing About Socrates's Nose." *Philosophy and Literature* 2 (2015): 322–37.

Sabl, Andrew. *Ruling Passions*. Princeton: Princeton University Press, 2002.

Sagar, Paul. "The State Without Sovereignty: Authority and Obligation in Hume's Political Philosophy." In *Opinion of Mankind*. Oxford, Princeton: Princeton University Press, 2018: 103–38.

Sagar, Paul. "Of Mushrooms and Method: History and the Family in Hobbes's Science of Politics." *European Journal of Political Theory* 14 (2015): 98–117.

Scaff, Lawrence A. *Weber and the Weberians*. New York: Palgrave Macmillan, 2004.

Schmitt, Carl. *The Concept of the Political*. Chicago: The Chicago University Press, 2007.

Schmitt, Carl. *Theory of the Partisan*. New York: Telos Press Publishing, 2007.

Shakespeare, William. *Measure for Measure. The New Cambridge Shakespeare*. Edited by Gibbons, Brian. Cambridge: Cambridge University Press, 1991.

Shakespeare, William. *The Tempest*. New Haven, London: Yale University Press, 2006.

Schabert, Tilo. "Ein klassischer Fürst. François Mitterrand im Spiegel einer vergleichenden Regierungslehre." In *Mitterrand und die Deutschen*. Edited by Sauzay, B. and von Thadden, R. Göttingen: Wallstein, 1998: 78–106.

Sheridan, Patricia. "Resisting the Scaffold: Self-Preservation and the Limits of Obligation in Hobbes' *Leviathan*." *Hobbes Studies* 24 (2011): 137–57.

Shklar, Judith. "The Liberalism of Fear." In *Liberalism and the Moral Life*. Edited by Rosenblum, Nancy L. Cambridge: Harvard University Press, 1989: 21–38.

Shuger, Debora Kuller. *Political Theologies in Shakespeare's England. The Sacred and the State in Measure for Measure*. New York: Palgrave MacMillan, 2001.

Sjoholm, Cecilia. "Naked Life; Arendt and the Exile at Colonus." In *Interrogating Antigone in Postmodern Philosophy and Criticism*. Edited by Wilmer, S. E. and Žukauskaitė, A. Oxford: Oxford University Press, 2010: 48–66.

Skinner, Quentin. "A Genealogy of the Modern State." *Proceedings of the British Academy* 162 (2008): 325–70.

Sophocles. *The Complete Greek Tragedies I*. Edited by Grene D. and Lattimore, R. Translated by Grene, David. Chicago, London: The Chicago University Press, 1991.

Spann, Othmar. *Der wahre Staat*. Leipzig: Quelle, 1921.

Strauss, Jonathan. *Private Lives, Public Deaths. Antigone and the Invention of Individuality*. New York: Fordham University Press, 2013.

Strawson, Galen. "The Self." In *Models of the Self*. Edited by Gallagher, S. and Shear, J. Thorverton: Imprint Academic, 1999: 3–45.

Sugrue, Michael. "Measure for Measure: The Bible Contra Puritanical Christianity." *Praesidium* 4 (2008), formerly available at www.literatevalues.org/prae-8.4.htm #measure.

Tampio, Nicholas. "A Defense of Political Constructivism." *Contemporary Political Theory* 3 (2012): 305–23.

Taylor, Gabriele. "Shame, Integrity, and Self-Respect." In *Dignity, Character and Self-respect*. Edited by Dillon, Robin S. New York: Routledge, 1995: 157–81.

Thomas, Alan. "Rawls and Political Realism: Realistic Utopianism or Judgement in Bad Faith?" *European Journal of Political Theory* 1 (2015): 1–21.

Tsouna, Voula, "What is the Subject of Plato's Charmides?" In *For a Skeptical Peripatetic. Festschrift in Honour of Johan Glucker*. Edited by Liebersohn, Y. Z., Ludlam, I., Edelheit, A., and Edelheit, S. Augustin: Academia Verlag, 2017: 34–63.

Tudor, Lucian. "Othmar Spann: A Catholic Radical Traditionalist." Accessed 14th February, 2020. https://archive.org/stream/EssaysByLucianTudor/OthmarSpann-A CatholicRadicalTraditionalist_djvu.txt

Tullock, Gordon and Buchanan, James. *The Calculus of Consent*. Ann Arbor: The University of Michigan Press, 1990.

Velleman, David. "The Genesis of Shame." *Philosophy and Public Affairs* 1 (2001): 27–52.

Vernant, Jean-Pierre and Vidal-Naquet, Pierre. *Myth and Tragedy in Ancient Greece*. New York: Zone Books, 1990.

Vibert, Frank. *The Rise of the Unelected. Democracy and the New Separation of Powers*. Cambridge: Cambridge University Press, 2007.

Waldron, Jeremy. "Separation of Powers in Thought and in Practice?" *Boston College Law Review* 2 (2013): 433–68.

Waldron, Jeremy. *Law and Disagreement*. Oxford: Oxford University Press, 1999.

Williams, Bernard. "Realism and Moralism in Political Theory." In *The Beginning Was The Deed. Realism and Moralism In Political Argument*. Edited by Hawthorn, G. Princeton NJ: Princeton University Press, 2005: 1–17.

Williams, Bernard. "Politics and Moral Character." In *Public and Private Morality*. Edited by Hampshire, S. et al. Cambridge: Cambridge University Press, 1978: 54–70.

Wilson, Jeffrey R. "'When Evil Deeds Have Their Permissive Pass': Broken Windows in William Shakespeare's Measure for Measure." *Law and Humanities* 2 (2017): 160–83.

Wolin, Sheldon. "Political Theory as a Vocation." *The American Political Science Review* 1 (1969): 1062–82.

Wood, Neal. "The Aesthetic Dimension of Burke's Political Thought." *Journal of British Studies* 1 (1964): 41–64.

Žižek, Slavoj. *Antigone*. London: Bloomsbury, 2016.

Žukauskaitė, Audrone. "Biopolitics: Antigone's Claim." In *Interrogating Antigone in Postmodern Philosophy and Criticism*. Edited by Wilmer, S. E. and Žukauskaitė, A. Oxford: Oxford University Press, 2010: 67–81.

# Index

# About the Author

**Zoltán Balázs** is professor of political science at the Corvinus University, Budapest, and advisor of the Center of Social Studies, L. Eotvos Research Network, Budapest. His interests are political phenomenology, theories of power, political theory in literature, and the thought of Aurel Kolnai. Besides publishing extensively in Hungarian, he has published numerous articles in English related to these topics. His previous book *The Principle of the Separation of Powers: A Defense* was published by Lexington Books (an imprint of Rowman and Littlefield) in 2016.